D•N•ANGEL

BY YUKIRU SUGISAKI

VOLUME 7

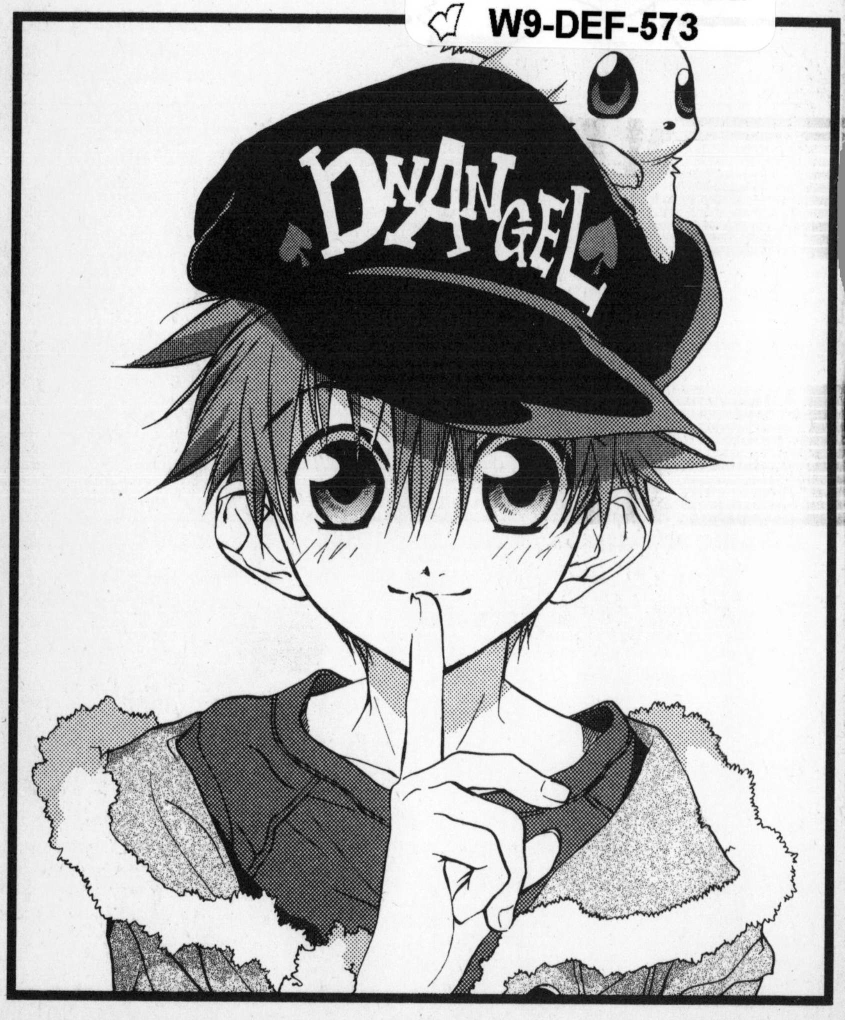
DNANGEL

& STORY

Daisuke and Dark's relationships with Riku and her sister Risa have gotten completely mixed up and complicated—but for now, at least Daisuke and Riku have finally made up and seem to be getting along fine. Things got more complicated however, when Satoshi's "other half" emerged and attacked Daisuke! Dark was able to rescue him, but it's beginning to look as though there's some strange connection between Dark and Satoshi...finally, when Dark and Daisuke went on their latest mission, to steal the "Second Hand of Time," it somehow came back to life and kidnapped Daisuke, pulling him into a mysterious world of snow!

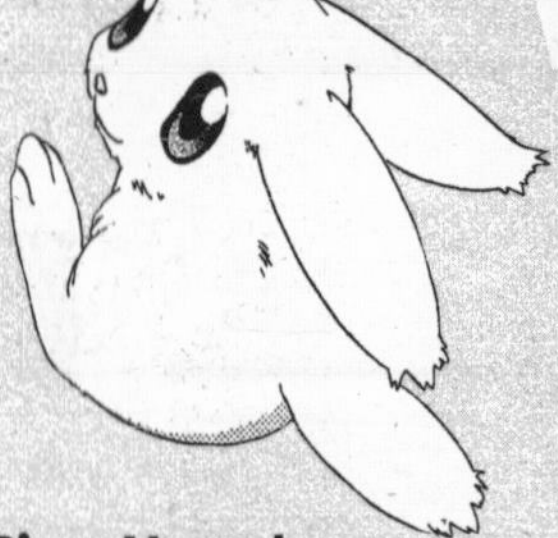

Wiz

A mysterious animal who acts as Dark's familiar and who can transform into many things, including Dark's black wings. He can also transform himself into Dark or Daisuke.

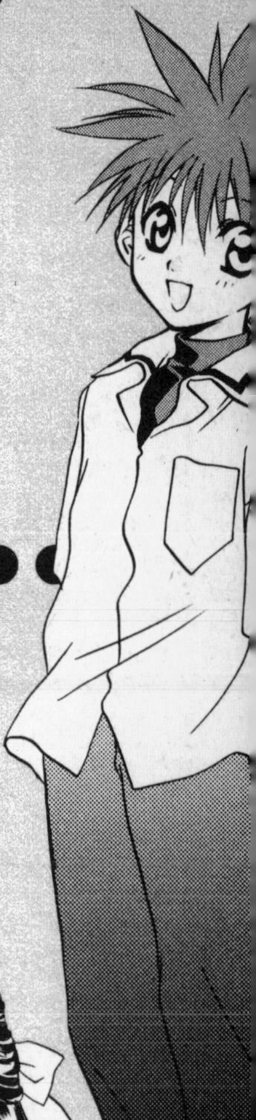

Risa Harada (younger sister)

Daisuke's first crush. Daisuke confessed his love to her...but she rejected him. She's been in love with Dark since the first time she saw him on TV.

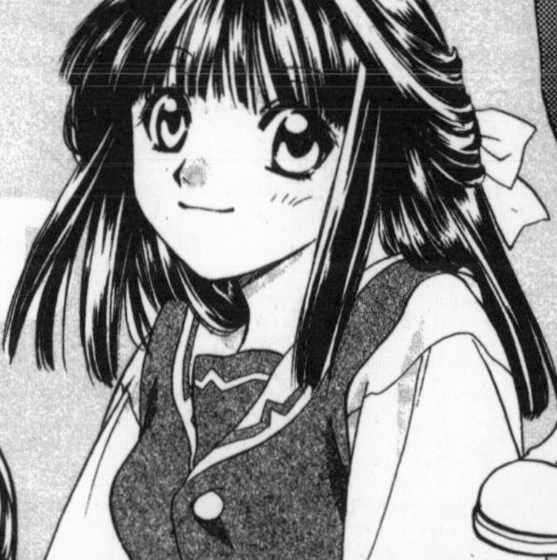

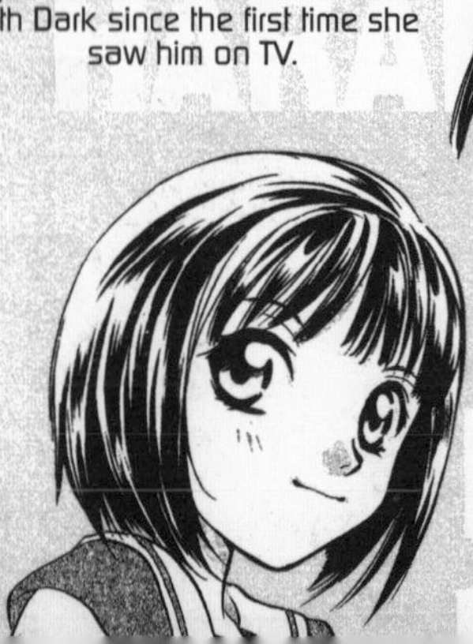

Riku Harada (older sister)

Risa's identical twin sister. She and Daisuke have fallen for each other.

Daisuke Niwa

A 14-year-old student at Azumano Middle School. He has a unique genetic condition that causes him to transform into the infamous Phantom Thief Dark whenever he has romantic feelings.

CHARACTERS

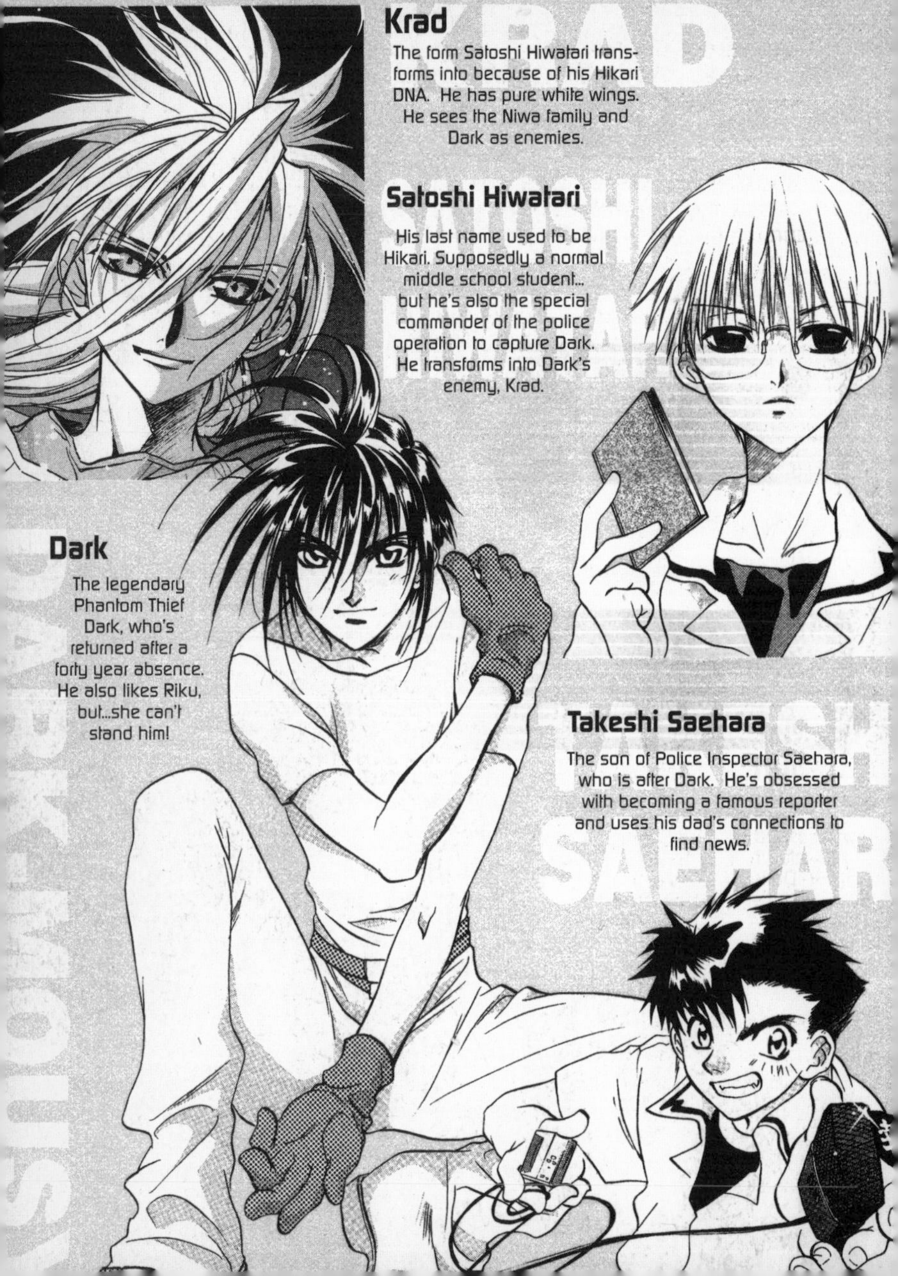

Krad

The form Satoshi Hiwatari transforms into because of his Hikari DNA. He has pure white wings. He sees the Niwa family and Dark as enemies.

Satoshi Hiwatari

His last name used to be Hikari. Supposedly a normal middle school student... but he's also the special commander of the police operation to capture Dark. He transforms into Dark's enemy, Krad.

Dark

The legendary Phantom Thief Dark, who's returned after a forty year absence. He also likes Riku, but...she can't stand him!

Takeshi Saehara

The son of Police Inspector Saehara, who is after Dark. He's obsessed with becoming a famous reporter and uses his dad's connections to find news.

D•N•ANGEL Vol. 7
Created by Yukiru Sugisaki

Translation - Alethea and Athena Nibley
English Adaptation - Sarah Dyer
Copy Editor - Peter Ahlstrom
Retouch and Lettering - Bowen Park
Production Artist - Eric Pineda
Cover Layout - Jennifer Nunn

Editor - Bryce P. Coleman
Digital Imaging Manager - Chris Buford
Pre-Press Manager - Antonio DePietro
Production Managers - Jennifer Miller and Mutsumi Miyazaki
Art Director - Matt Alford
Managing Editor - Jill Freshney
VP of Production - Ron Klamert
Editor-in-Chief - Mike Kiley
President and C.O.O. - John Parker
Publisher and C.E.O. - Stuart Levy

A  Manga

TOKYOPOP Inc.
5900 Wilshire Blvd. Suite 2000
Los Angeles, CA 90036

E-mail: info@TOKYOPOP.com
Come visit us online at www.TOKYOPOP.com

ISBN: 1-59182-956-9

First TOKYOPOP printing: April 2005
10 9 8 7 6 5 4 3
Printed in the USA

D·N·ANGEL

Volume 7

By

Yukiru Sugisaki

HAMBURG // LONDON // LOS ANGELES // TOKYO

CONTENTS

THE SECOND HAND OF TIME PART 3

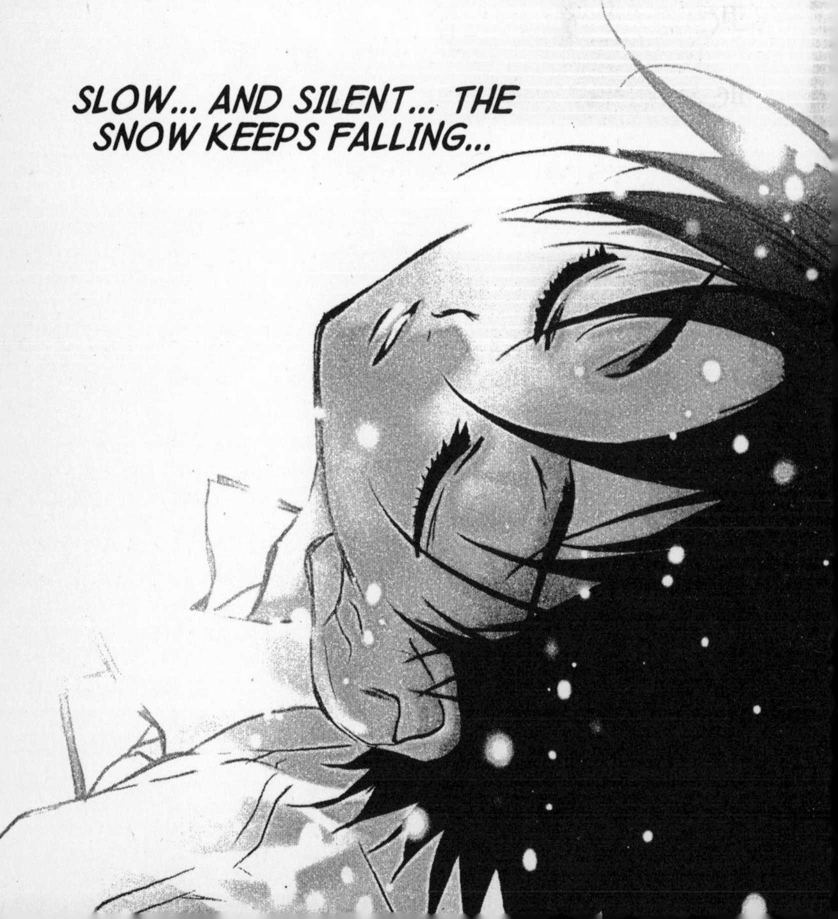
SLOW... AND SILENT... THE SNOW KEEPS FALLING...

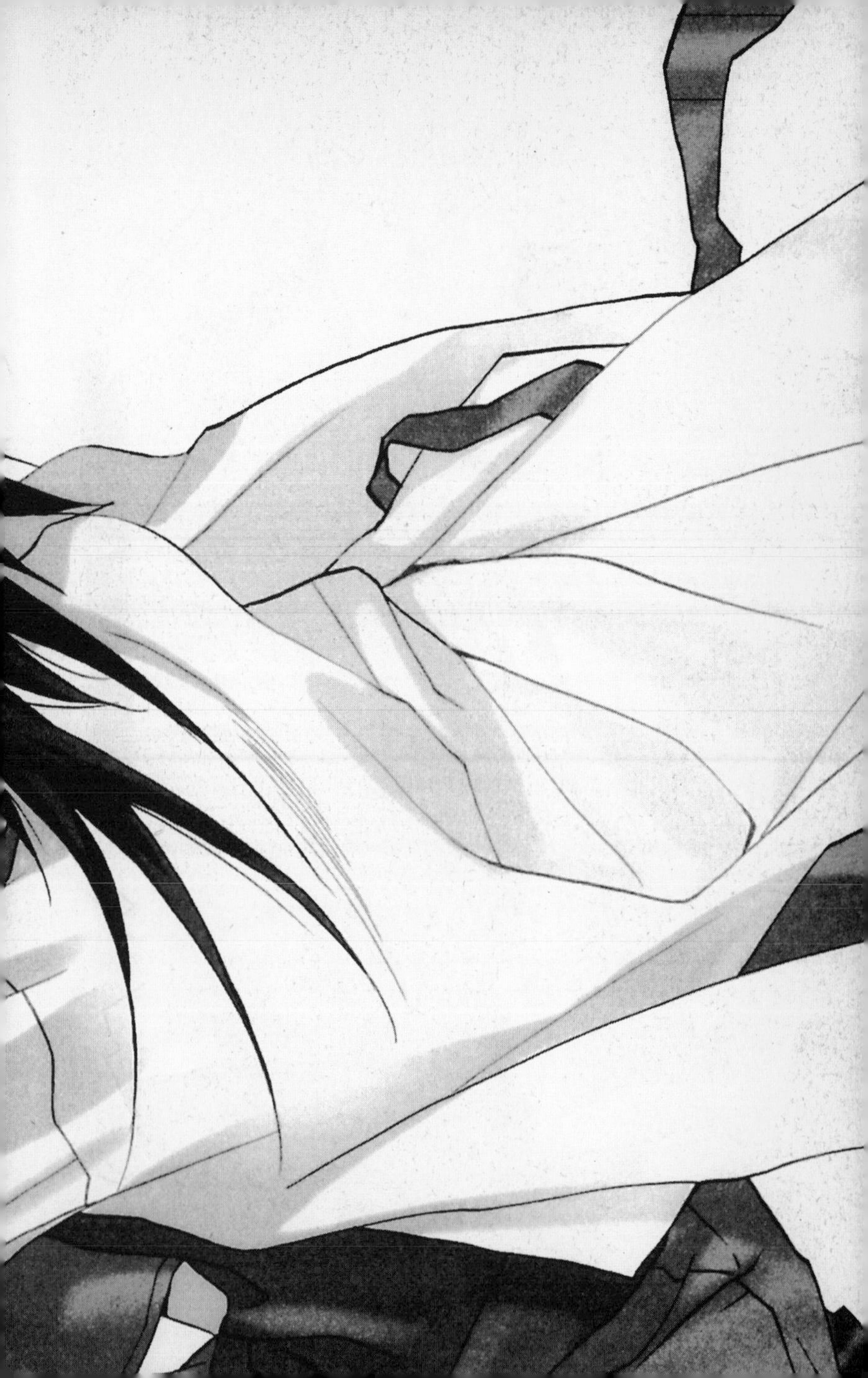

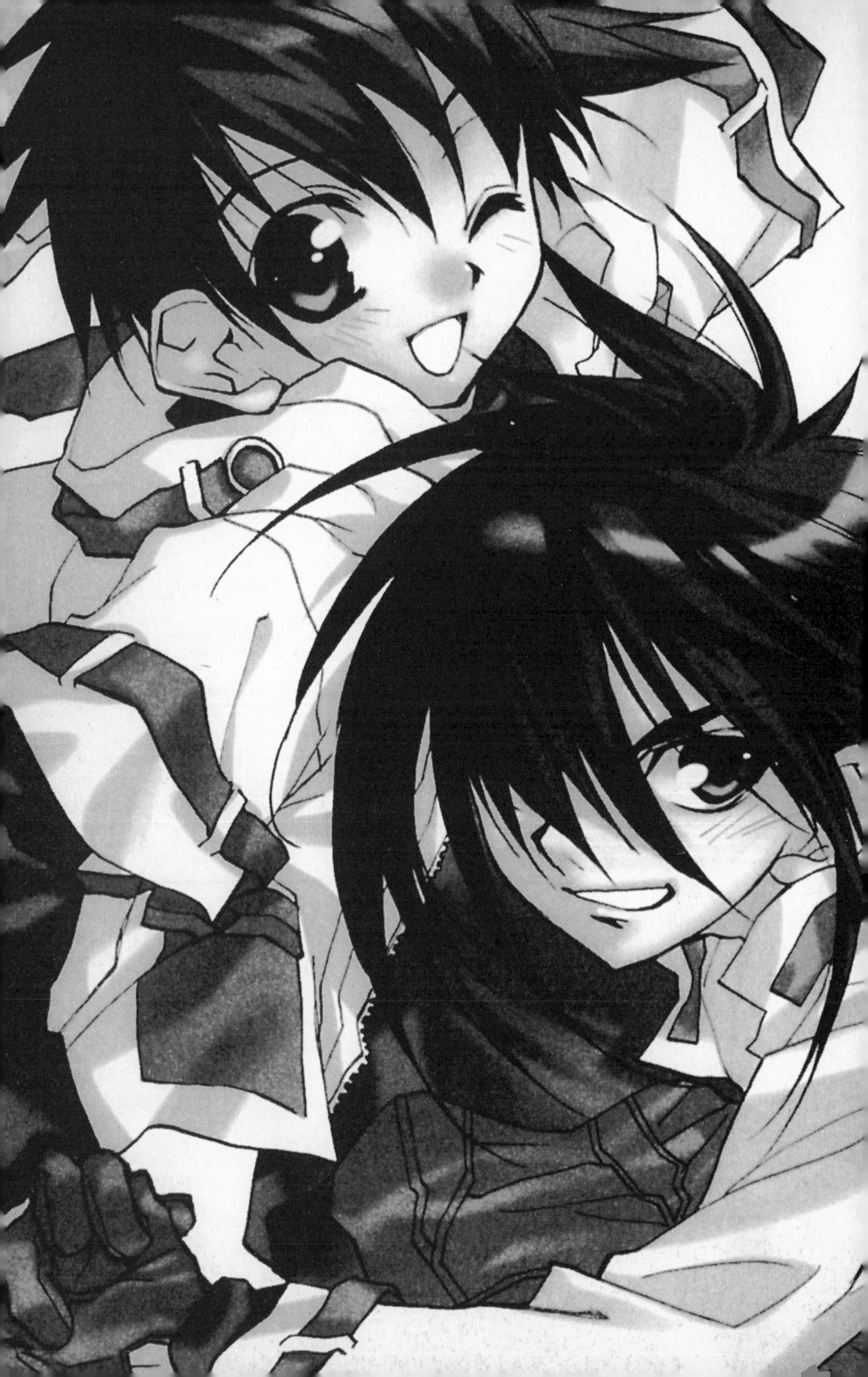

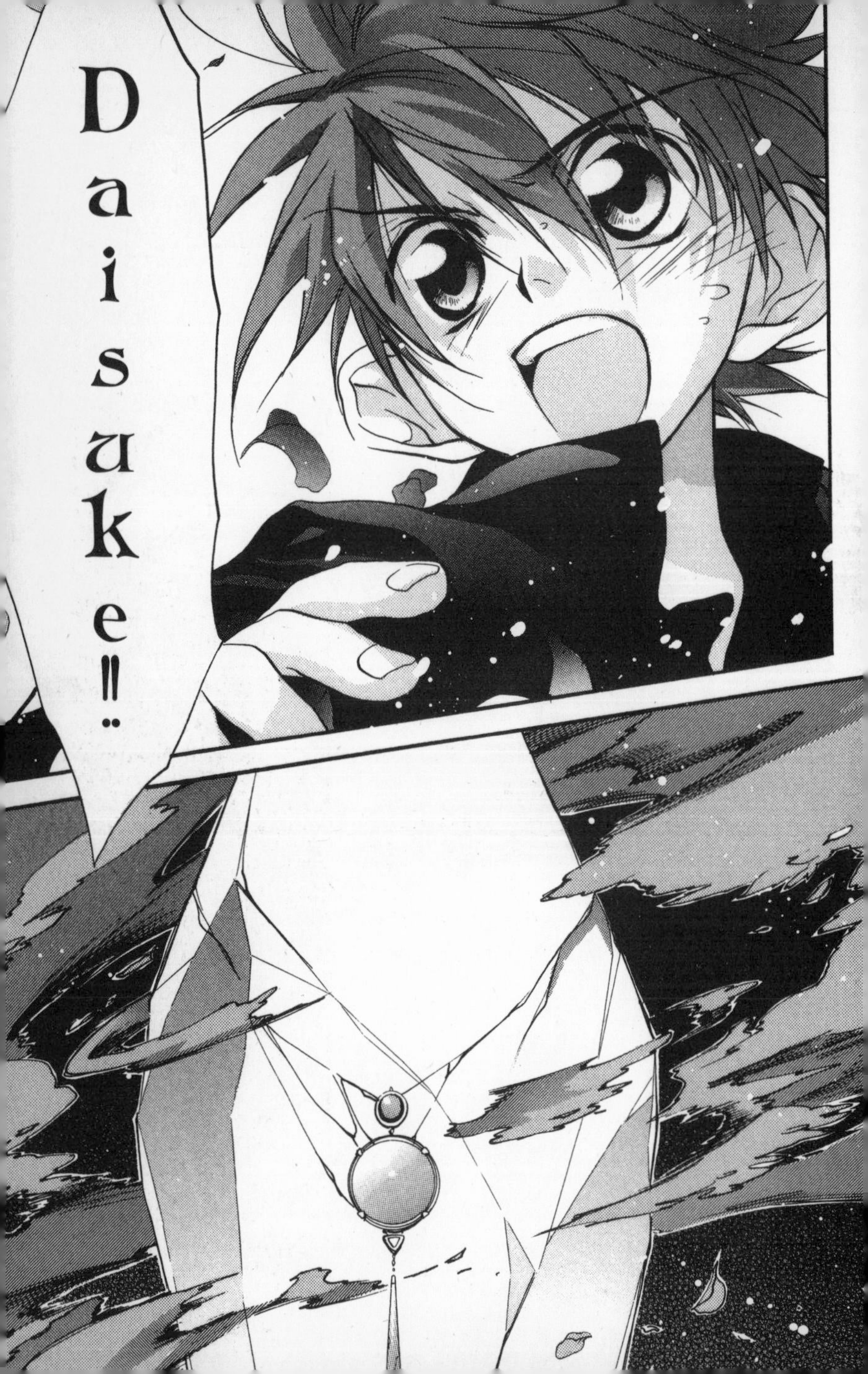
Daisuke!!

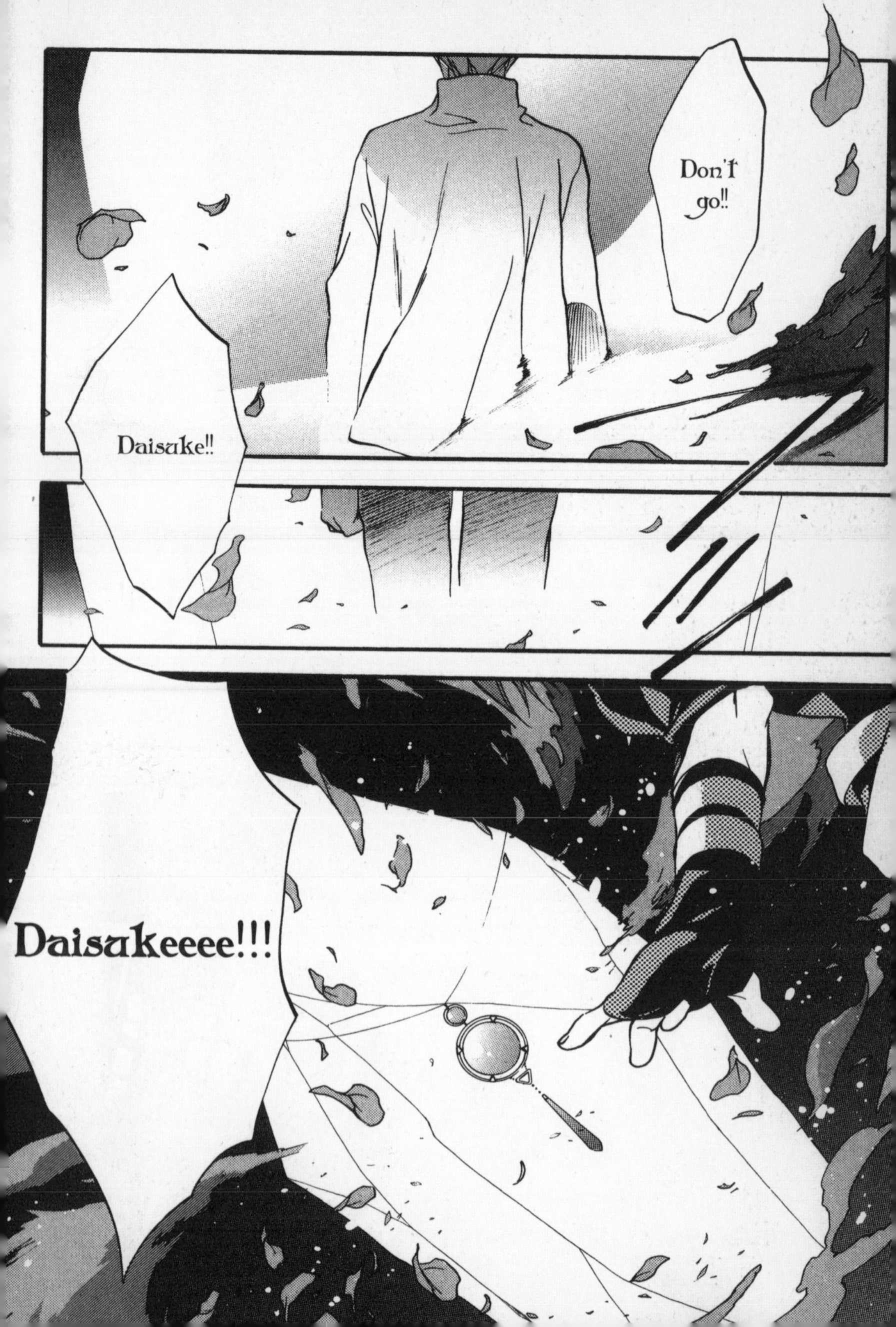
Don't go!!
Daisuke!!
Daisukeeee!!!

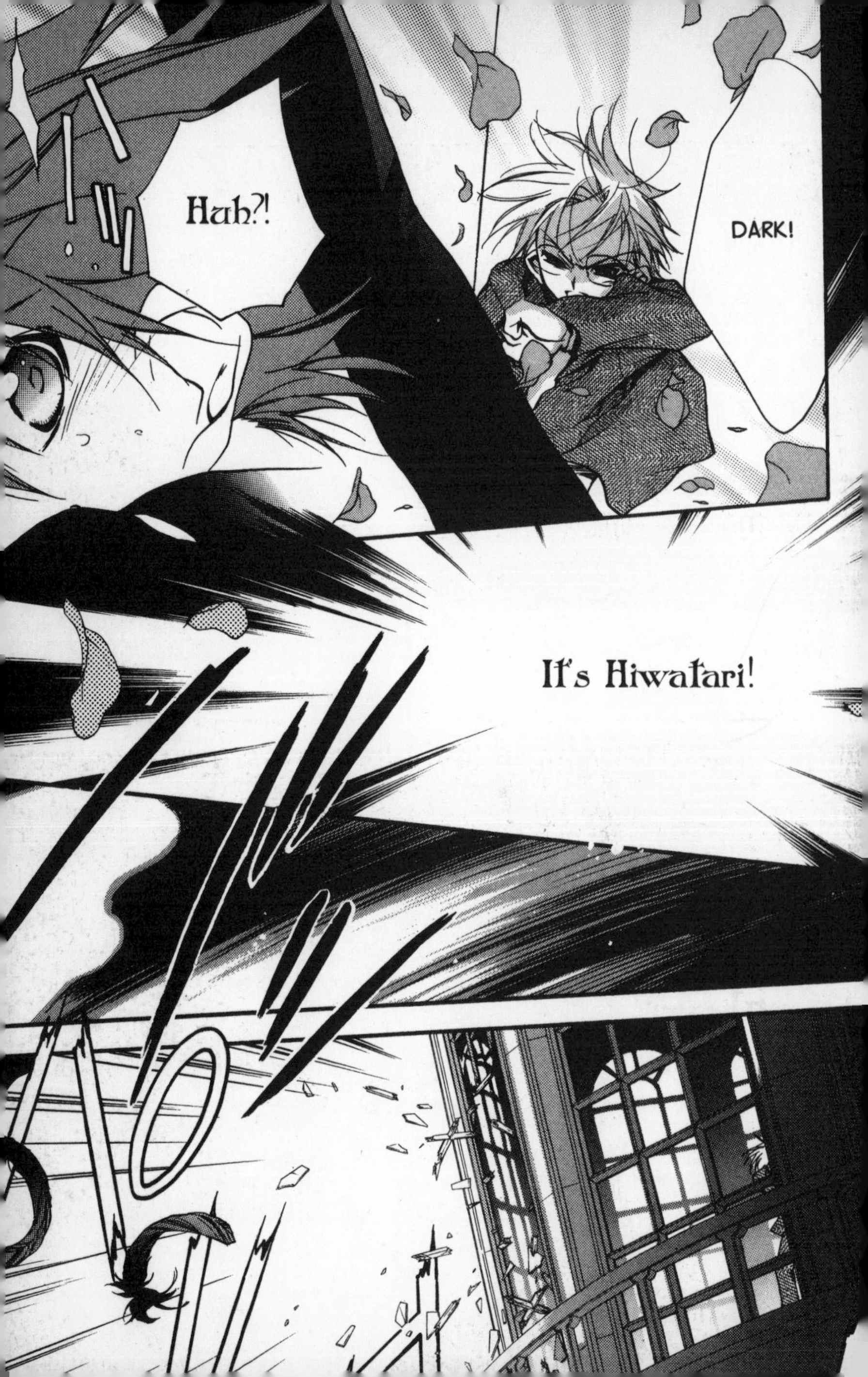
DARK!
Huh?!
It's Hiwatari!

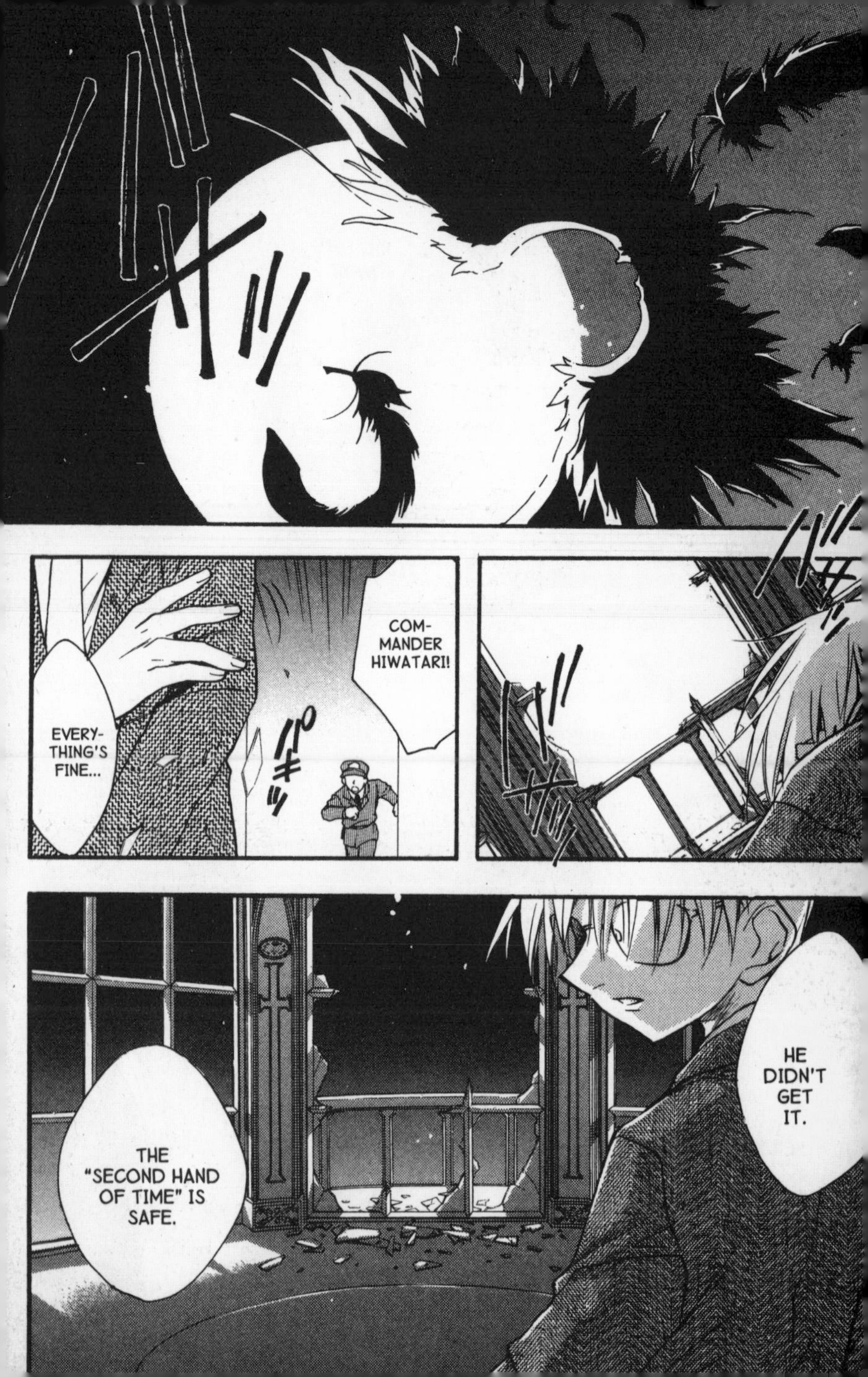
COM-
MANDER
HIWATARI!
EVERY-
THING'S
FINE...
HE
DIDN'T
GET
IT.
THE
"SECOND HAND
OF TIME" IS
SAFE.

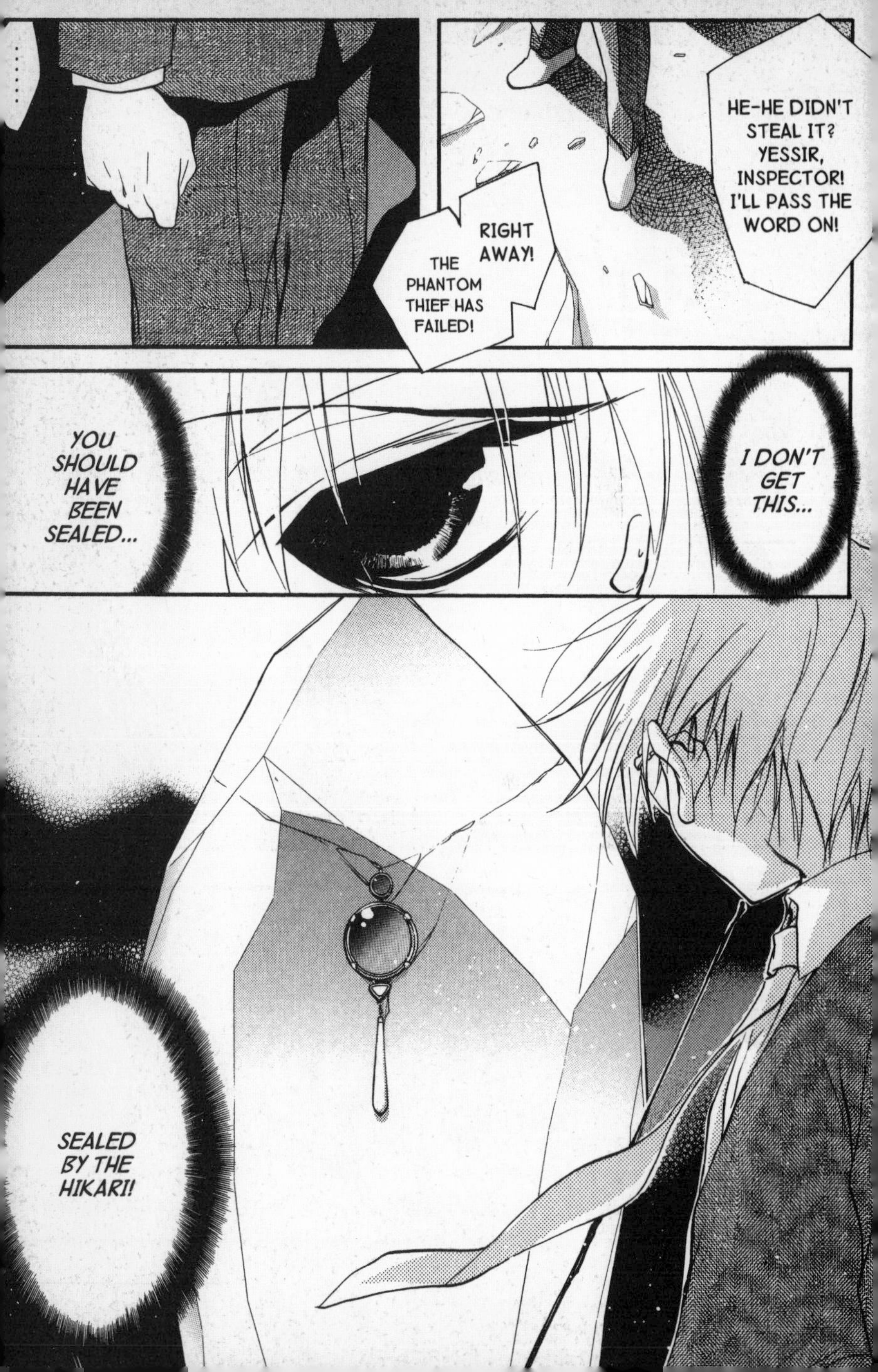
HE-HE DIDN'T STEAL IT? YESSIR, INSPECTOR! I'LL PASS THE WORD ON!
RIGHT AWAY! THE PHANTOM THIEF HAS FAILED!
I DON'T GET THIS...
YOU SHOULD HAVE BEEN SEALED...
SEALED BY THE HIKARI!

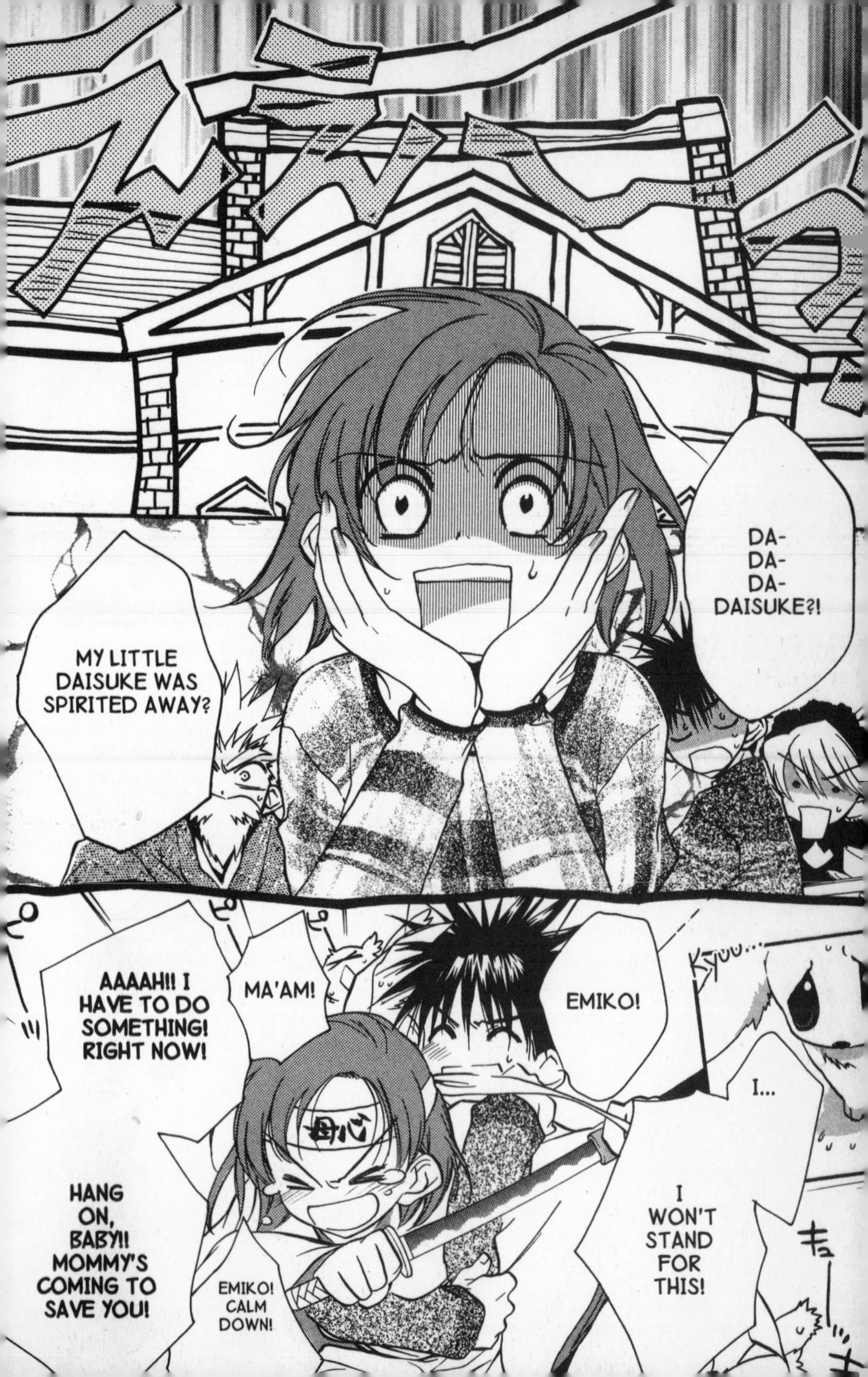
DA-DA-DA-DAISUKE?!
MY LITTLE DAISUKE WAS SPIRITED AWAY?
Kyuu...
EMIKO!
MA'AM!
AAAAH!! I HAVE TO DO SOMETHING! RIGHT NOW!
I...
I WON'T STAND FOR THIS!
HANG ON, BABY!! MOMMY'S COMING TO SAVE YOU!
EMIKO! CALM DOWN!

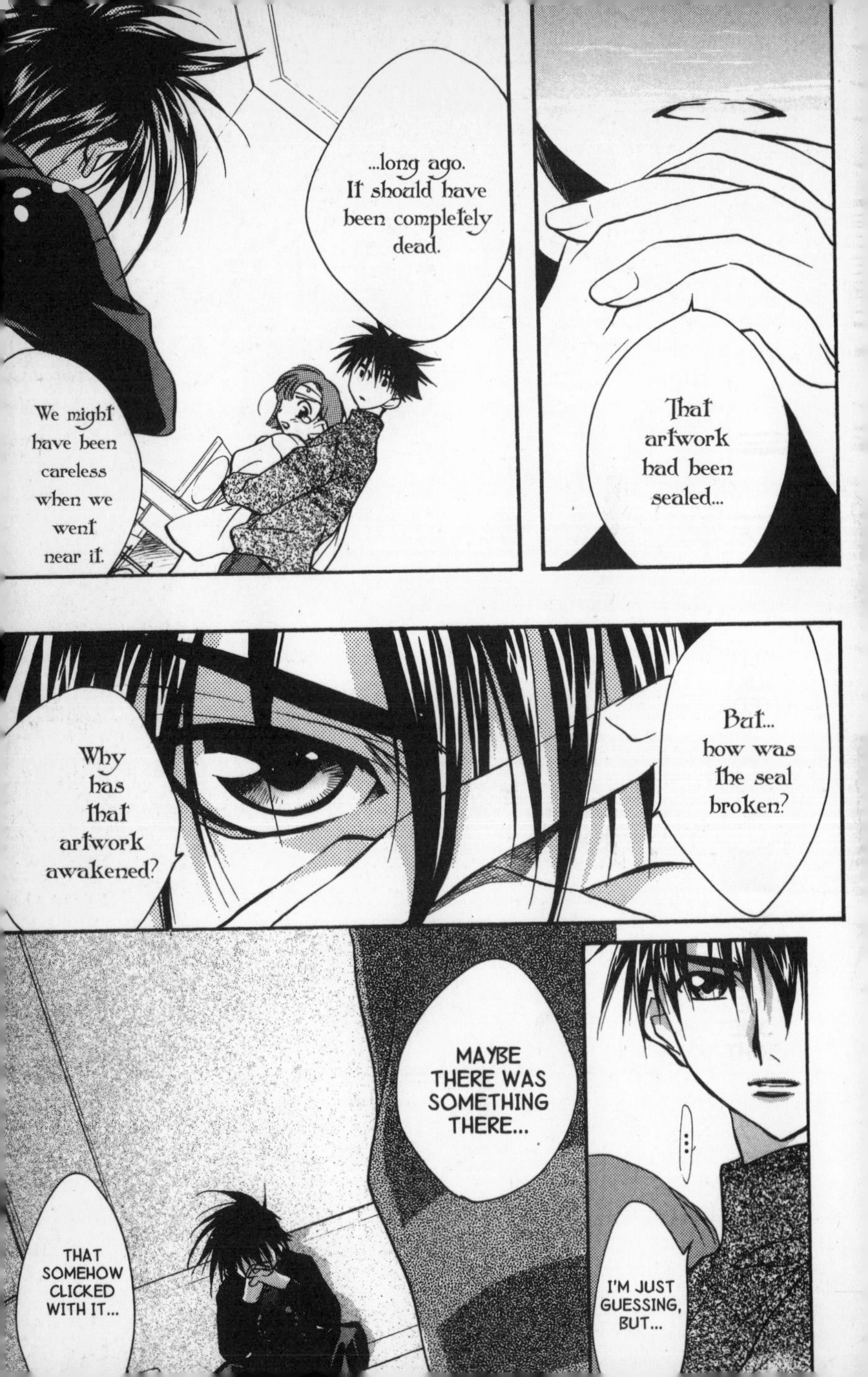
That artwork had been sealed...
...long ago. It should have been completely dead.
We might have been careless when we went near it.
But... how was the seal broken?
Why has that artwork awakened?
...
I'M JUST GUESSING, BUT...
MAYBE THERE WAS SOMETHING THERE...
THAT SOMEHOW CLICKED WITH IT...

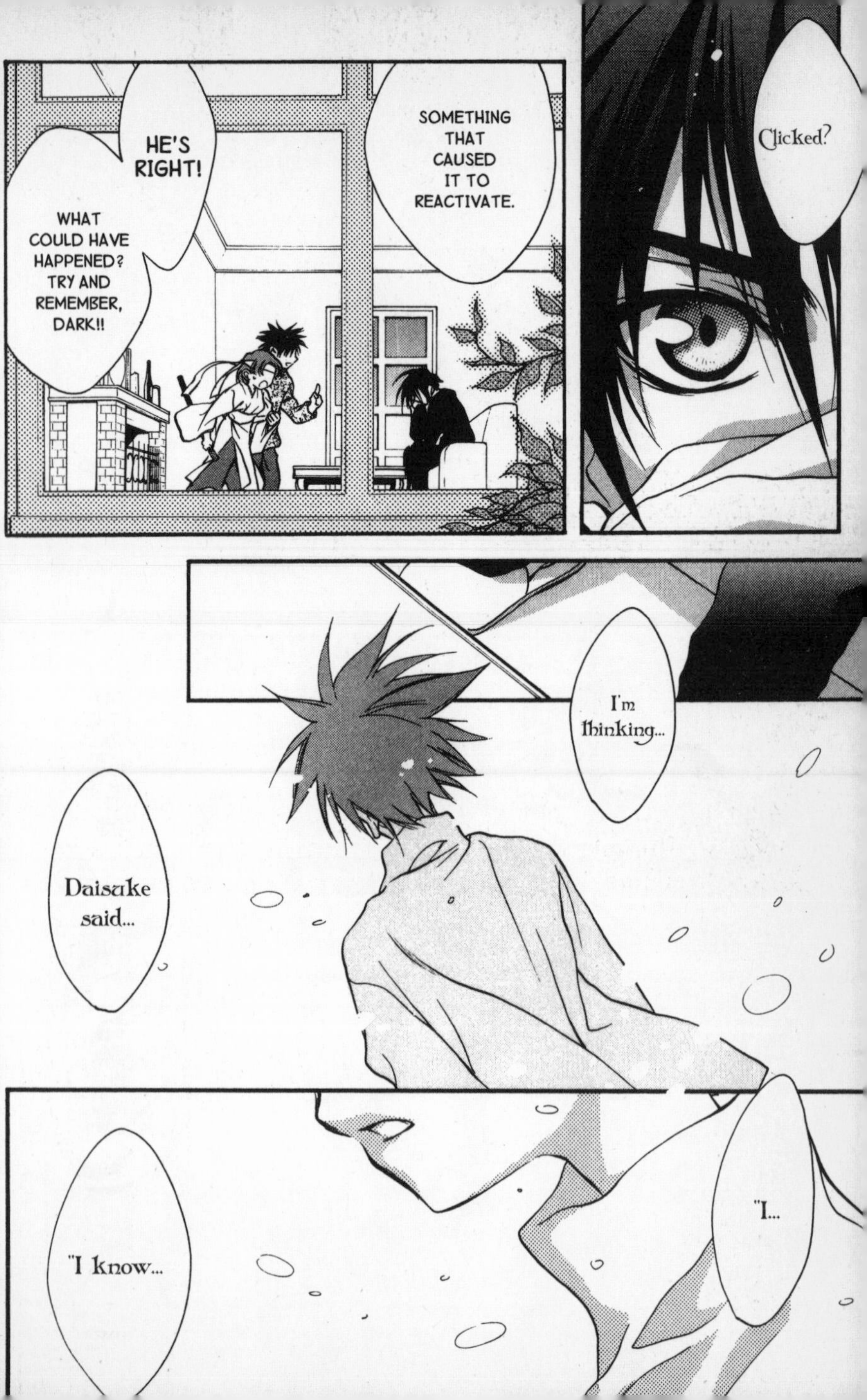
Clicked?
SOMETHING THAT CAUSED IT TO REACTIVATE.
HE'S RIGHT!
WHAT COULD HAVE HAPPENED? TRY AND REMEMBER, DARK!!
I'm thinking...
Daisuke said...
"I...
"I know...

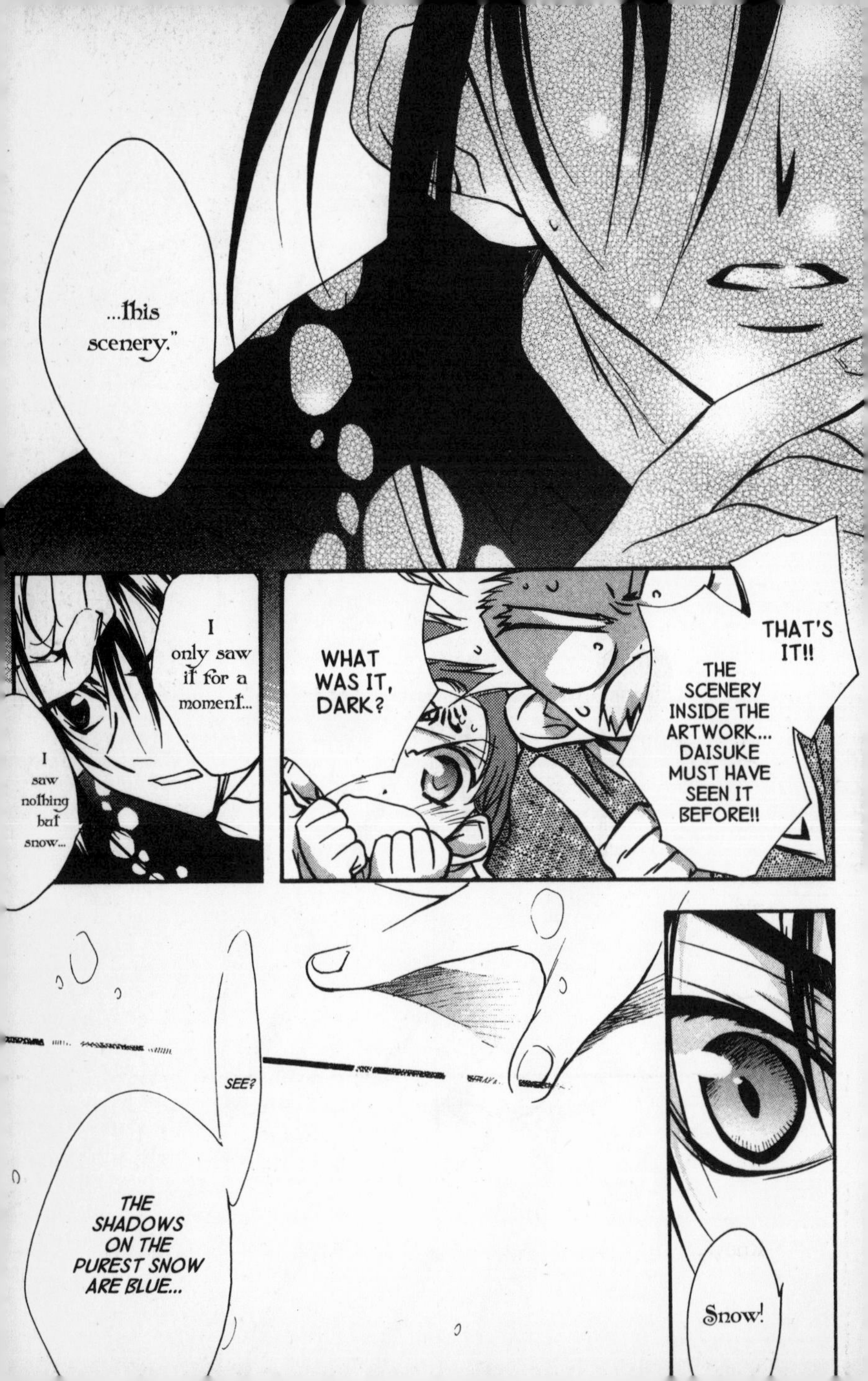
...this scenery."
THAT'S IT!!
THE SCENERY INSIDE THE ARTWORK... DAISUKE MUST HAVE SEEN IT BEFORE!!
WHAT WAS IT, DARK?
I only saw it for a moment...
I saw nothing but snow...
Snow!
SEE?
THE SHADOWS ON THE PUREST SNOW ARE BLUE...

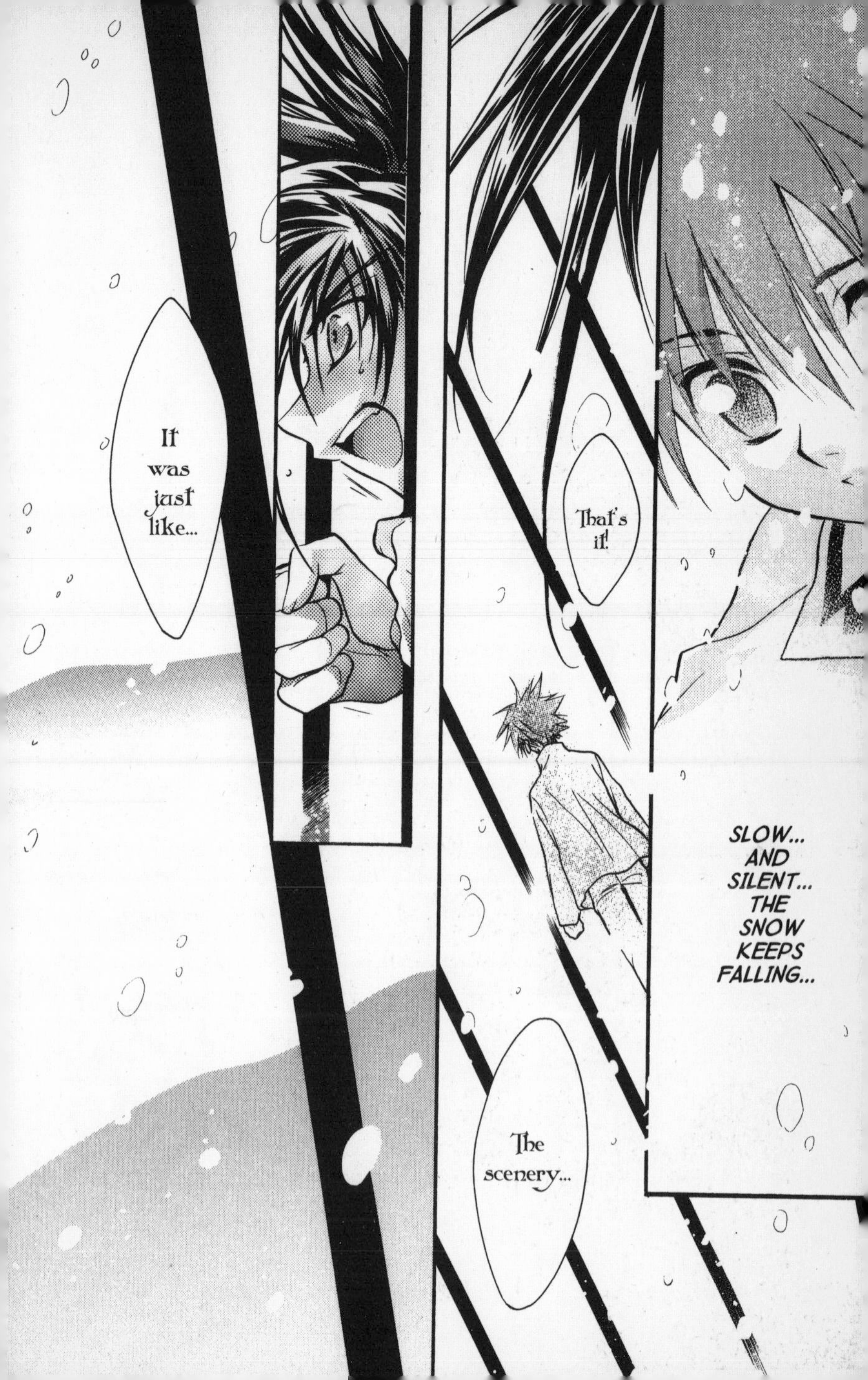
SLOW... AND SILENT... THE SNOW KEEPS FALLING...
That's it!
The scenery...
It was just like...

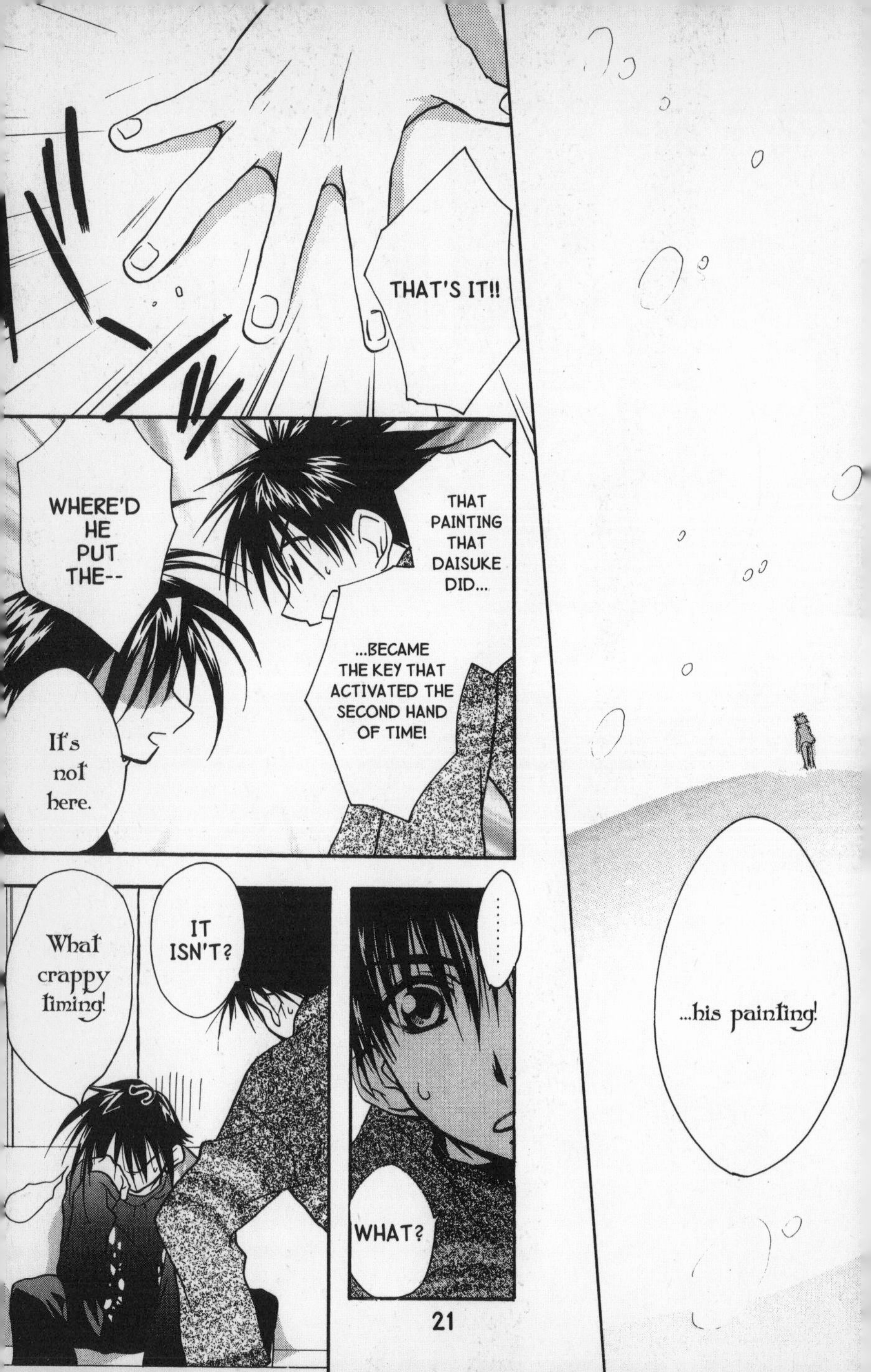
...his painting!
THAT'S IT!!
THAT PAINTING THAT DAISUKE DID...
...BECAME THE KEY THAT ACTIVATED THE SECOND HAND OF TIME!
WHERE'D HE PUT THE--
It's not here.
......
WHAT?
IT ISN'T?
What crappy timing!

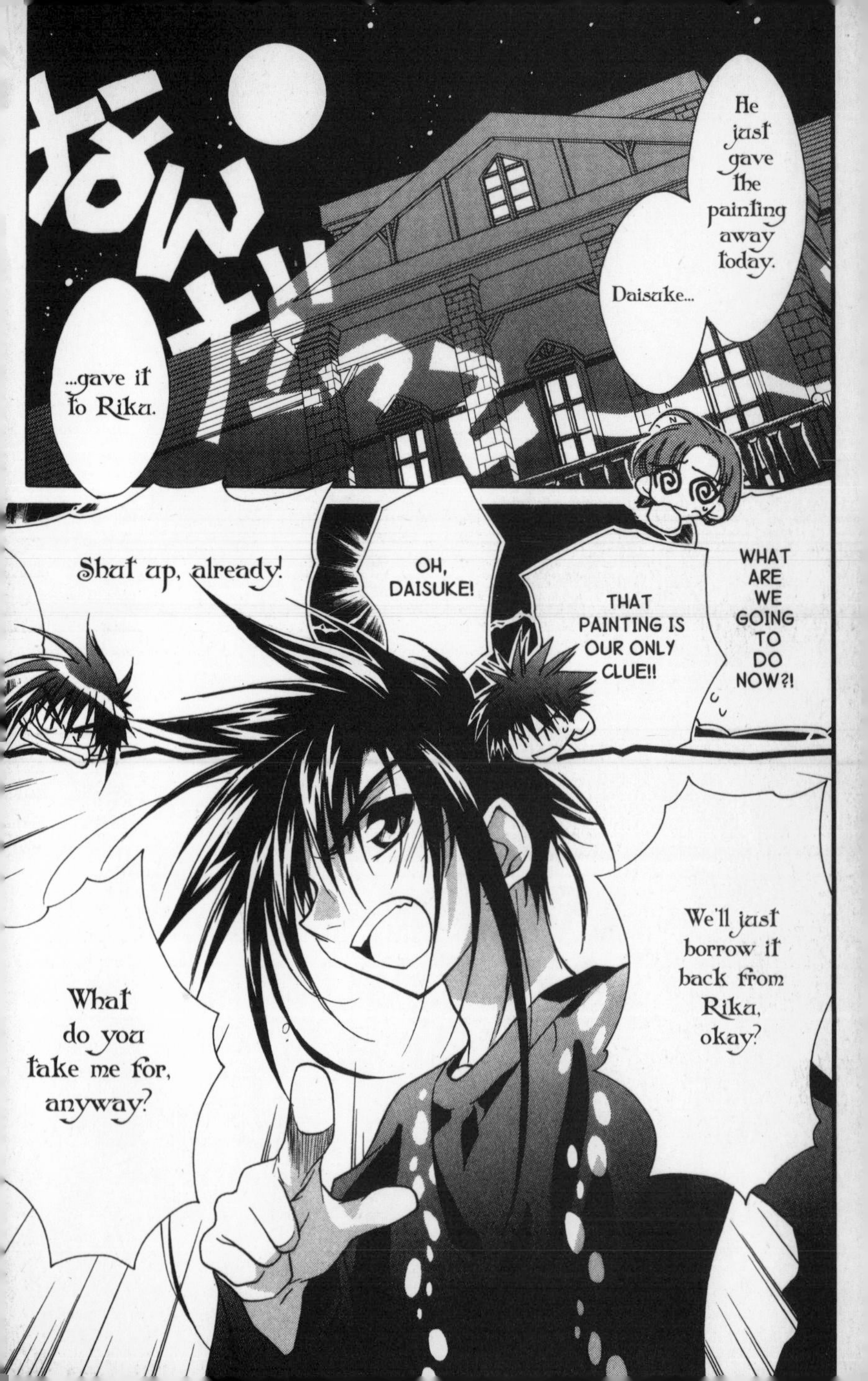
He just gave the painting away today.
Daisuke...
...gave it to Riku.
WHAT ARE WE GOING TO DO NOW?!
THAT PAINTING IS OUR ONLY CLUE!!
OH, DAISUKE!
Shut up, already!
We'll just borrow it back from Riku, okay?
What do you take me for, anyway?

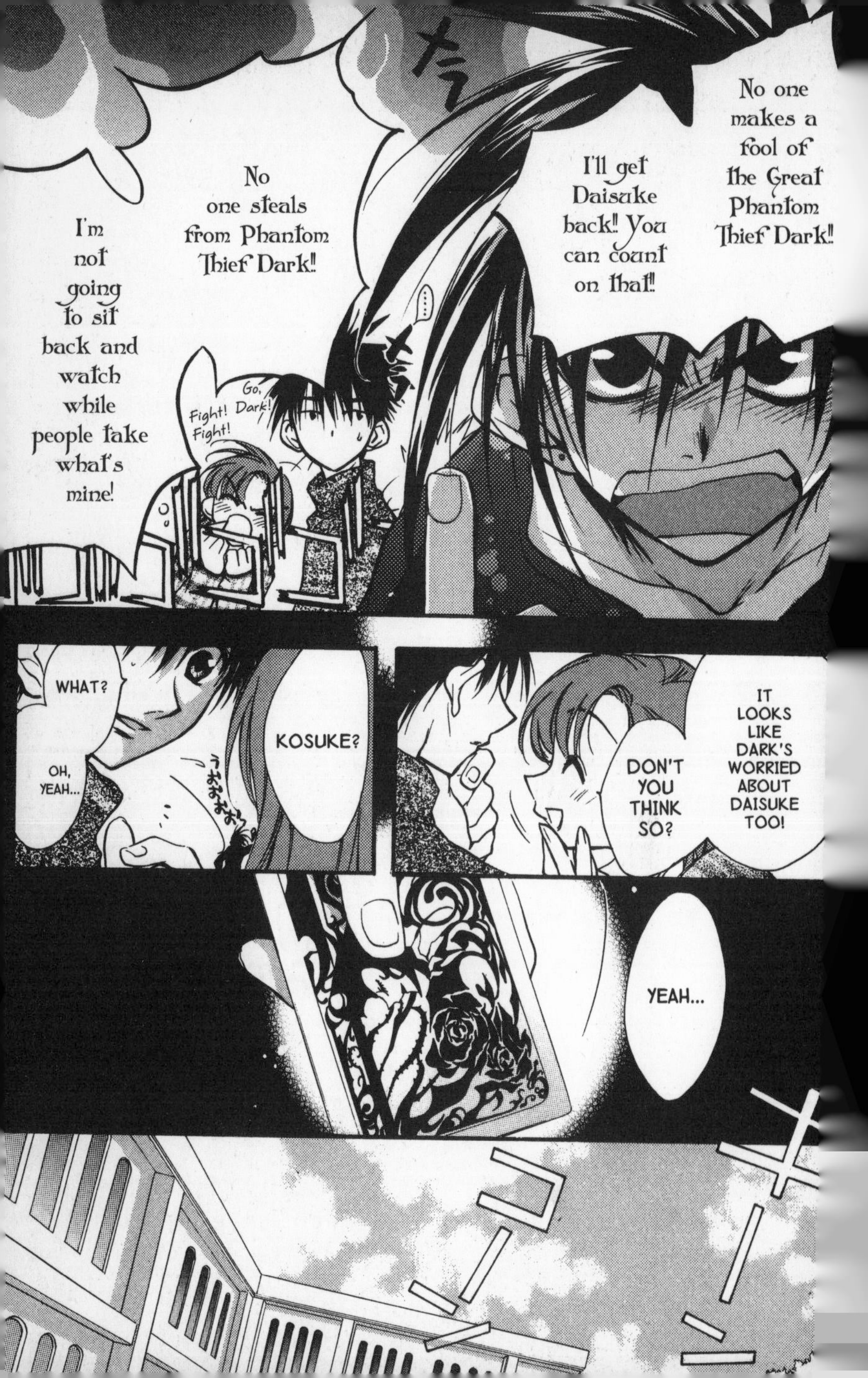
No one makes a fool of the Great Phantom Thief Dark!!
I'll get Daisuke back!! You can count on that!!
No one steals from Phantom Thief Dark!!
I'm not going to sit back and watch while people take what's mine!
Go, Dark!
Fight! Fight!
IT LOOKS LIKE DARK'S WORRIED ABOUT DAISUKE TOO!
DON'T YOU THINK SO?
KOSUKE?
WHAT?
OH, YEAH...
YEAH...

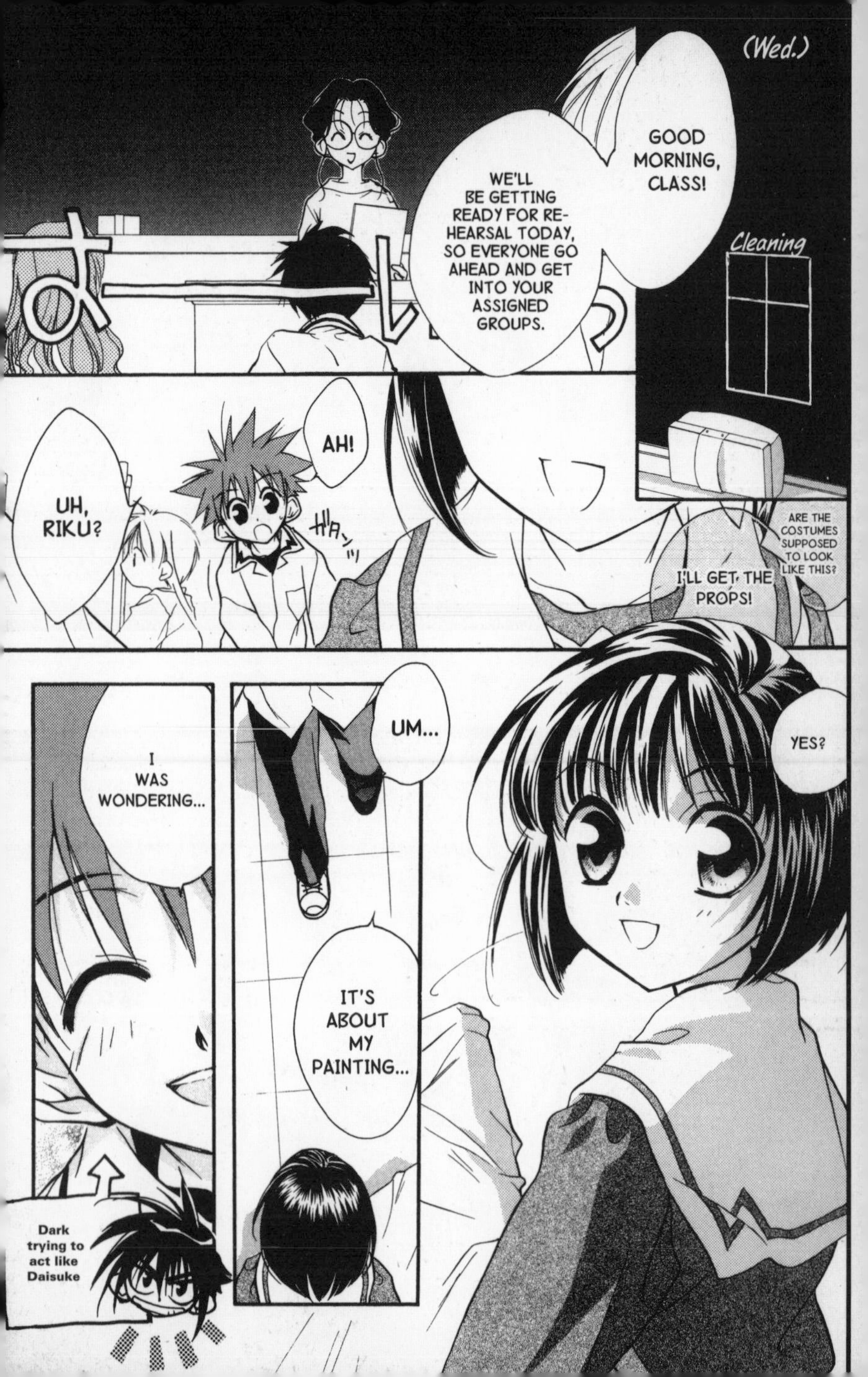
(Wed.)
GOOD MORNING, CLASS!
WE'LL BE GETTING READY FOR RE-HEARSAL TODAY, SO EVERYONE GO AHEAD AND GET INTO YOUR ASSIGNED GROUPS.
Cleaning
ARE THE COSTUMES SUPPOSED TO LOOK LIKE THIS?
I'LL GET THE PROPS!
AH!
UH, RIKU?
YES?
UM...
IT'S ABOUT MY PAINTING...
I WAS WONDERING...
Dark trying to act like Daisuke

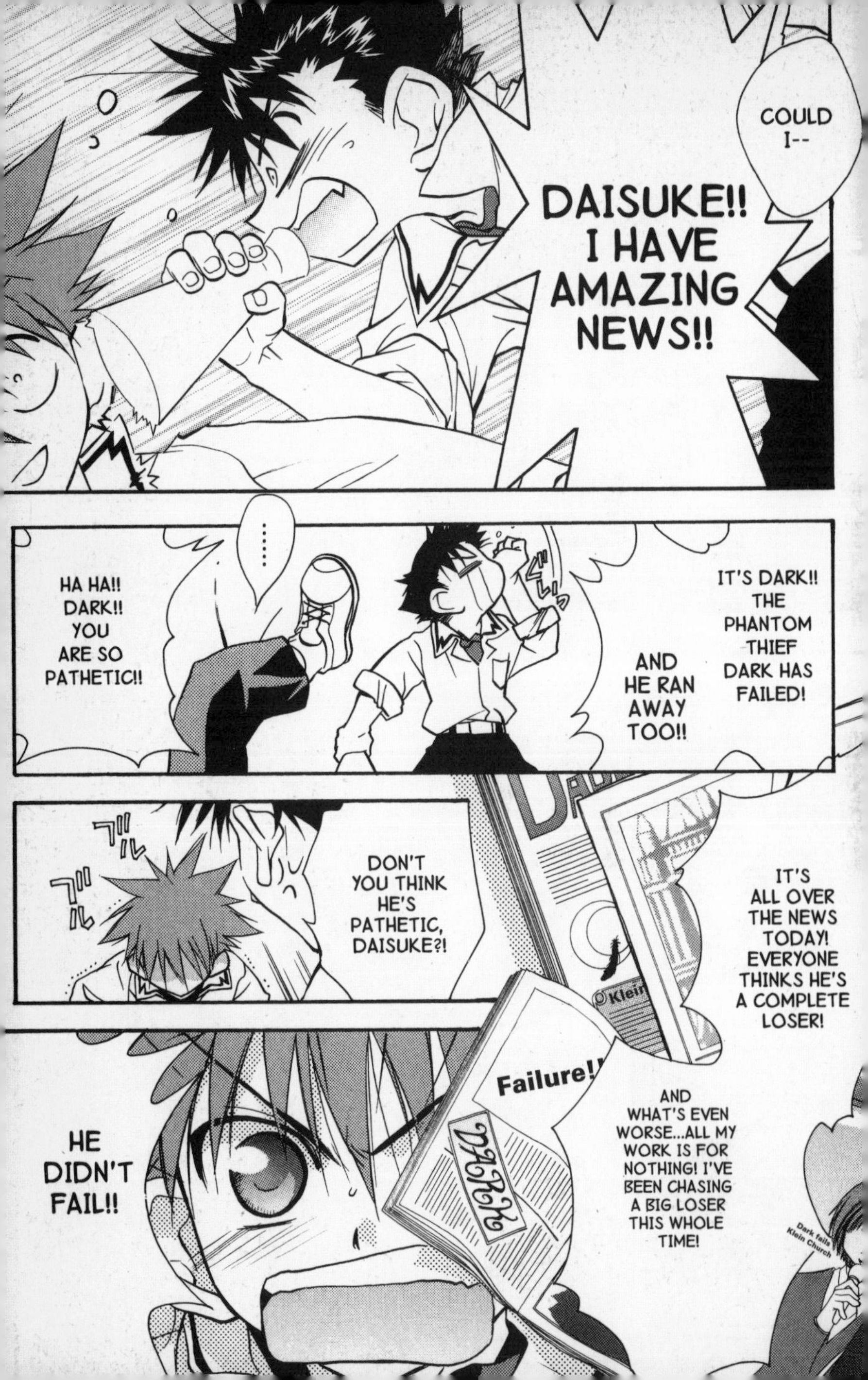
COULD I--
DAISUKE!! I HAVE AMAZING NEWS!!
IT'S DARK!! THE PHANTOM THIEF DARK HAS FAILED!
AND HE RAN AWAY TOO!!
HA HA!! DARK!! YOU ARE SO PATHETIC!!
......
IT'S ALL OVER THE NEWS TODAY! EVERYONE THINKS HE'S A COMPLETE LOSER!
DON'T YOU THINK HE'S PATHETIC, DAISUKE?!
ブル
ブル
Klein
Dark fails Klein Church
AND WHAT'S EVEN WORSE...ALL MY WORK IS FOR NOTHING! I'VE BEEN CHASING A BIG LOSER THIS WHOLE TIME!
Failure!!
HE DIDN'T FAIL!!

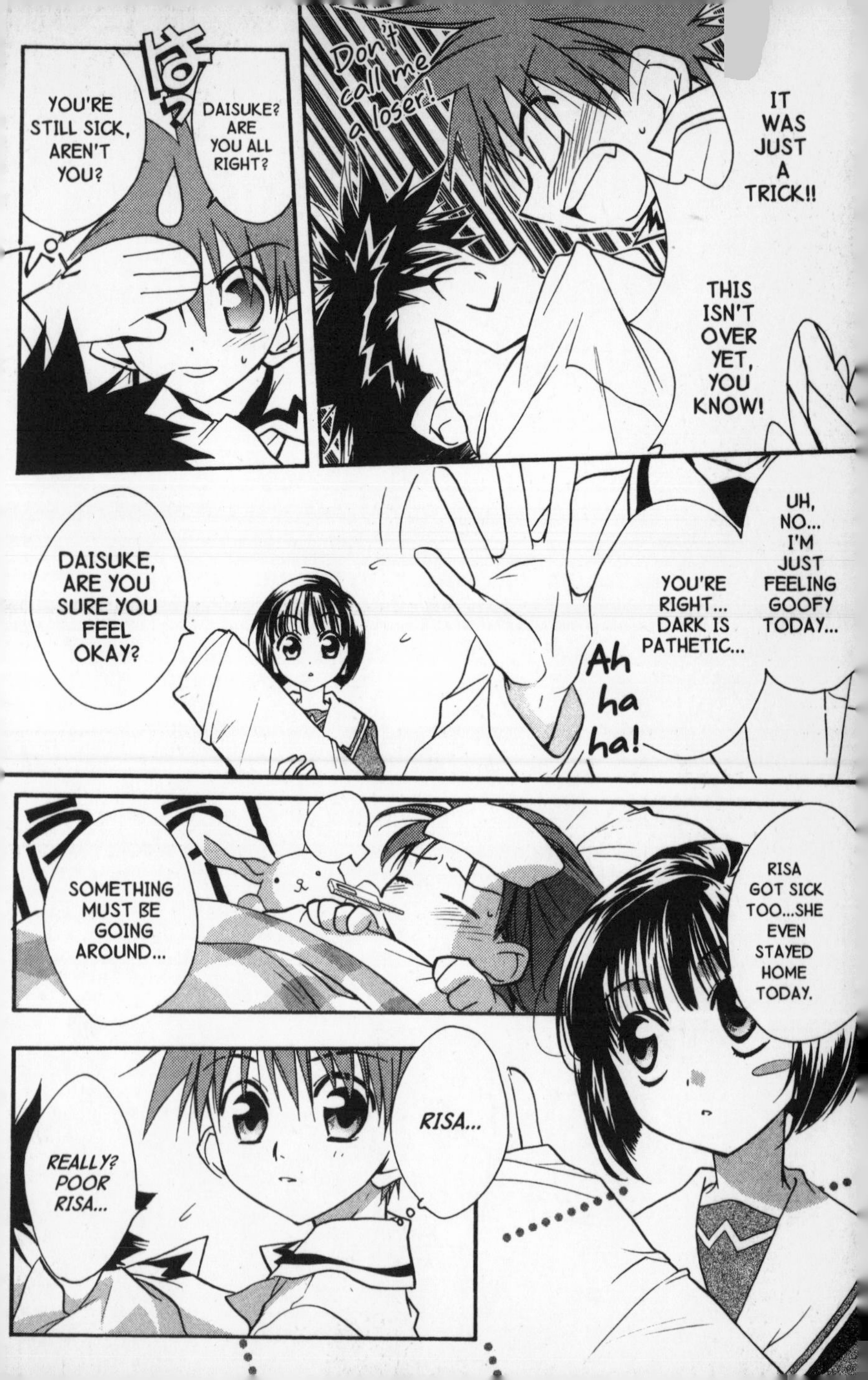
Don't call me a loser!
IT WAS JUST A TRICK!!
THIS ISN'T OVER YET, YOU KNOW!
DAISUKE? ARE YOU ALL RIGHT?
YOU'RE STILL SICK, AREN'T YOU?
UH, NO... I'M JUST FEELING GOOFY TODAY...
YOU'RE RIGHT... DARK IS PATHETIC...
Ah ha ha!
DAISUKE, ARE YOU SURE YOU FEEL OKAY?
RISA GOT SICK TOO...SHE EVEN STAYED HOME TODAY.
SOMETHING MUST BE GOING AROUND...
RISA...
REALLY? POOR RISA...

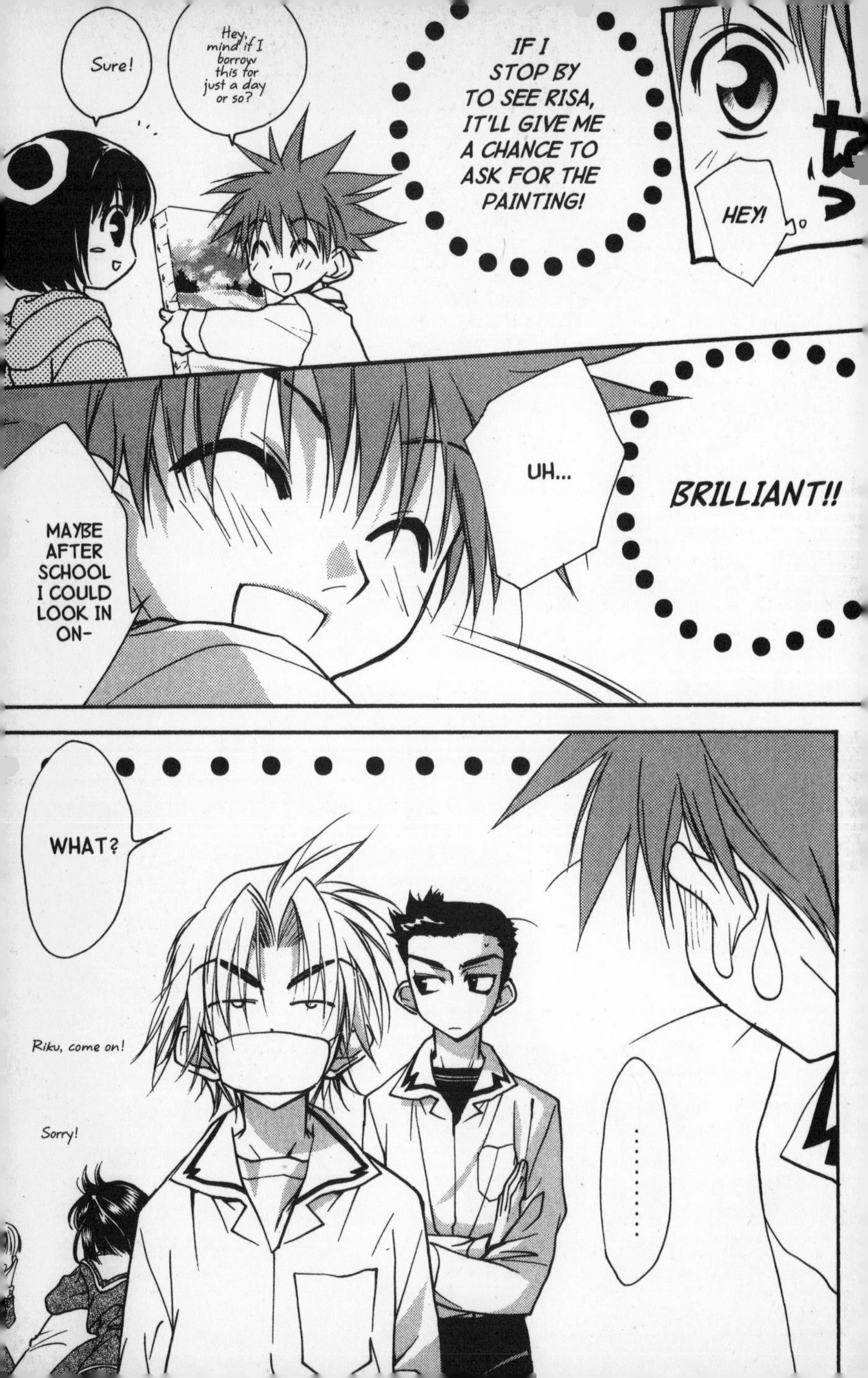
HEY!
IF I STOP BY TO SEE RISA, IT'LL GIVE ME A CHANCE TO ASK FOR THE PAINTING!
Hey, mind if I borrow this for just a day or so?
Sure!
BRILLIANT!!
UH...
MAYBE AFTER SCHOOL I COULD LOOK IN ON-
......
WHAT?
Riku, come on!
Sorry!

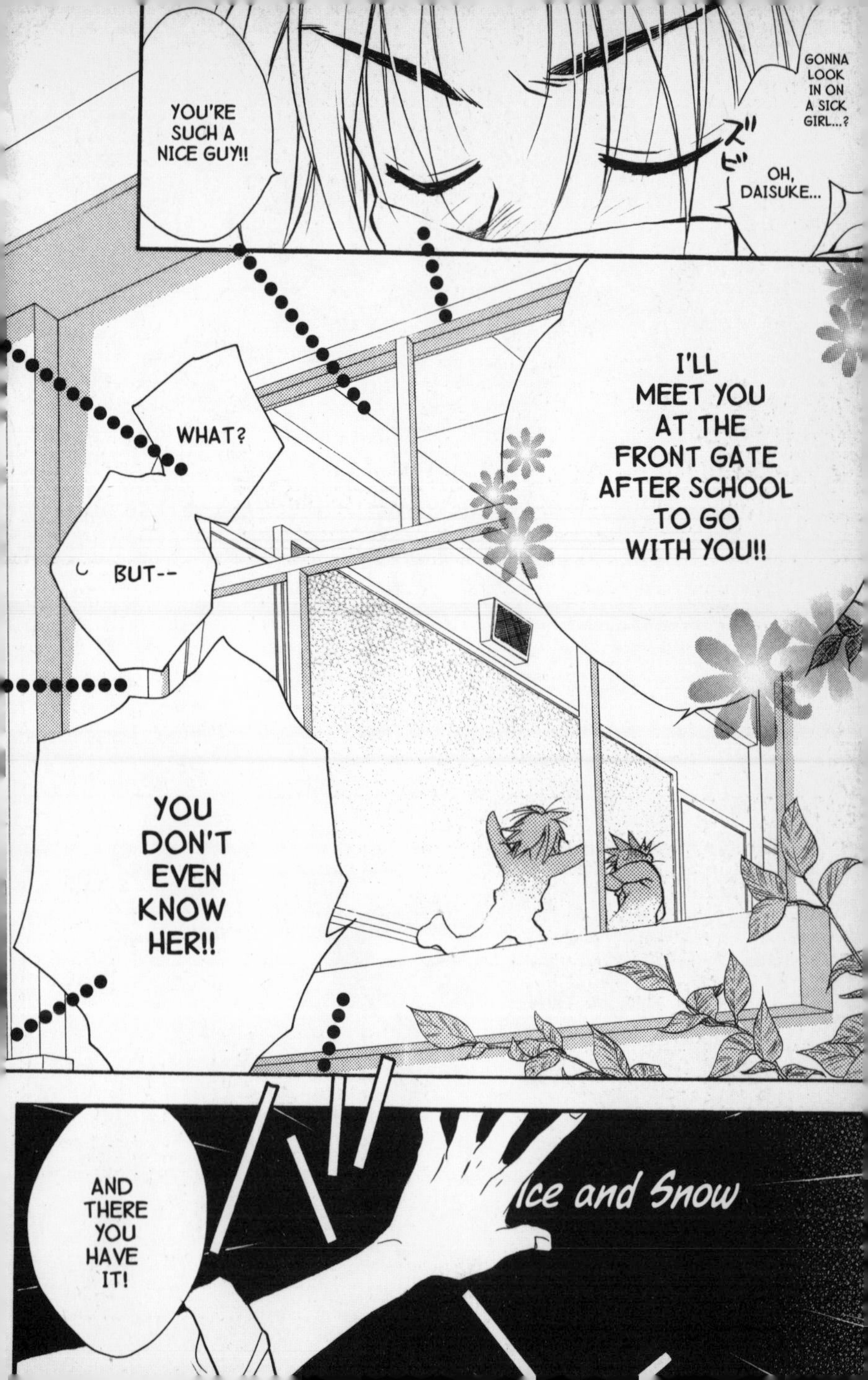
GONNA LOOK IN ON A SICK GIRL...?
ズビ
OH, DAISUKE...
YOU'RE SUCH A NICE GUY!!
I'LL MEET YOU AT THE FRONT GATE AFTER SCHOOL TO GO WITH YOU!!
WHAT?
BUT--
YOU DON'T EVEN KNOW HER!!
Ice and Snow
AND THERE YOU HAVE IT!

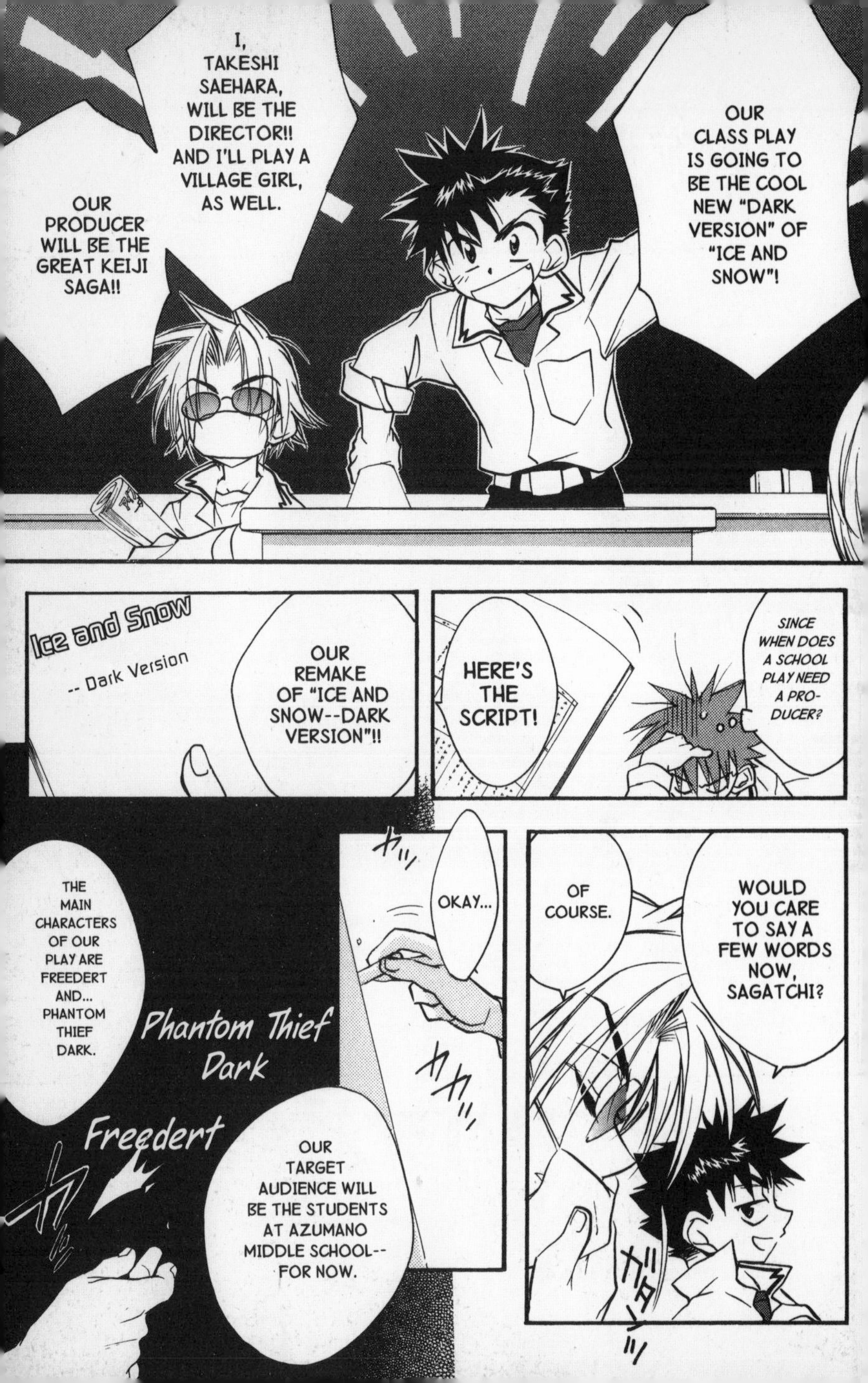
OUR CLASS PLAY IS GOING TO BE THE COOL NEW "DARK VERSION" OF "ICE AND SNOW"!
I, TAKESHI SAEHARA, WILL BE THE DIRECTOR!! AND I'LL PLAY A VILLAGE GIRL, AS WELL.
OUR PRODUCER WILL BE THE GREAT KEIJI SAGA!!
SINCE WHEN DOES A SCHOOL PLAY NEED A PRO-DUCER?
HERE'S THE SCRIPT!
OUR REMAKE OF "ICE AND SNOW--DARK VERSION"!!
Ice and Snow
-- Dark Version
WOULD YOU CARE TO SAY A FEW WORDS NOW, SAGATCHI?
OF COURSE.
OKAY...
THE MAIN CHARACTERS OF OUR PLAY ARE FREEDERT AND... PHANTOM THIEF DARK.
Phantom Thief Dark
Freedert
OUR TARGET AUDIENCE WILL BE THE STUDENTS AT AZUMANO MIDDLE SCHOOL--FOR NOW.

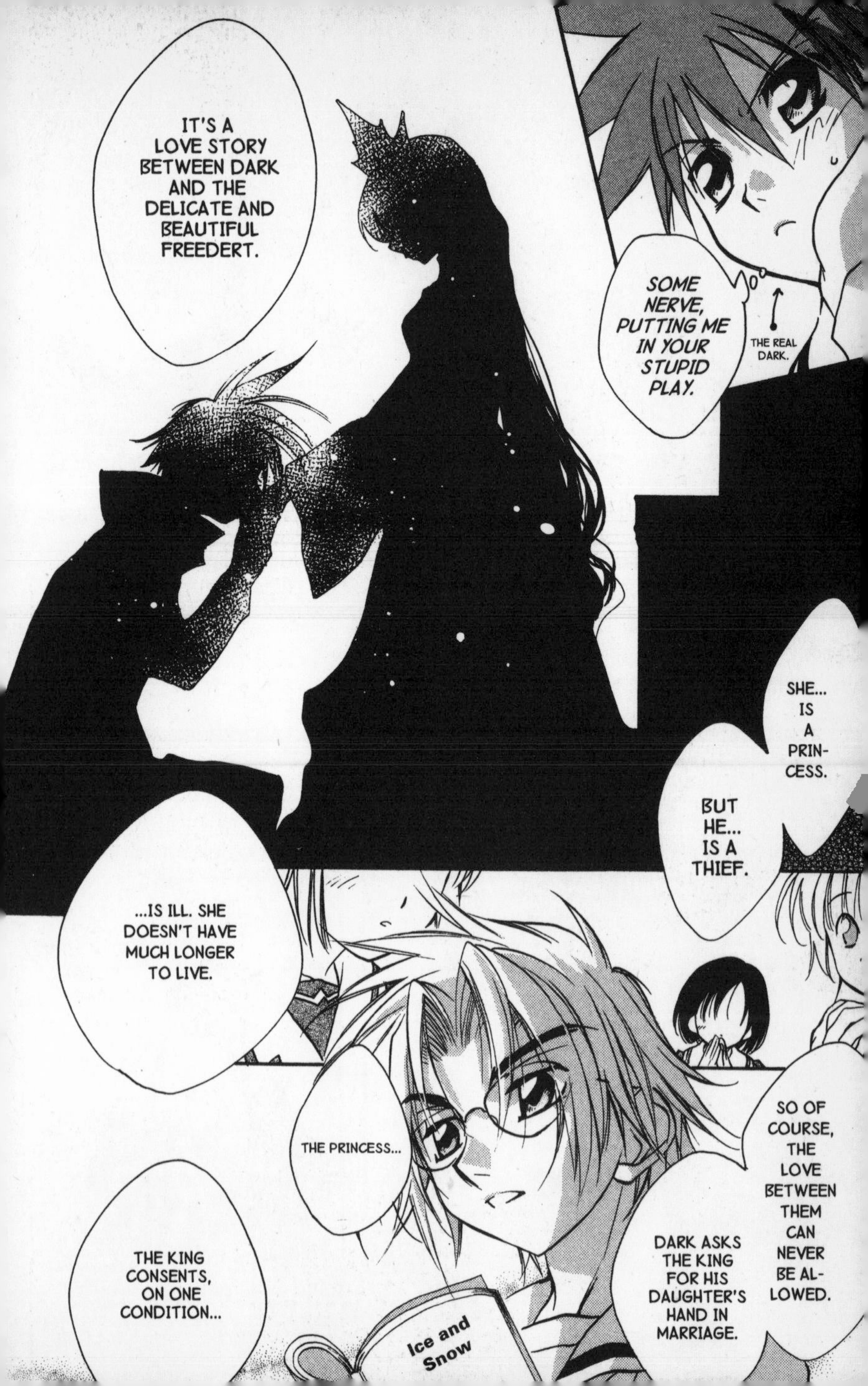
IT'S A LOVE STORY BETWEEN DARK AND THE DELICATE AND BEAUTIFUL FREEDERT.
SOME NERVE, PUTTING ME IN YOUR STUPID PLAY.
THE REAL DARK.
SHE... IS A PRIN-CESS.
BUT HE... IS A THIEF.
SO OF COURSE, THE LOVE BETWEEN THEM CAN NEVER BE AL-LOWED.
THE PRINCESS...
...IS ILL. SHE DOESN'T HAVE MUCH LONGER TO LIVE.
DARK ASKS THE KING FOR HIS DAUGHTER'S HAND IN MARRIAGE.
THE KING CONSENTS, ON ONE CONDITION...
Ice and Snow

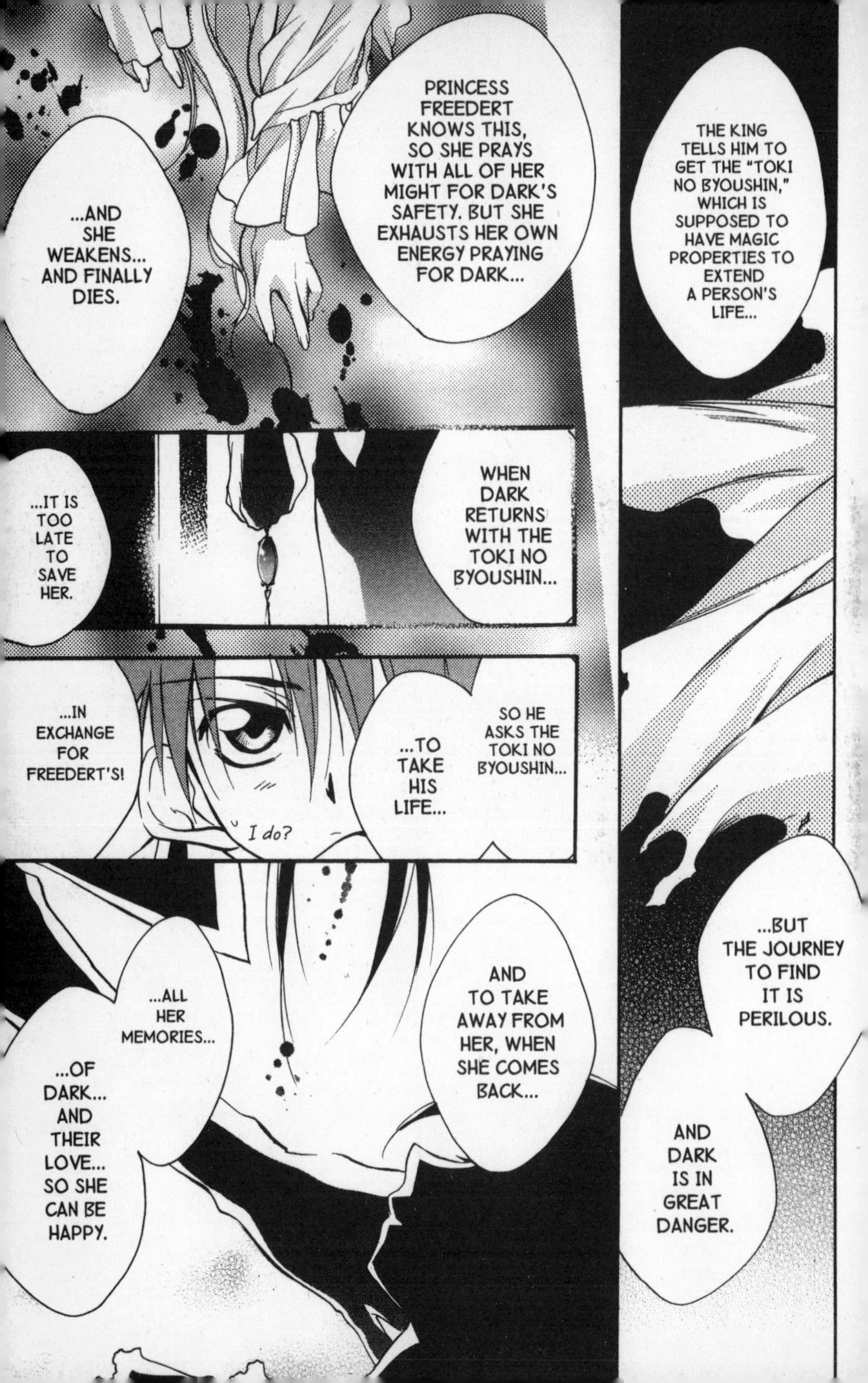
THE KING TELLS HIM TO GET THE "TOKI NO BYOUSHIN," WHICH IS SUPPOSED TO HAVE MAGIC PROPERTIES TO EXTEND A PERSON'S LIFE...
...BUT THE JOURNEY TO FIND IT IS PERILOUS.
AND DARK IS IN GREAT DANGER.
PRINCESS FREEDERT KNOWS THIS, SO SHE PRAYS WITH ALL OF HER MIGHT FOR DARK'S SAFETY. BUT SHE EXHAUSTS HER OWN ENERGY PRAYING FOR DARK...
...AND SHE WEAKENS... AND FINALLY DIES.
WHEN DARK RETURNS WITH THE TOKI NO BYOUSHIN...
...IT IS TOO LATE TO SAVE HER.
SO HE ASKS THE TOKI NO BYOUSHIN...
...TO TAKE HIS LIFE...
I do?
...IN EXCHANGE FOR FREEDERT'S!
AND TO TAKE AWAY FROM HER, WHEN SHE COMES BACK...
...ALL HER MEMORIES...
...OF DARK... AND THEIR LOVE... SO SHE CAN BE HAPPY.

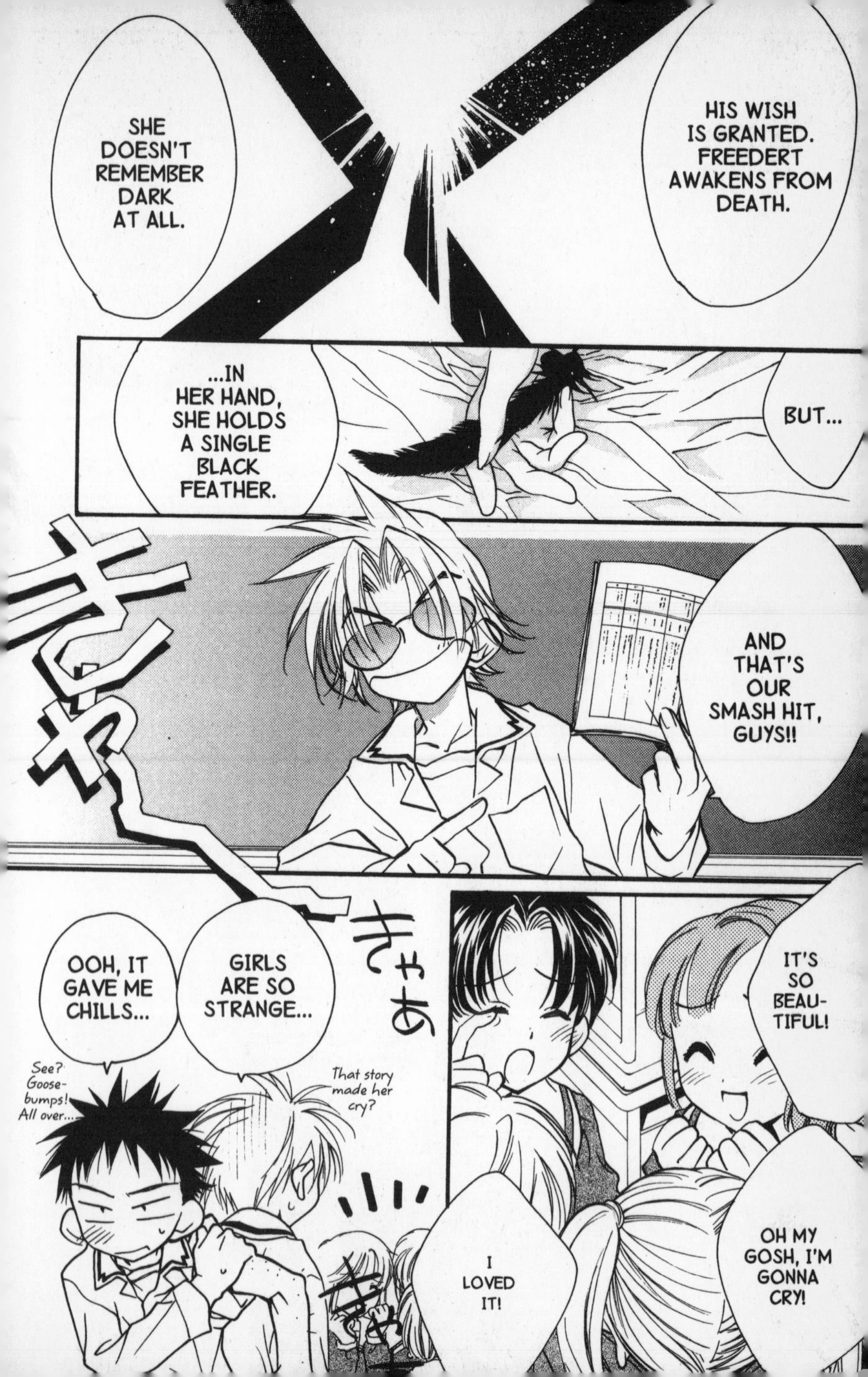
HIS WISH IS GRANTED. FREEDERT AWAKENS FROM DEATH.
SHE DOESN'T REMEMBER DARK AT ALL.
BUT...
...IN HER HAND, SHE HOLDS A SINGLE BLACK FEATHER.
AND THAT'S OUR SMASH HIT, GUYS!!
きゃ
IT'S SO BEAU-TIFUL!
OH MY GOSH, I'M GONNA CRY!
I LOVED IT!
きゃあ
GIRLS ARE SO STRANGE...
OOH, IT GAVE ME CHILLS...
That story made her cry?
See? Goose-bumps! All over...

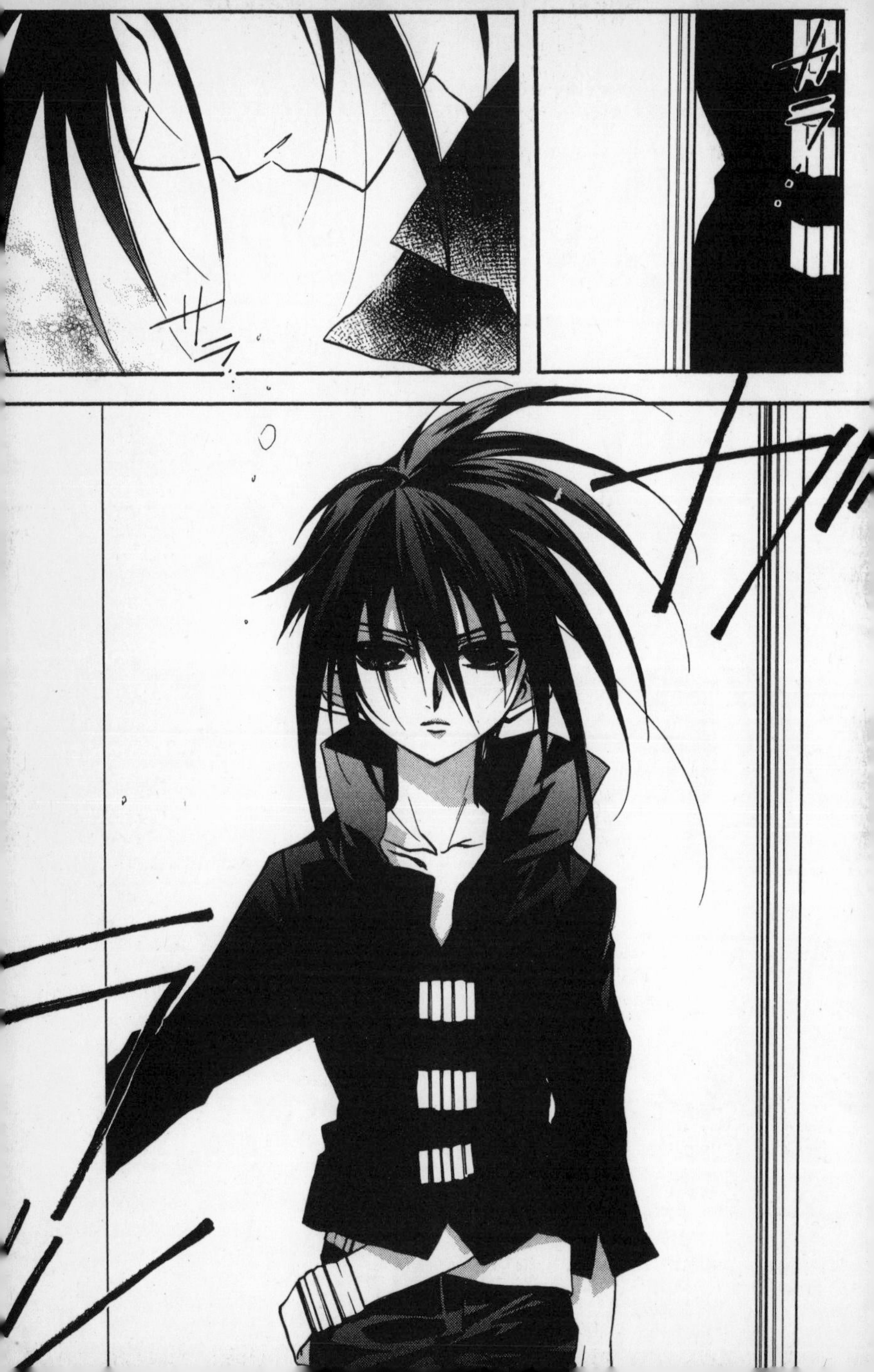
カラ
サラ

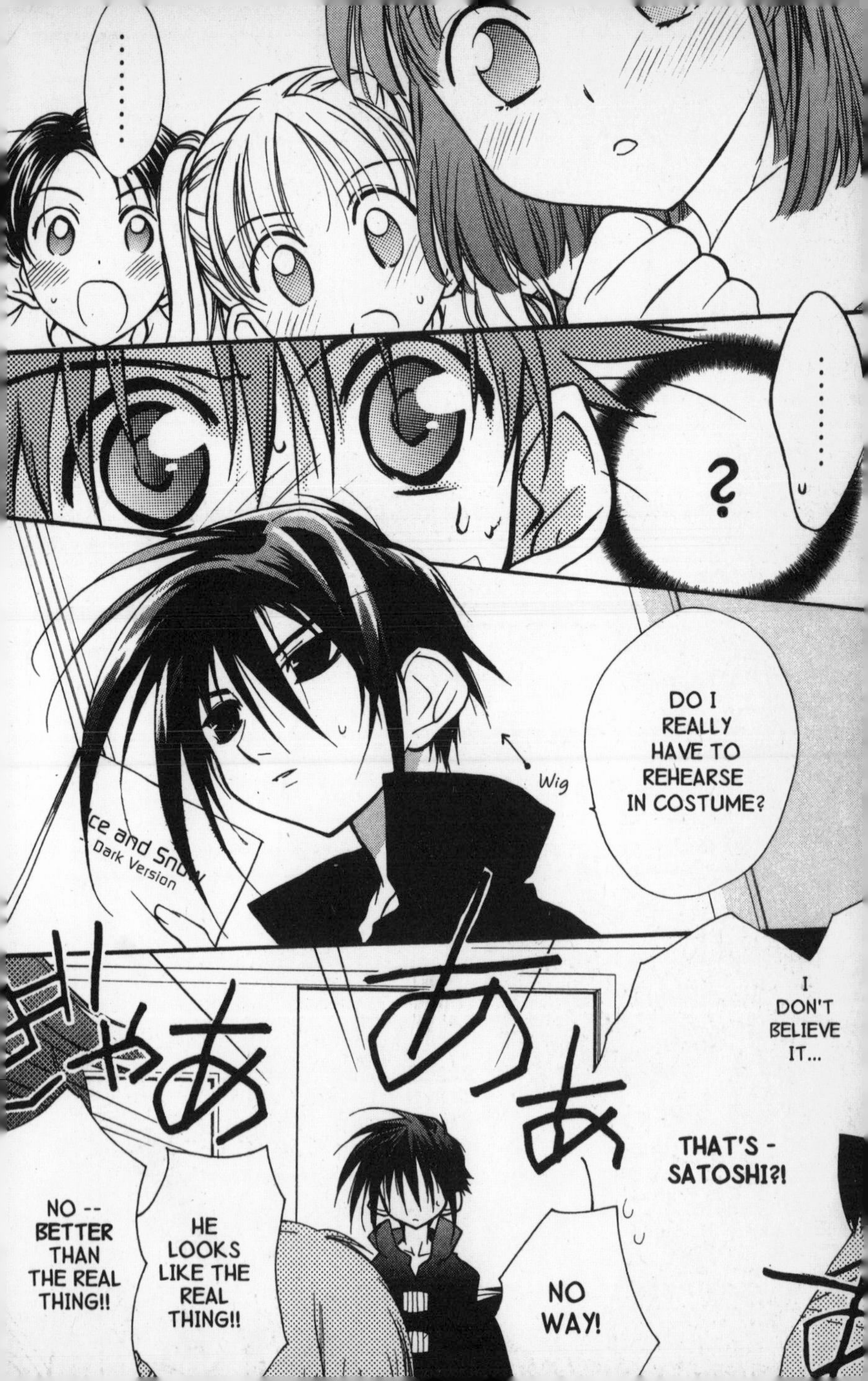

......
......
?
DO I REALLY HAVE TO REHEARSE IN COSTUME?
Wig
Ice and Snow - Dark Version
I DON'T BELIEVE IT...
THAT'S - SATOSHI?!
ああ
きゃあ
NO WAY!
HE LOOKS LIKE THE REAL THING!!
NO -- BETTER THAN THE REAL THING!!

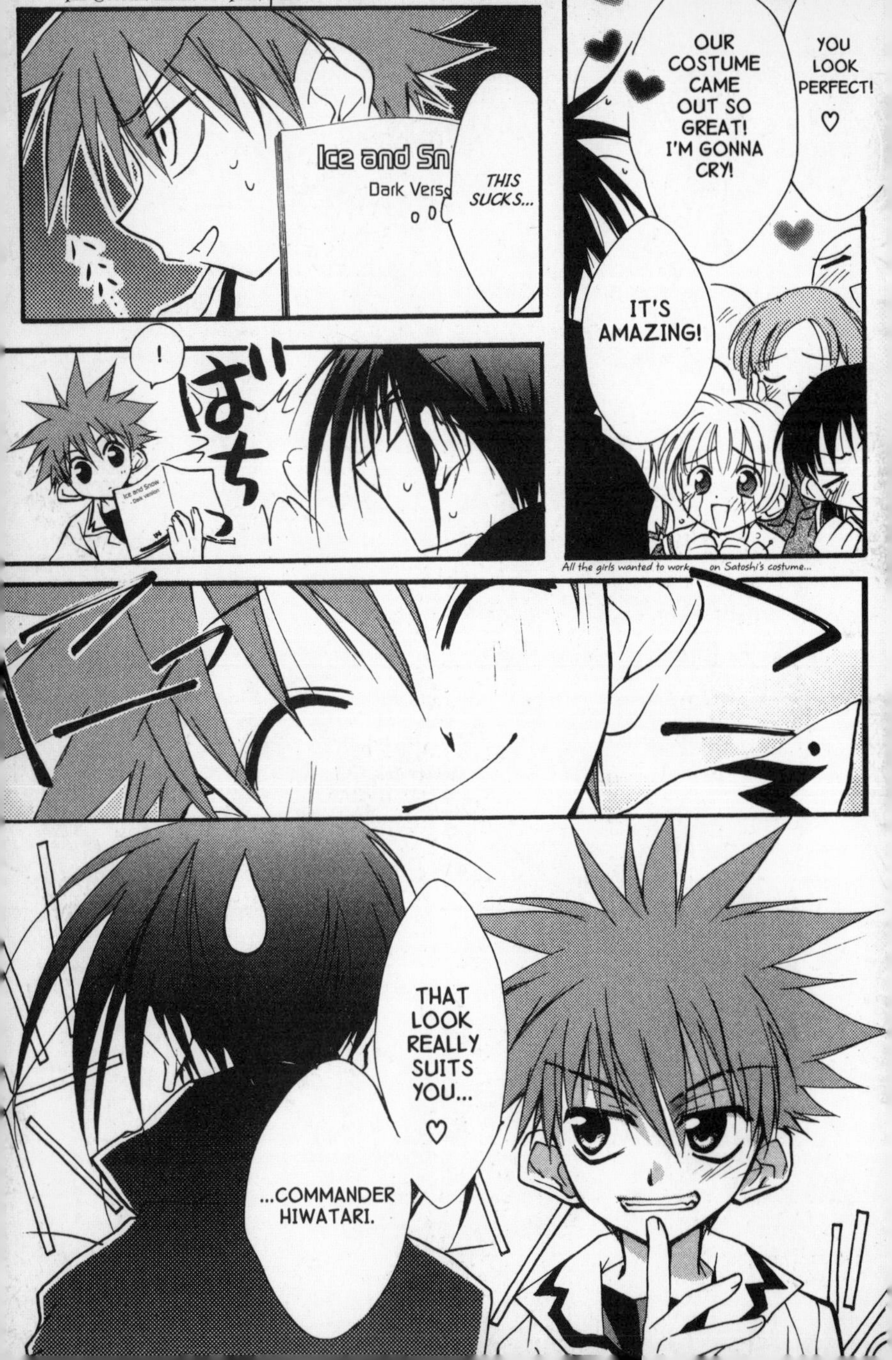
YOU LOOK PERFECT! ♡
OUR COSTUME CAME OUT SO GREAT! I'M GONNA CRY!
IT'S AMAZING!
All the girls wanted to work on Satoshi's costume...
Ice and Sn
Dark Vers
THIS SUCKS...
!
ぱち
Ice and Snow
- Dark Version
THAT LOOK REALLY SUITS YOU... ♡
...COMMANDER HIWATARI.

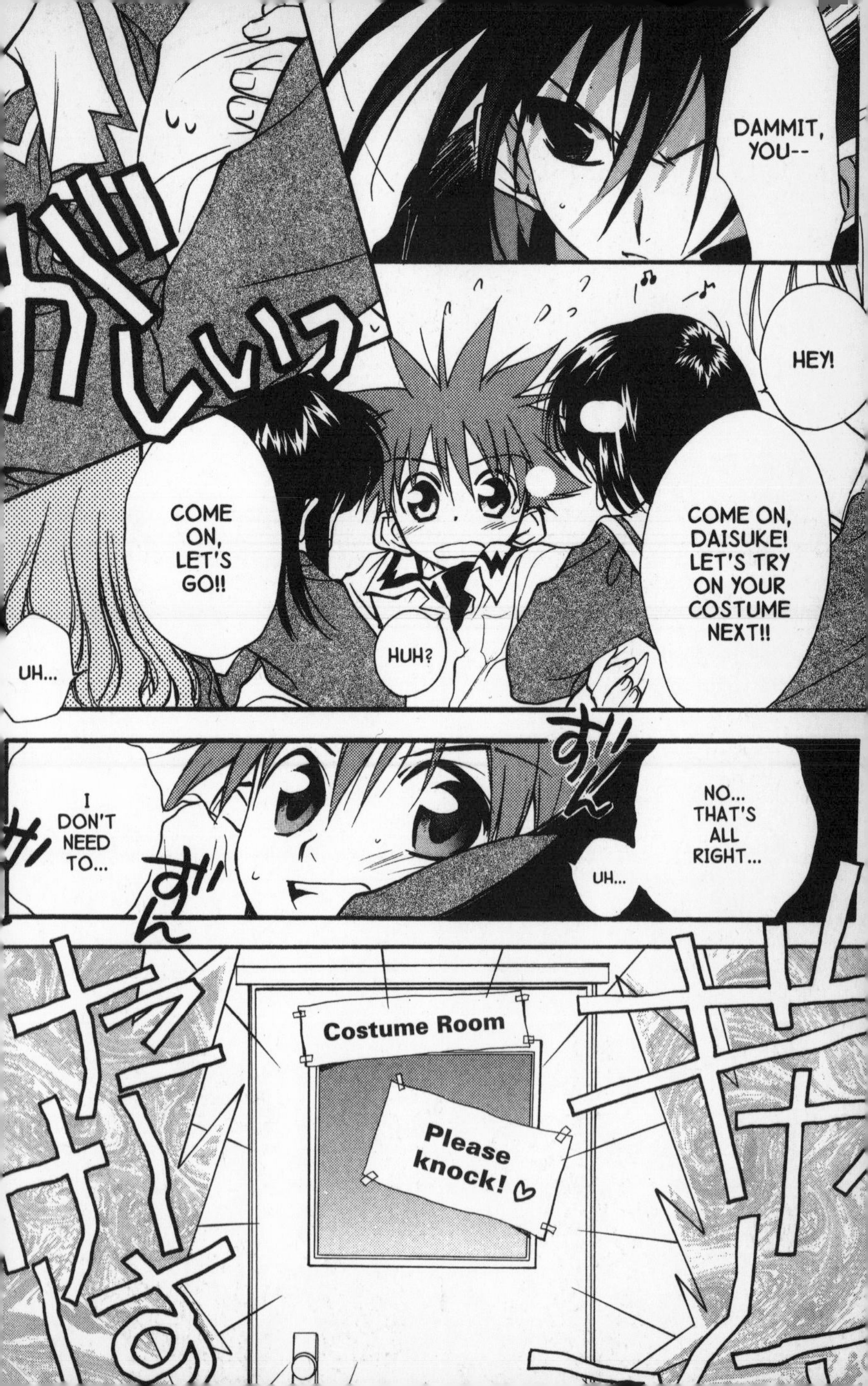
DAMMIT, YOU--
HEY!
COME ON, DAISUKE! LET'S TRY ON YOUR COSTUME NEXT!!
HUH?
COME ON, LET'S GO!!
UH...
NO... THAT'S ALL RIGHT...
UH...
I DON'T NEED TO...
Costume Room
Please knock! ♡

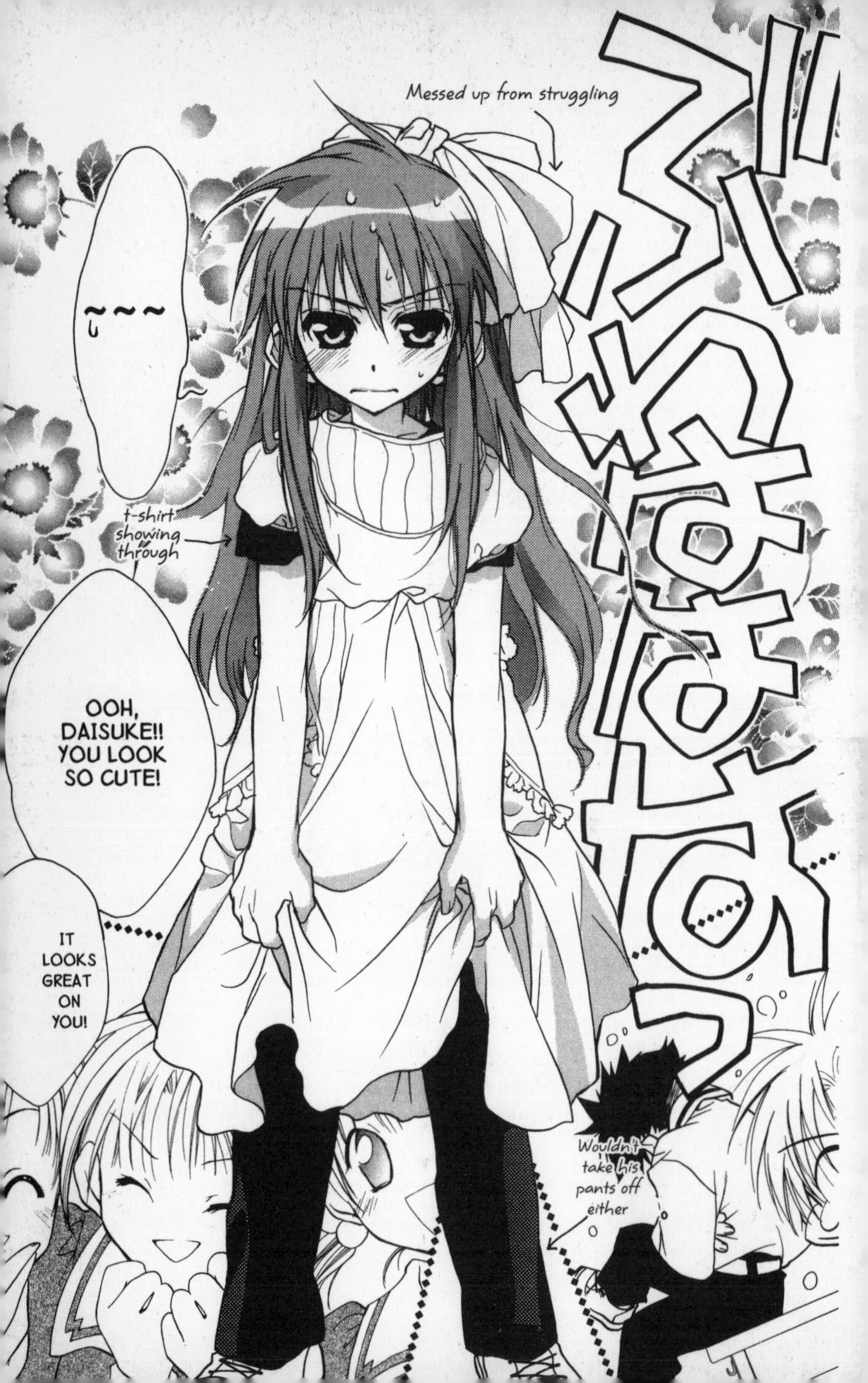
Messed up from struggling
~~~
t-shirt showing through
OOH, DAISUKE!! YOU LOOK SO CUTE!
Wouldn't take his pants off either
IT LOOKS GREAT ON YOU!
~~~

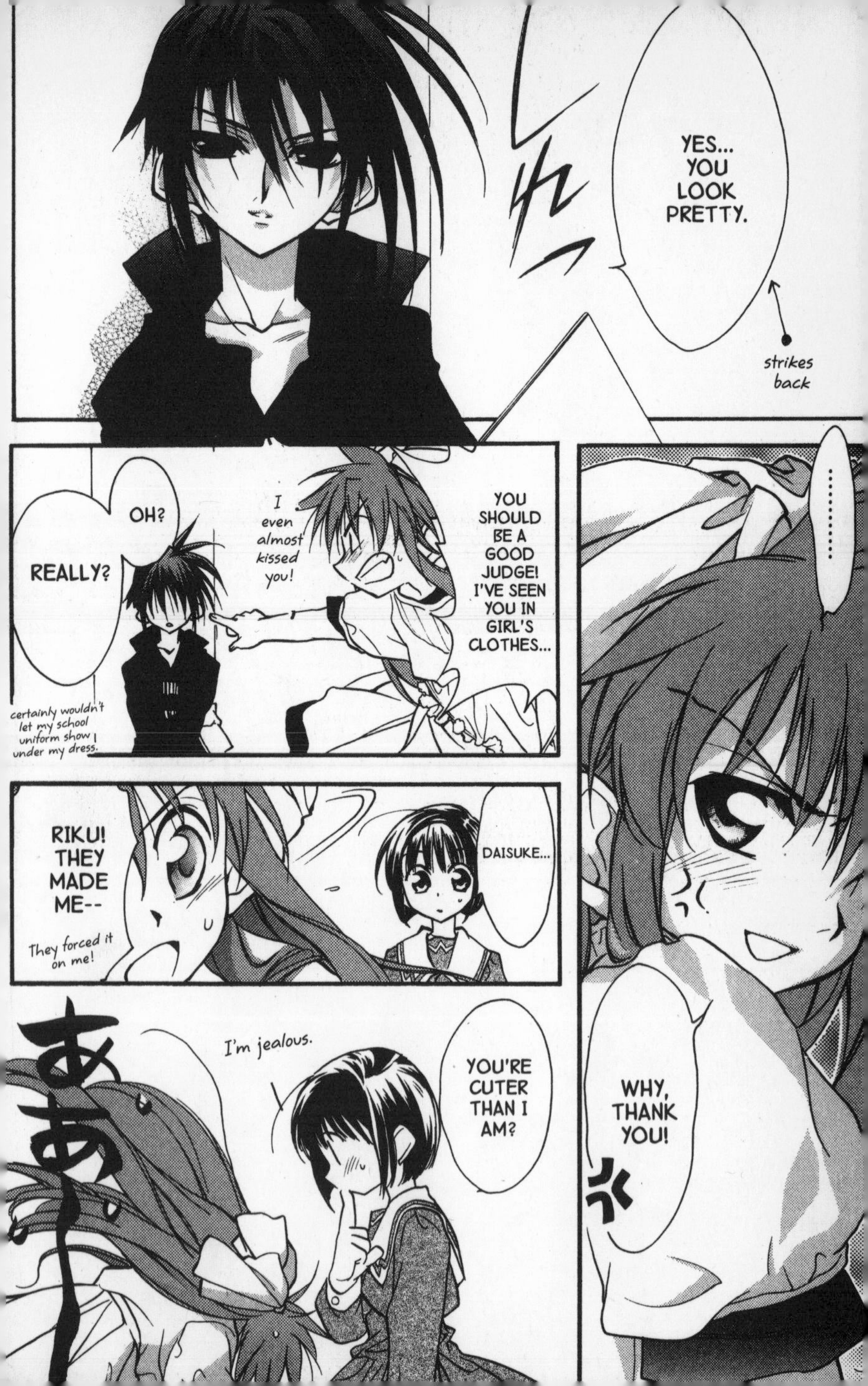
YES... YOU LOOK PRETTY.
strikes back
......
WHY, THANK YOU!
YOU SHOULD BE A GOOD JUDGE! I'VE SEEN YOU IN GIRL'S CLOTHES...
I even almost kissed you!
OH? REALLY?
certainly wouldn't let my school uniform show under my dress.
DAISUKE...
RIKU! THEY MADE ME--
They forced it on me!
YOU'RE CUTER THAN I AM?
I'm jealous.
ああ

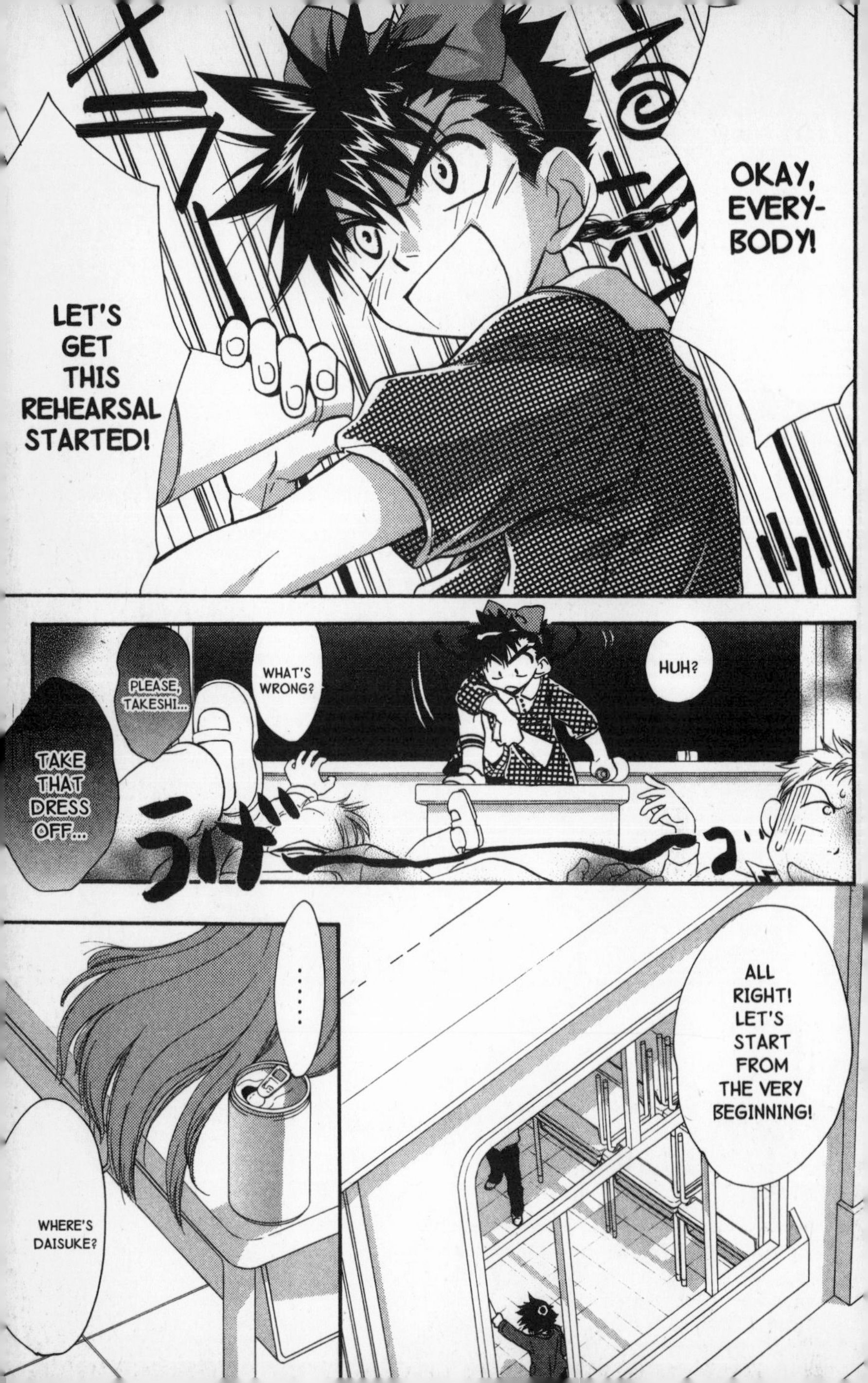
OKAY, EVERY-BODY!
LET'S GET THIS REHEARSAL STARTED!
HUH?
WHAT'S WRONG?
PLEASE, TAKESHI...
TAKE THAT DRESS OFF...
ALL RIGHT! LET'S START FROM THE VERY BEGINNING!
......
WHERE'S DAISUKE?

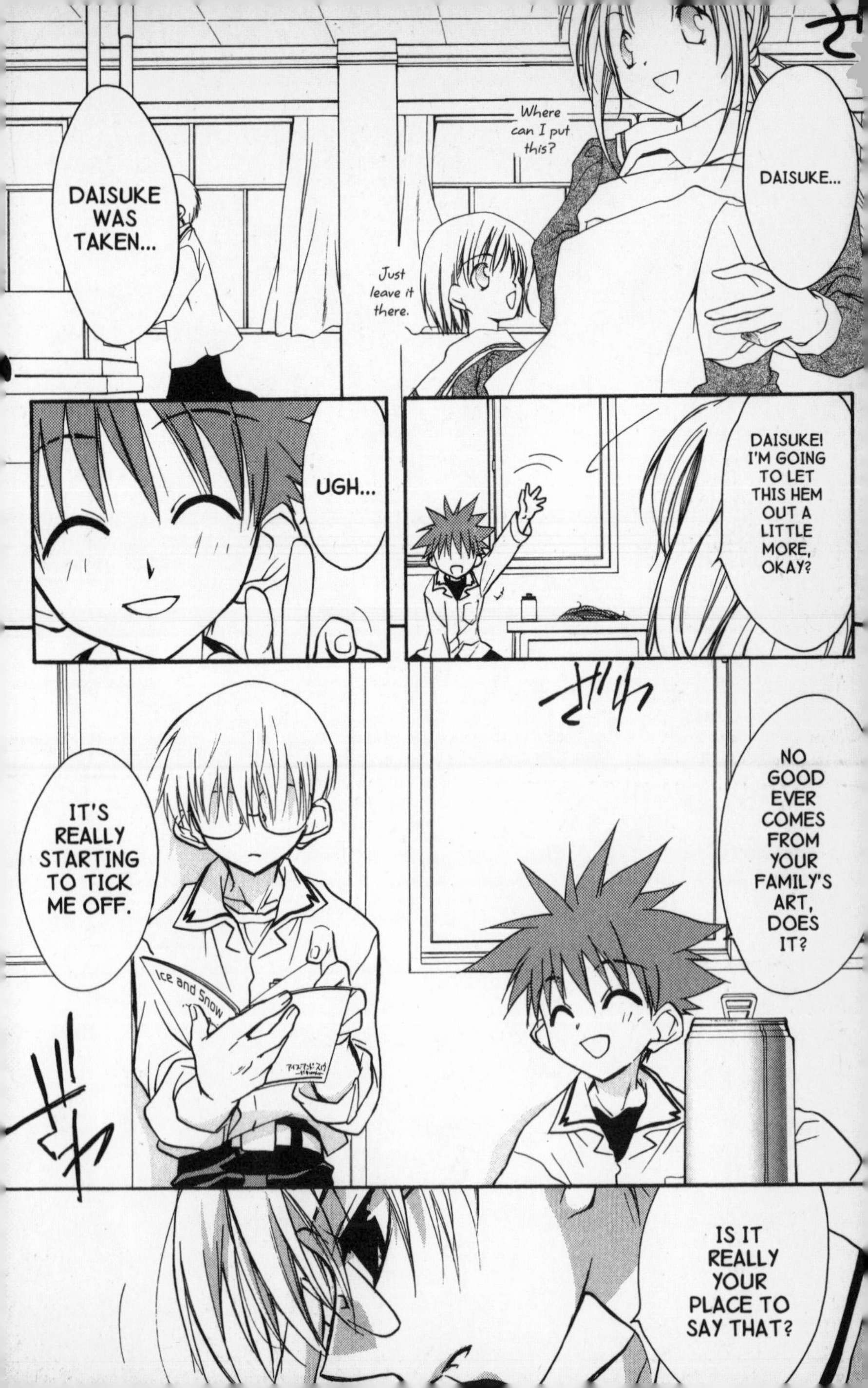
DAISUKE...
Where can I put this?
Just leave it there.
DAISUKE WAS TAKEN...
DAISUKE! I'M GOING TO LET THIS HEM OUT A LITTLE MORE, OKAY?
UGH...
ざわ
NO GOOD EVER COMES FROM YOUR FAMILY'S ART, DOES IT?
IT'S REALLY STARTING TO TICK ME OFF.
Ice and Snow
ざわ
IS IT REALLY YOUR PLACE TO SAY THAT?

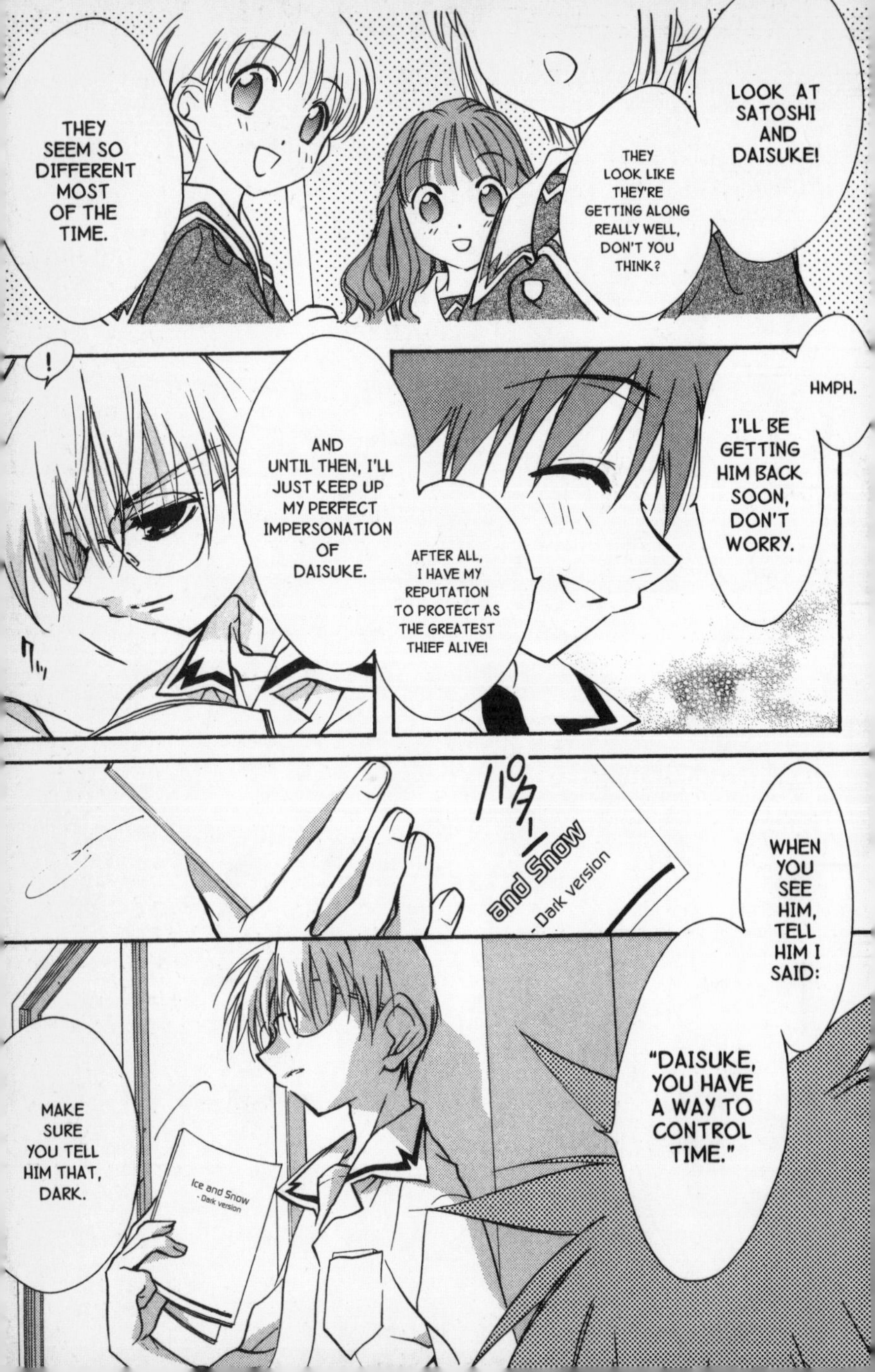
LOOK AT SATOSHI AND DAISUKE!
THEY LOOK LIKE THEY'RE GETTING ALONG REALLY WELL, DON'T YOU THINK?
THEY SEEM SO DIFFERENT MOST OF THE TIME.
HMPH.
I'LL BE GETTING HIM BACK SOON, DON'T WORRY.
AFTER ALL, I HAVE MY REPUTATION TO PROTECT AS THE GREATEST THIEF ALIVE!
AND UNTIL THEN, I'LL JUST KEEP UP MY PERFECT IMPERSONATION OF DAISUKE.
!
WHEN YOU SEE HIM, TELL HIM I SAID:
and Snow
- Dark version
"DAISUKE, YOU HAVE A WAY TO CONTROL TIME."
MAKE SURE YOU TELL HIM THAT, DARK.
Ice and Snow
- Dark version

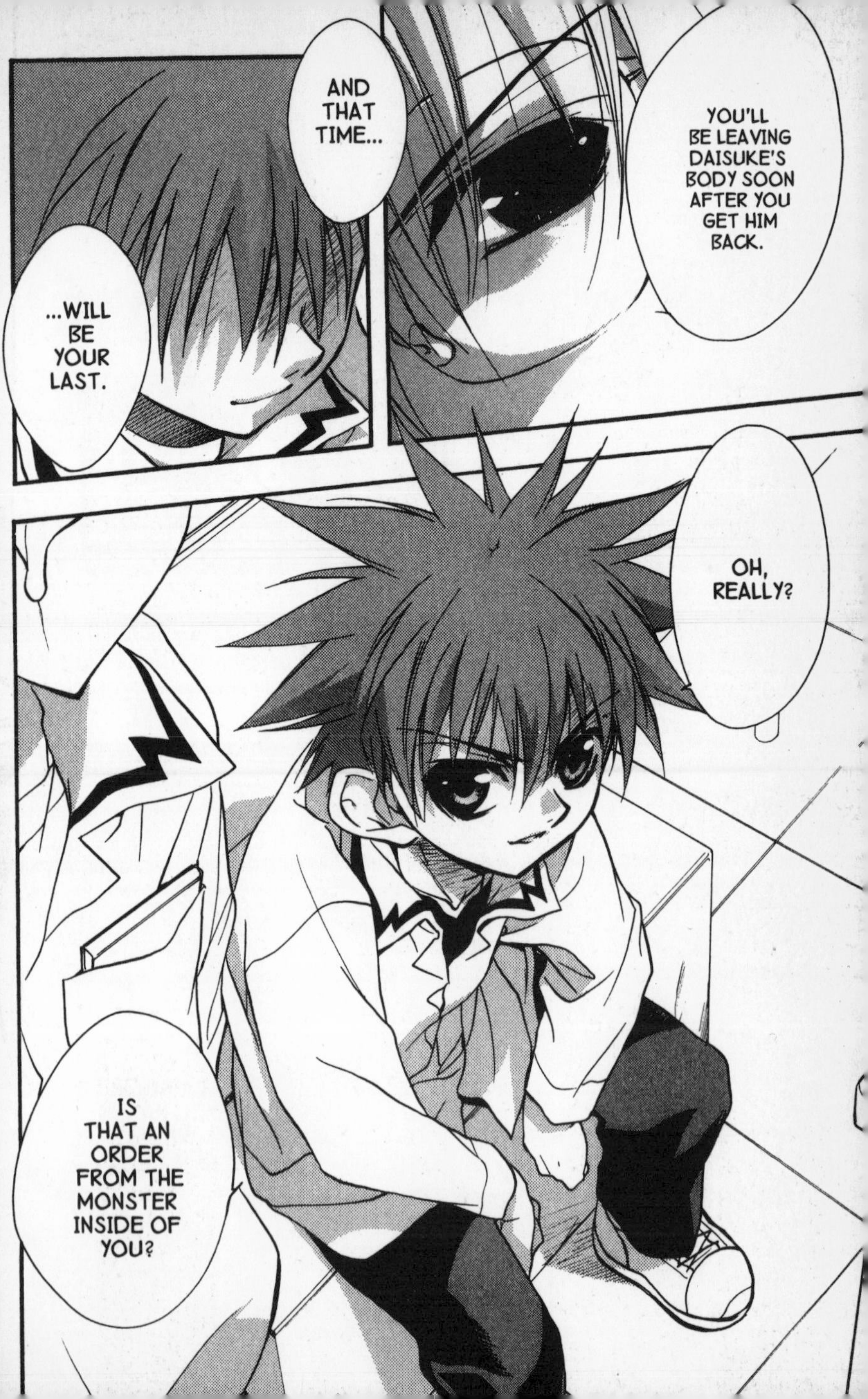
YOU'LL BE LEAVING DAISUKE'S BODY SOON AFTER YOU GET HIM BACK.
AND THAT TIME...
...WILL BE YOUR LAST.
OH, REALLY?
IS THAT AN ORDER FROM THE MONSTER INSIDE OF YOU?

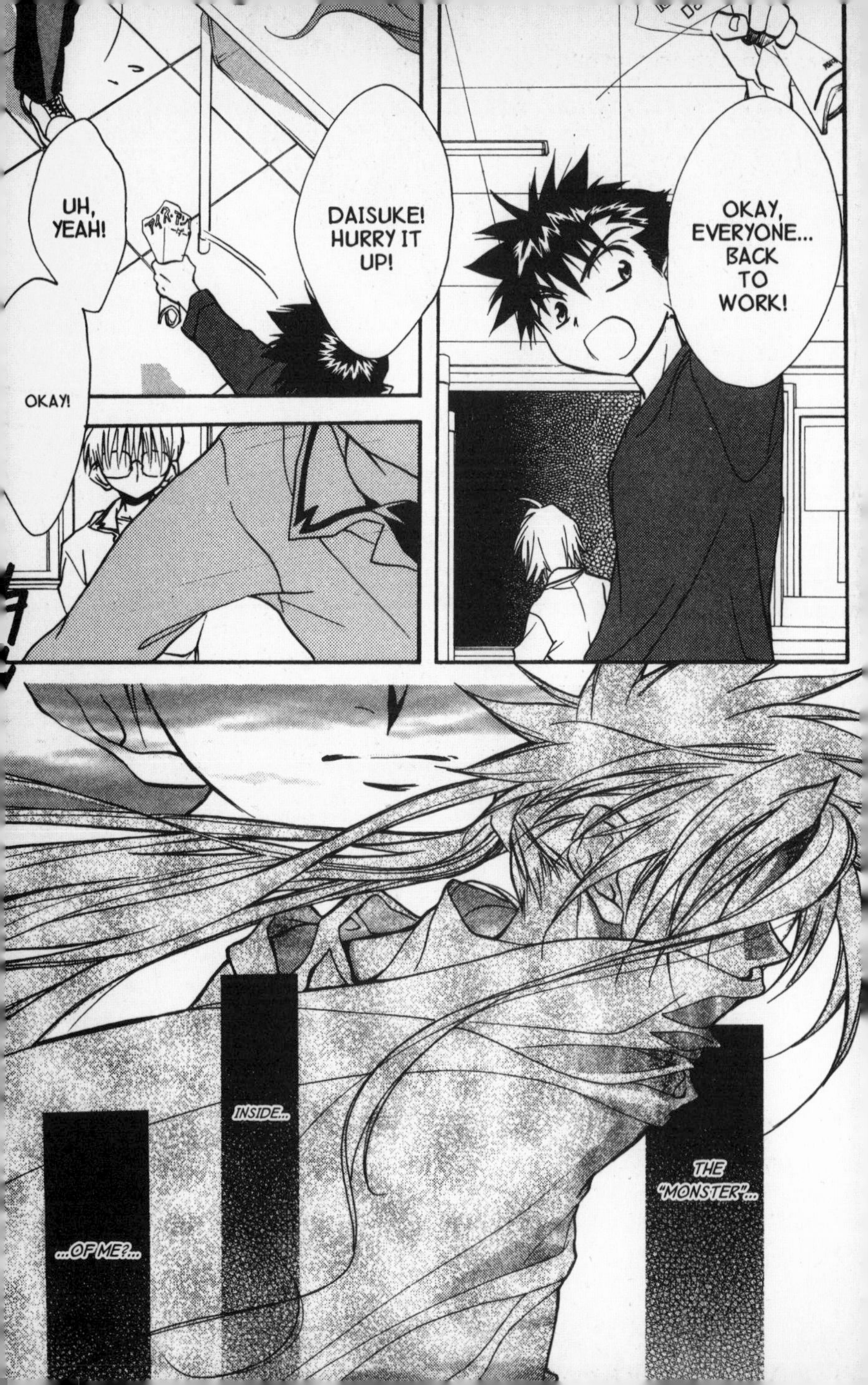
OKAY, EVERYONE... BACK TO WORK!
DAISUKE! HURRY IT UP!
UH, YEAH!
OKAY!
THE "MONSTER"...
INSIDE...
...OF ME?...

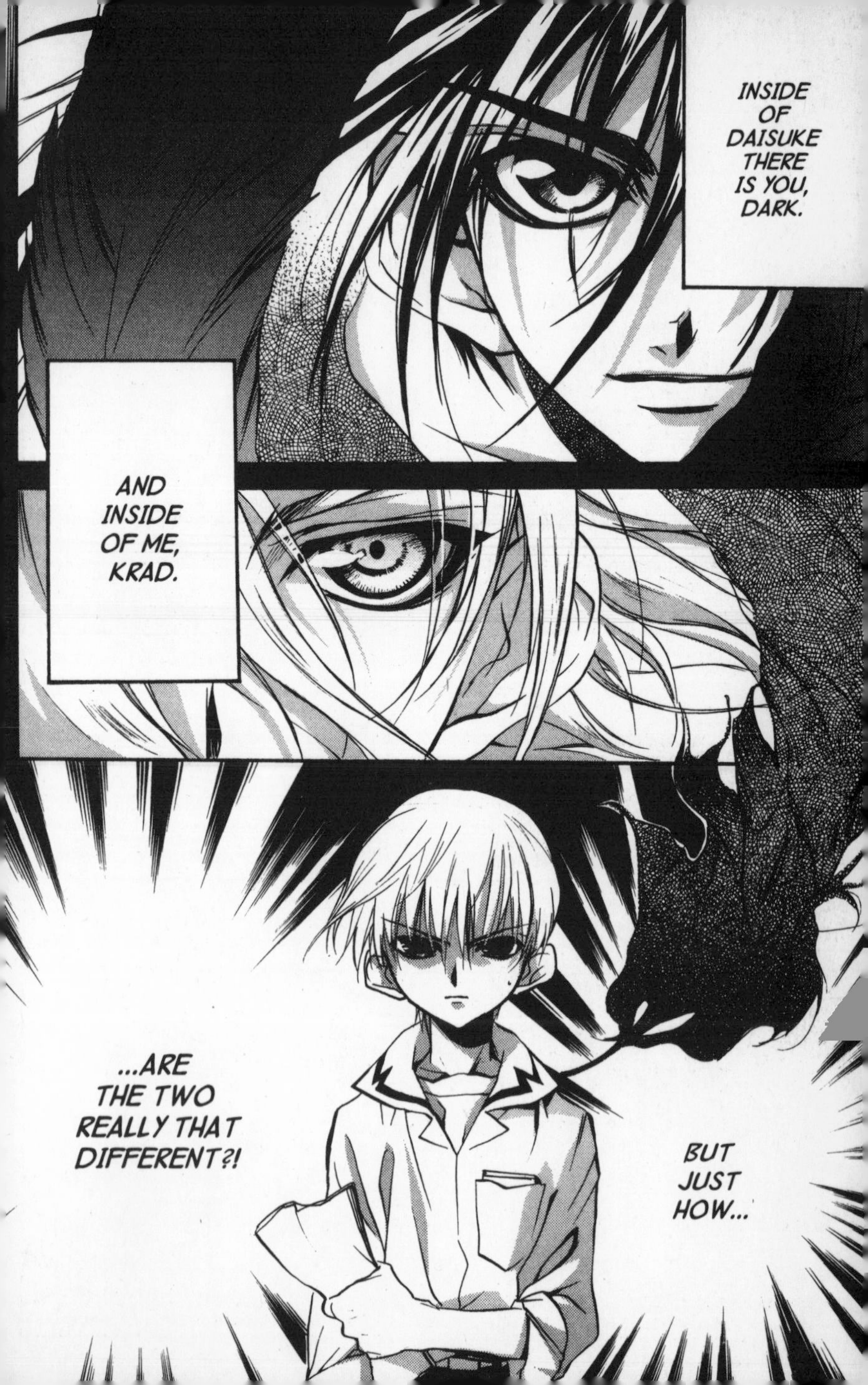
INSIDE OF DAISUKE THERE IS YOU, DARK.
AND INSIDE OF ME, KRAD.
BUT JUST HOW...
...ARE THE TWO REALLY THAT DIFFERENT?!

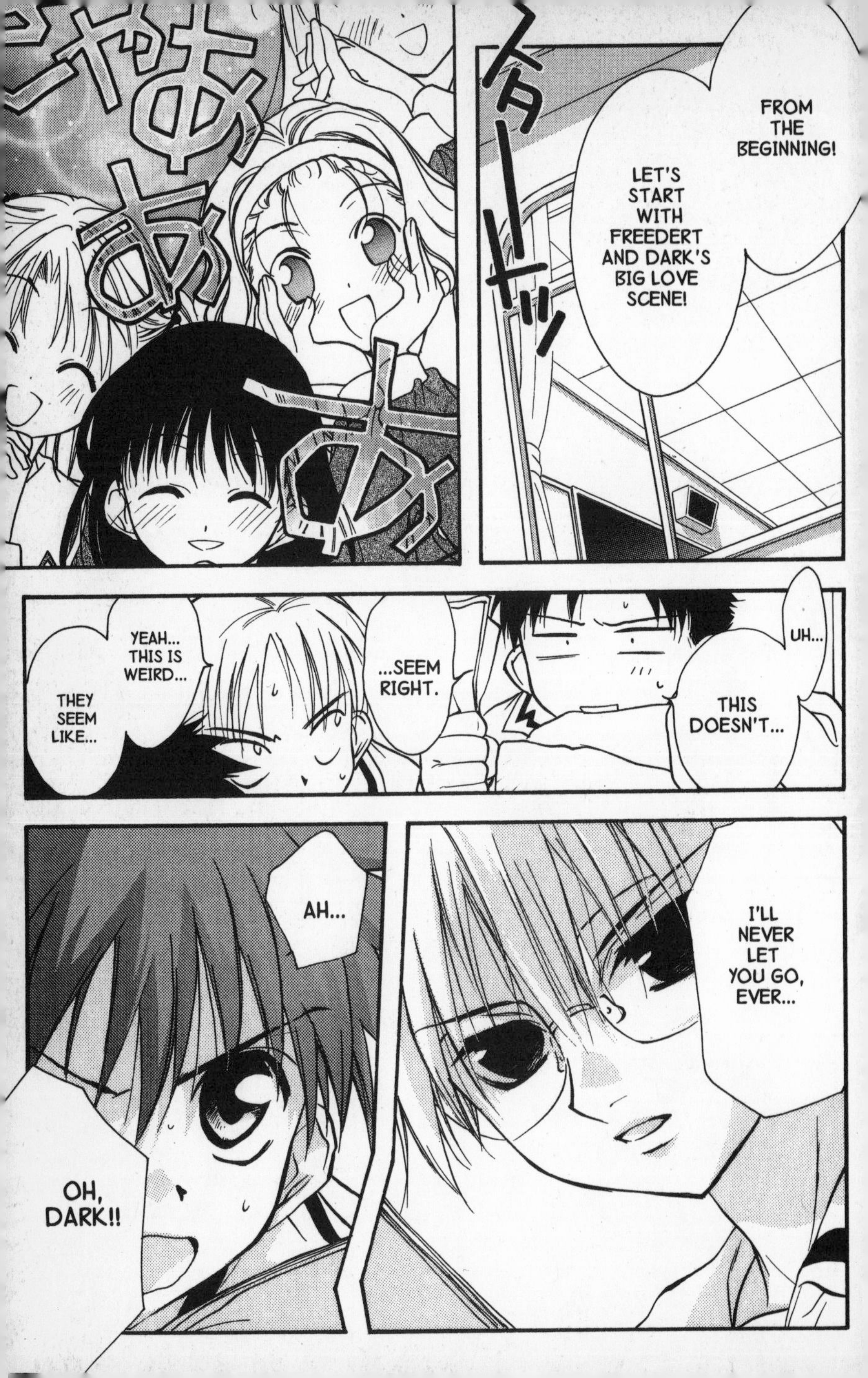
FROM THE BEGINNING!
LET'S START WITH FREEDERT AND DARK'S BIG LOVE SCENE!
UH...
THIS DOESN'T...
...SEEM RIGHT.
YEAH... THIS IS WEIRD...
THEY SEEM LIKE...
I'LL NEVER LET YOU GO, EVER...
AH...
OH, DARK!!

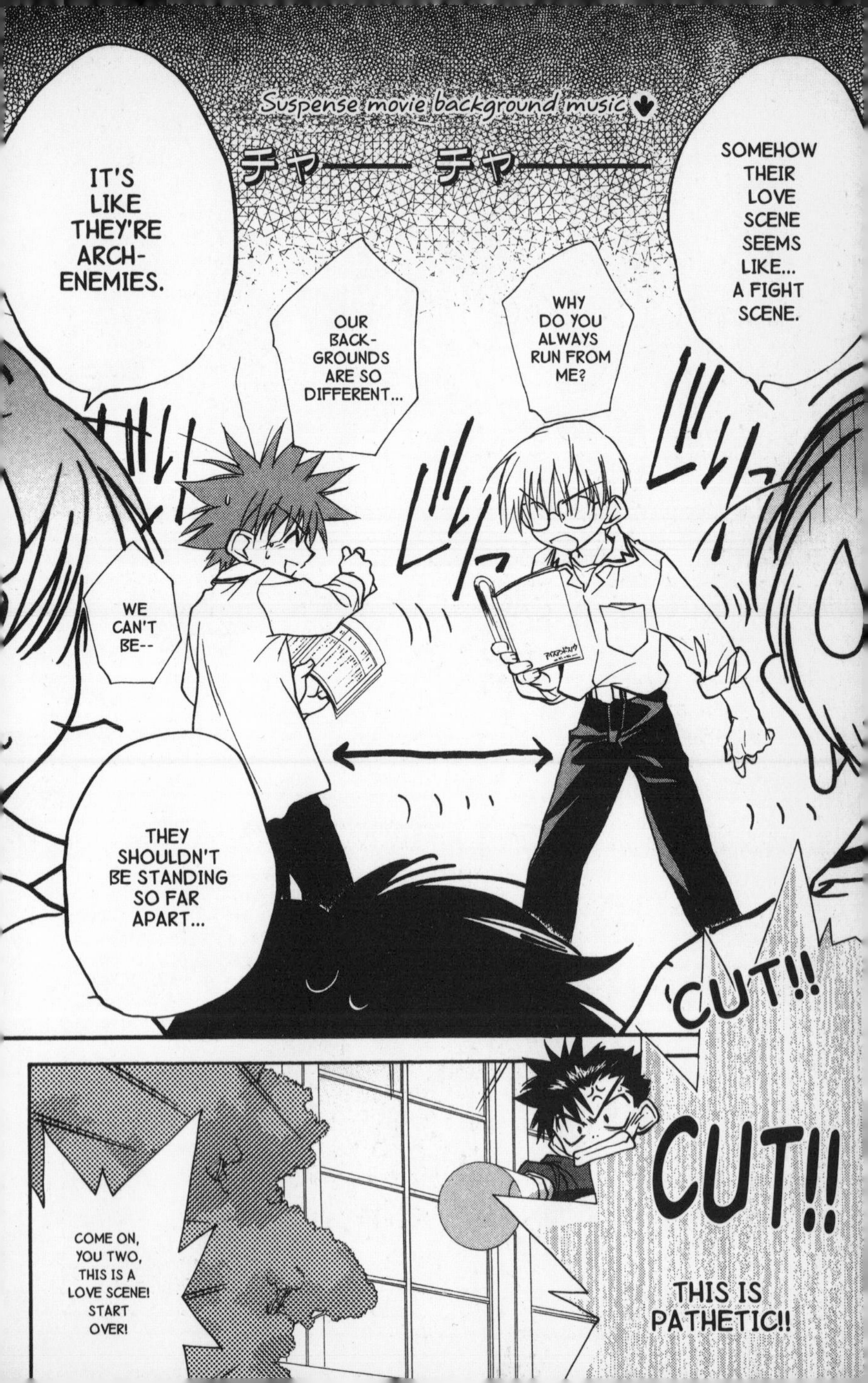
Suspense movie background music ♥
チャ―― チャ――――
SOMEHOW THEIR LOVE SCENE SEEMS LIKE... A FIGHT SCENE.
WHY DO YOU ALWAYS RUN FROM ME?
OUR BACK-GROUNDS ARE SO DIFFERENT...
IT'S LIKE THEY'RE ARCH-ENEMIES.
WE CAN'T BE--
THEY SHOULDN'T BE STANDING SO FAR APART...
CUT!!
CUT!!
THIS IS PATHETIC!!
COME ON, YOU TWO, THIS IS A LOVE SCENE! START OVER!

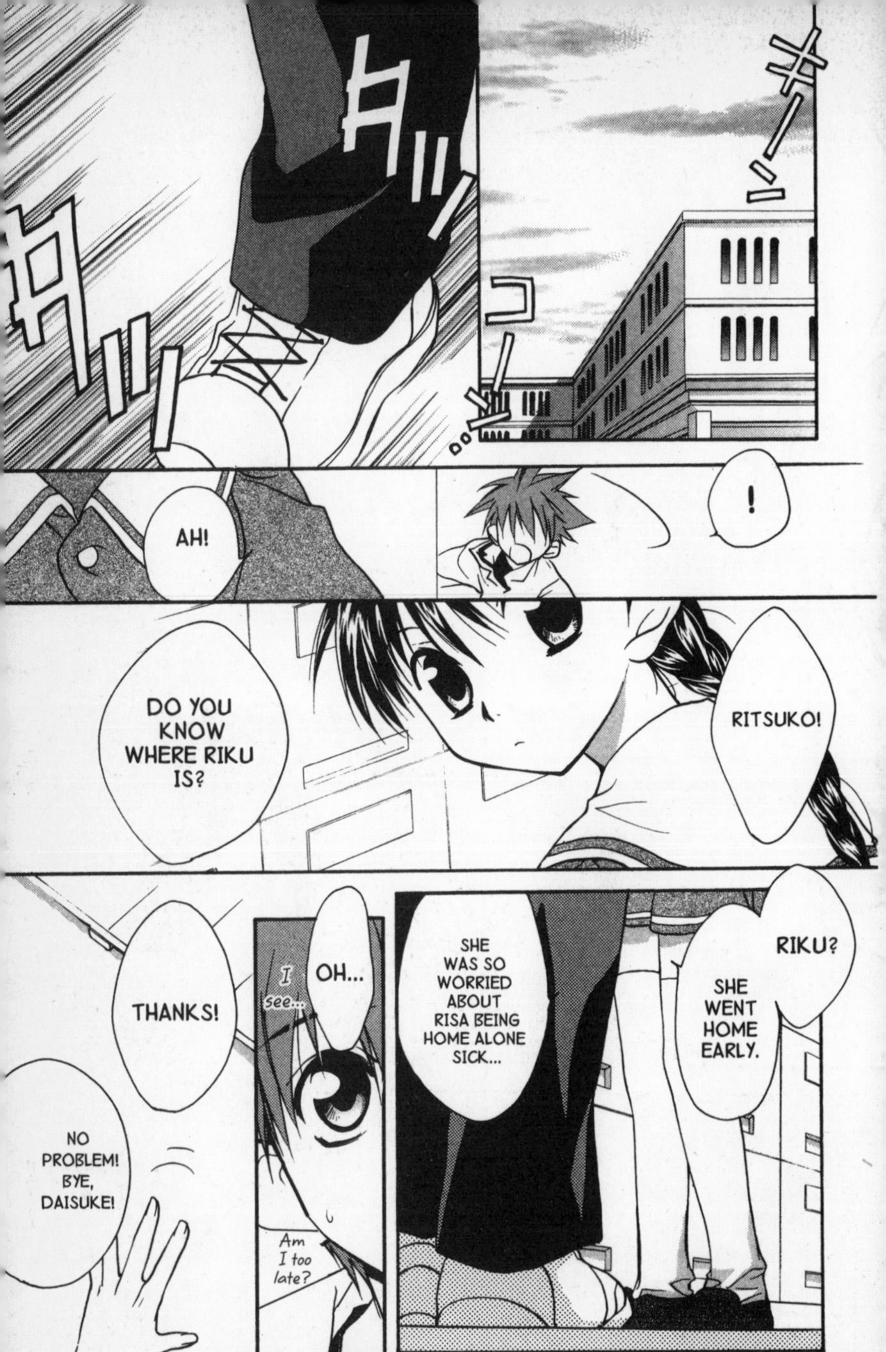

!
AH!
RITSUKO!
DO YOU KNOW WHERE RIKU IS?
RIKU?
SHE WENT HOME EARLY.
SHE WAS SO WORRIED ABOUT RISA BEING HOME ALONE SICK...
OH...
I see...
Am I too late?
THANKS!
NO PROBLEM! BYE, DAISUKE!

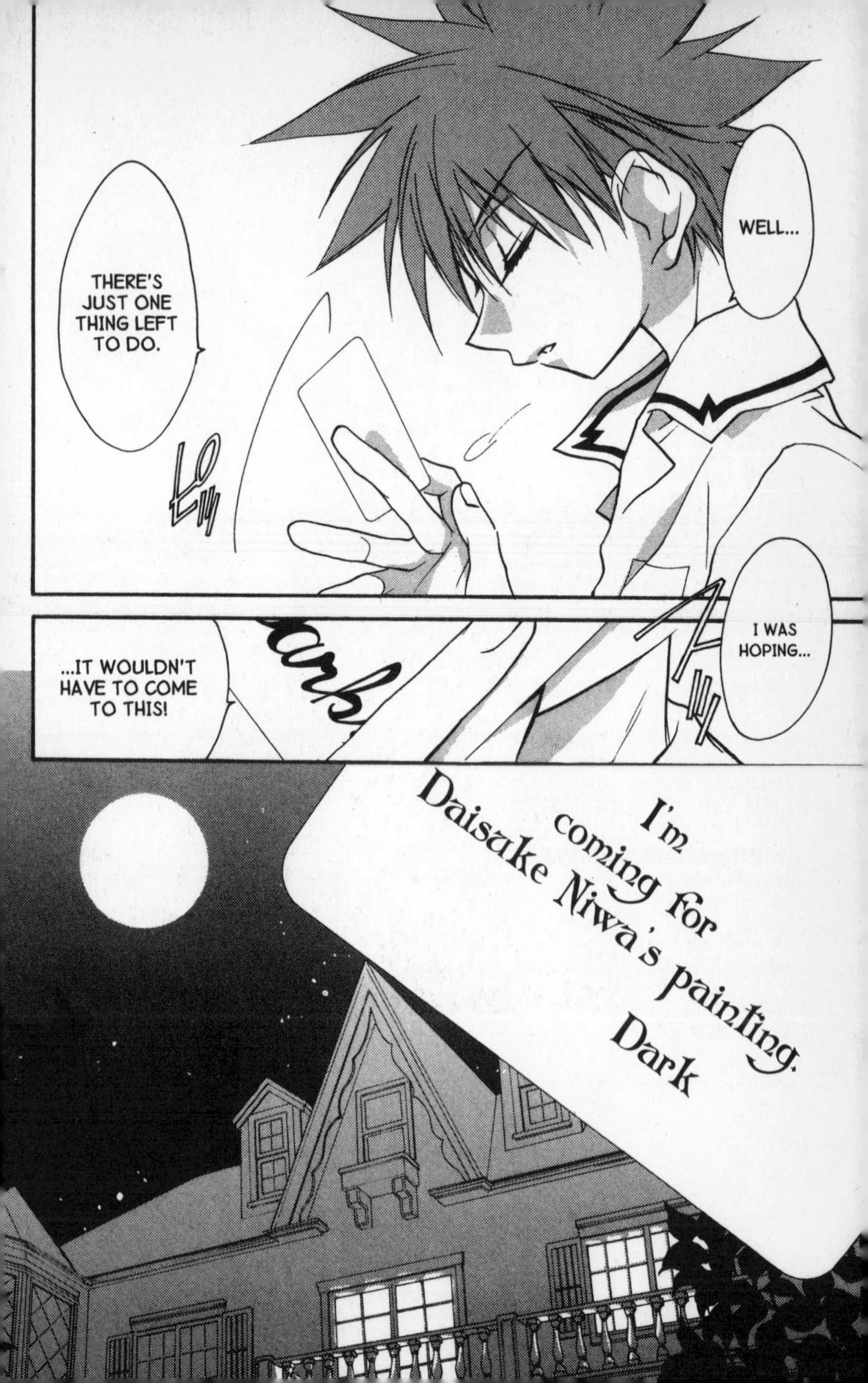
WELL...
THERE'S JUST ONE THING LEFT TO DO.
I WAS HOPING...
...IT WOULDN'T HAVE TO COME TO THIS!
I'm coming for Daisuke Niwa's painting.
Dark

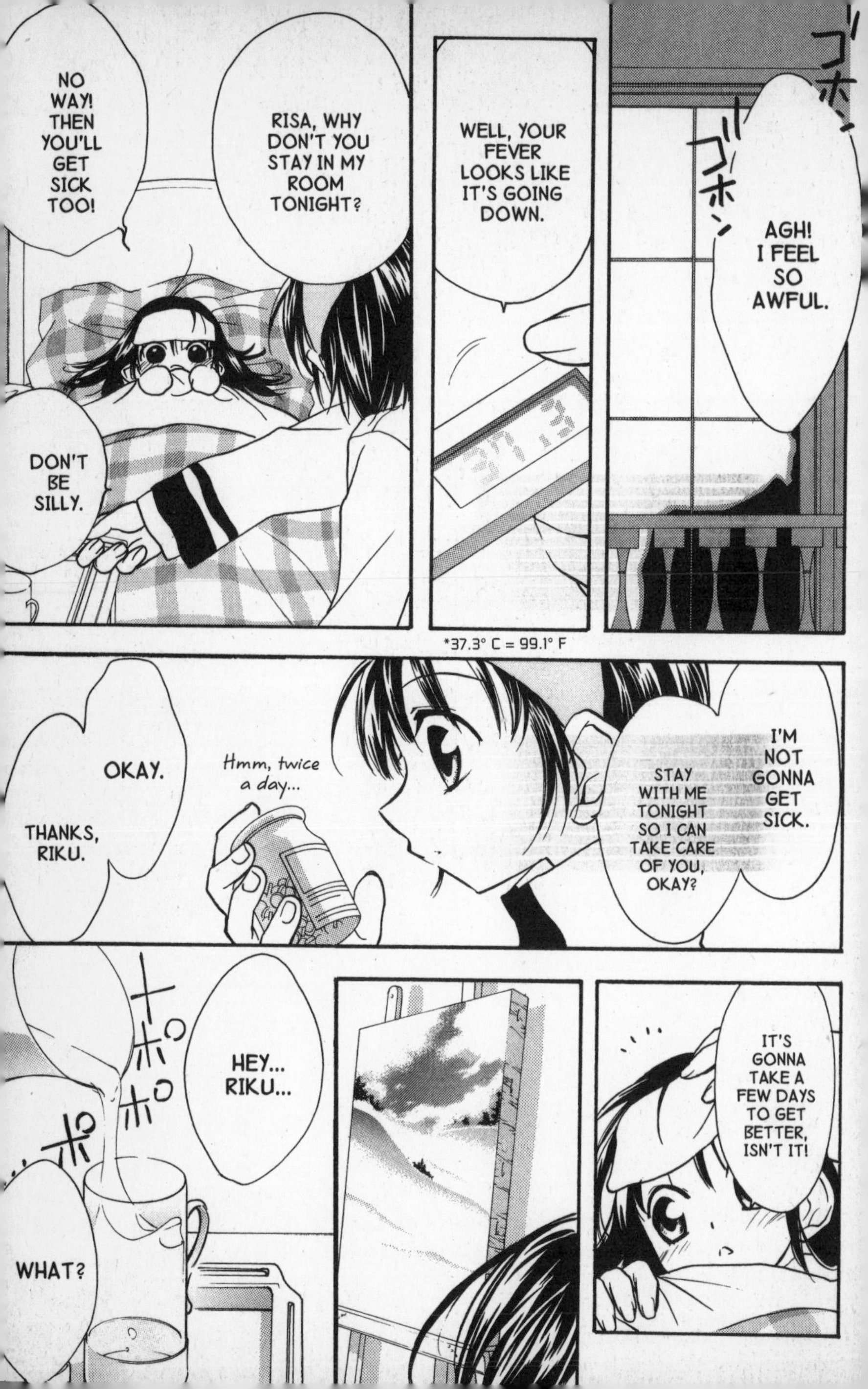
ゴホ
ゴホン
AGH! I FEEL SO AWFUL.
WELL, YOUR FEVER LOOKS LIKE IT'S GOING DOWN.
37.3
RISA, WHY DON'T YOU STAY IN MY ROOM TONIGHT?
NO WAY! THEN YOU'LL GET SICK TOO!
DON'T BE SILLY.
I'M NOT GONNA GET SICK.
STAY WITH ME TONIGHT SO I CAN TAKE CARE OF YOU, OKAY?
Hmm, twice a day...
OKAY.
THANKS, RIKU.
IT'S GONNA TAKE A FEW DAYS TO GET BETTER, ISN'T IT!
HEY... RIKU...
WHAT?
*37.3° C = 99.1° F

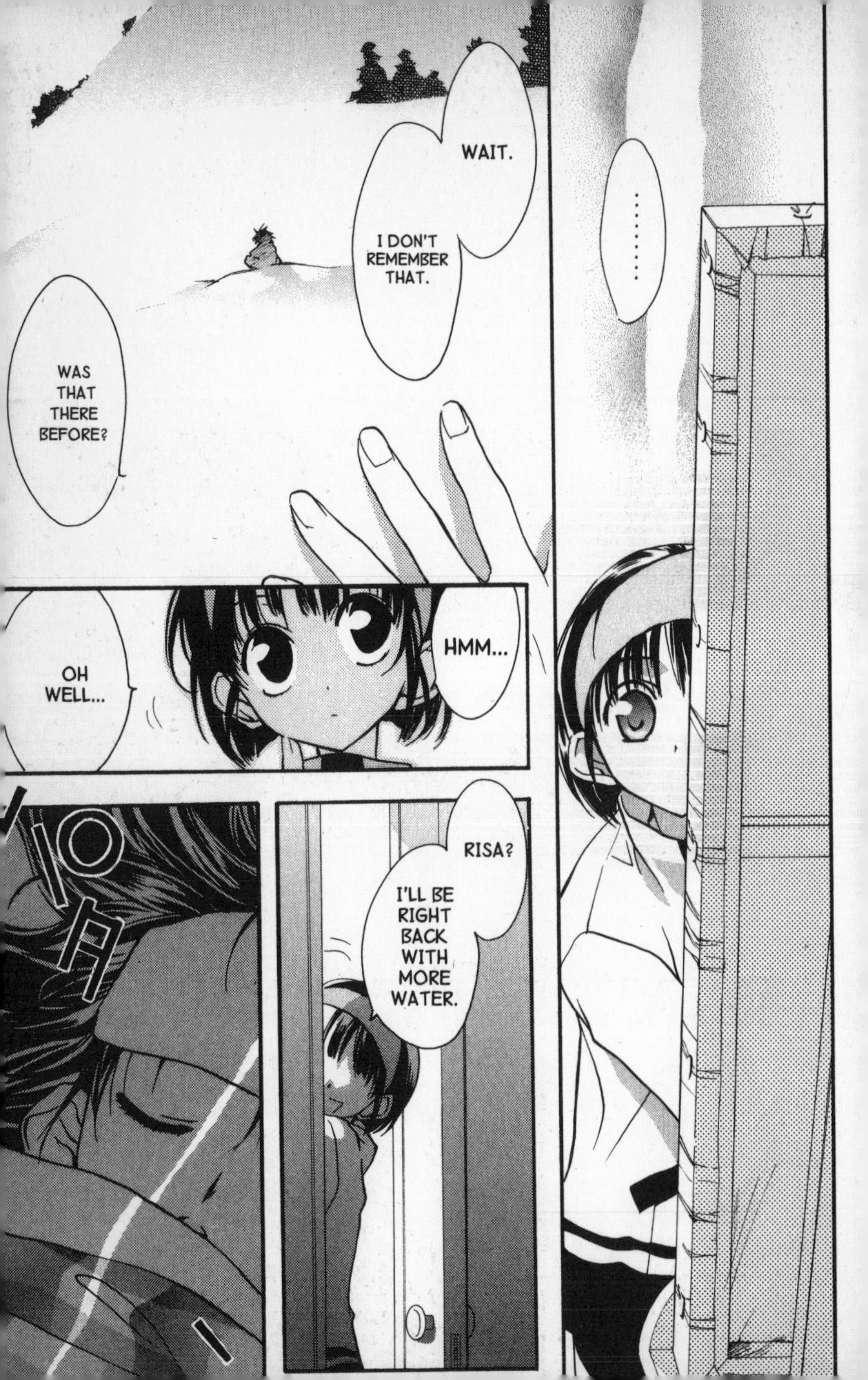
......
WAIT.
I DON'T REMEMBER THAT.
WAS THAT THERE BEFORE?
HMM...
OH WELL...
RISA?
I'LL BE RIGHT BACK WITH MORE WATER.

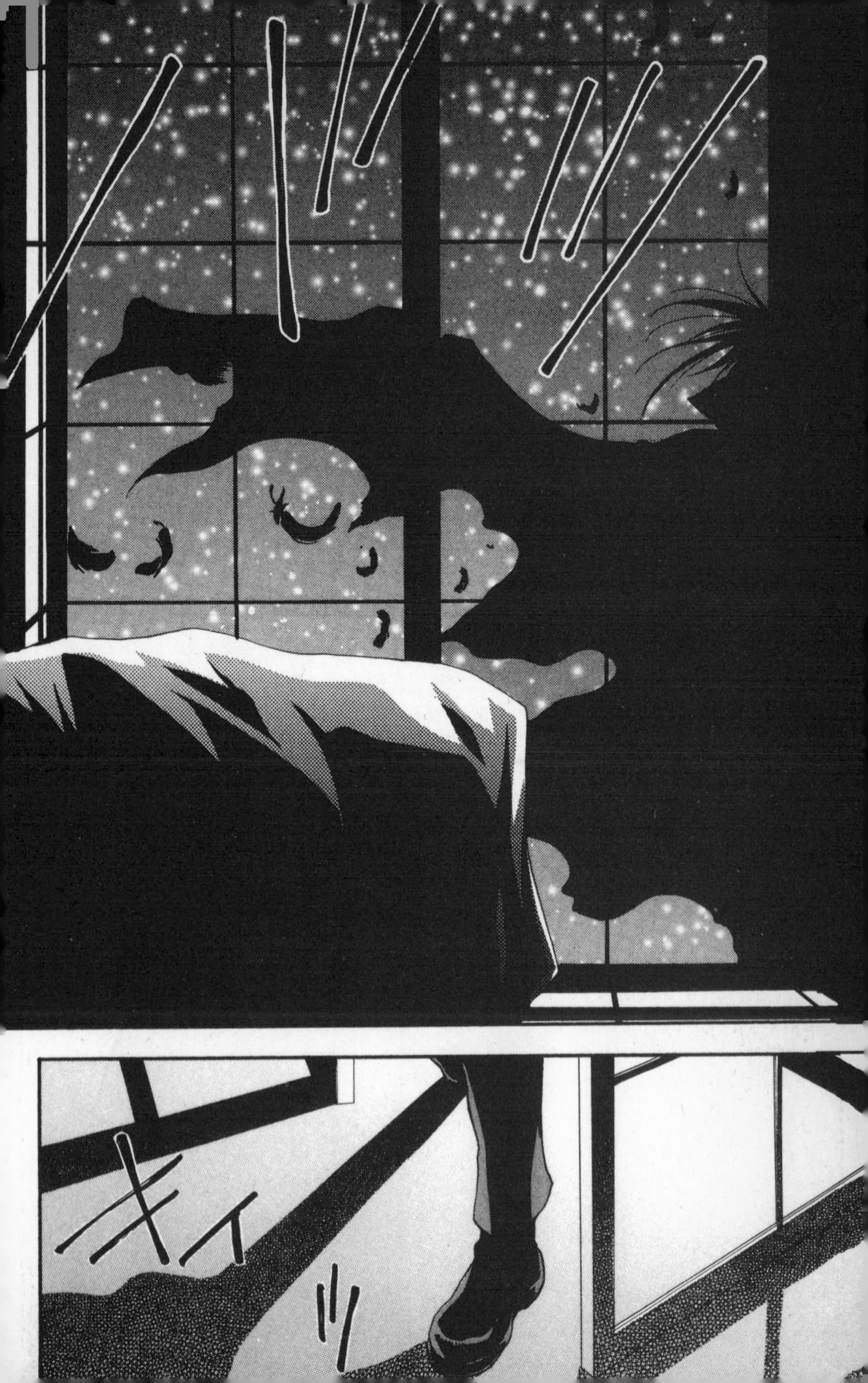
キイッ

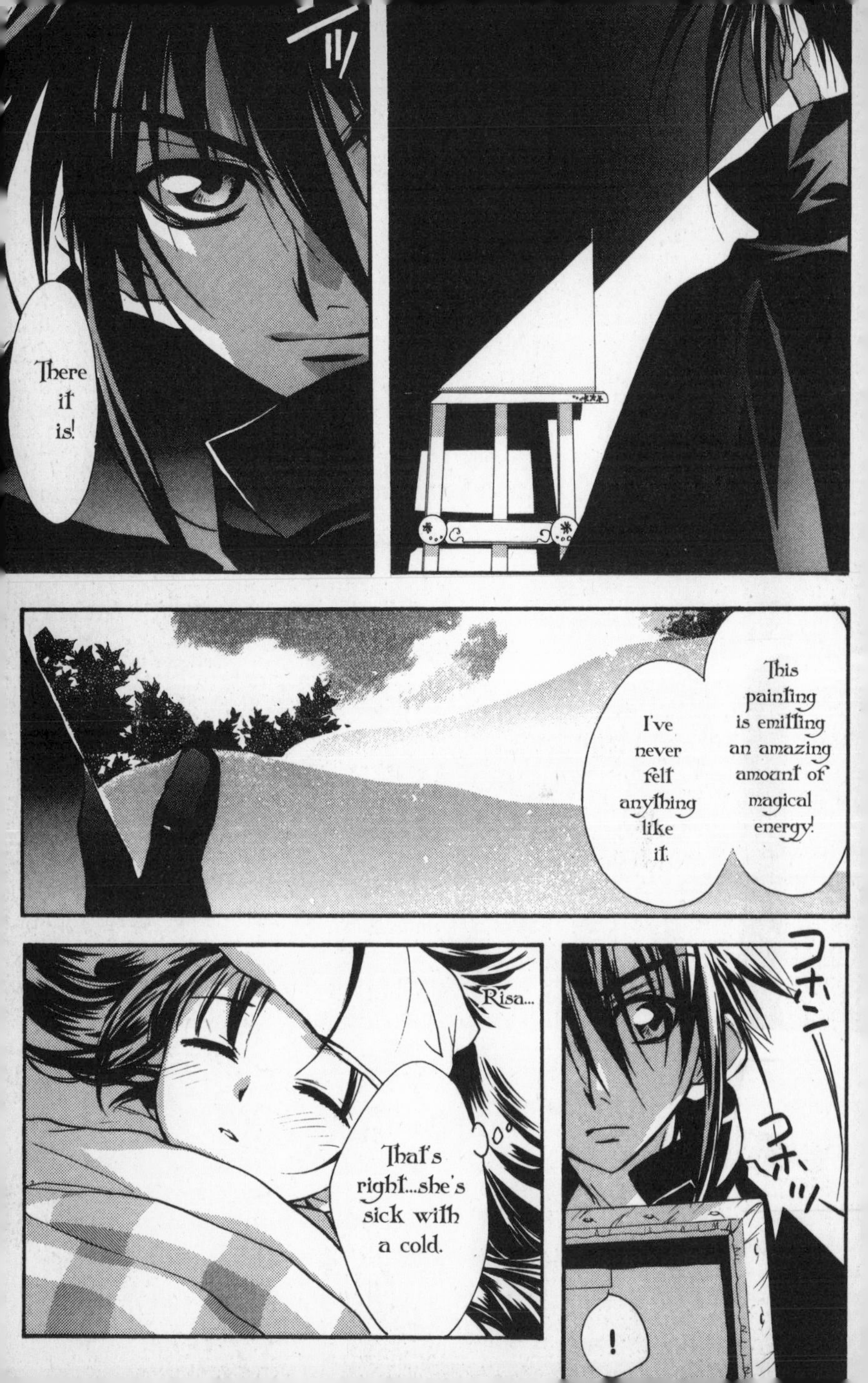
There it is!
This painting is emitting an amazing amount of magical energy!
I've never felt anything like it.
!
Risa...
That's right...she's sick with a cold.

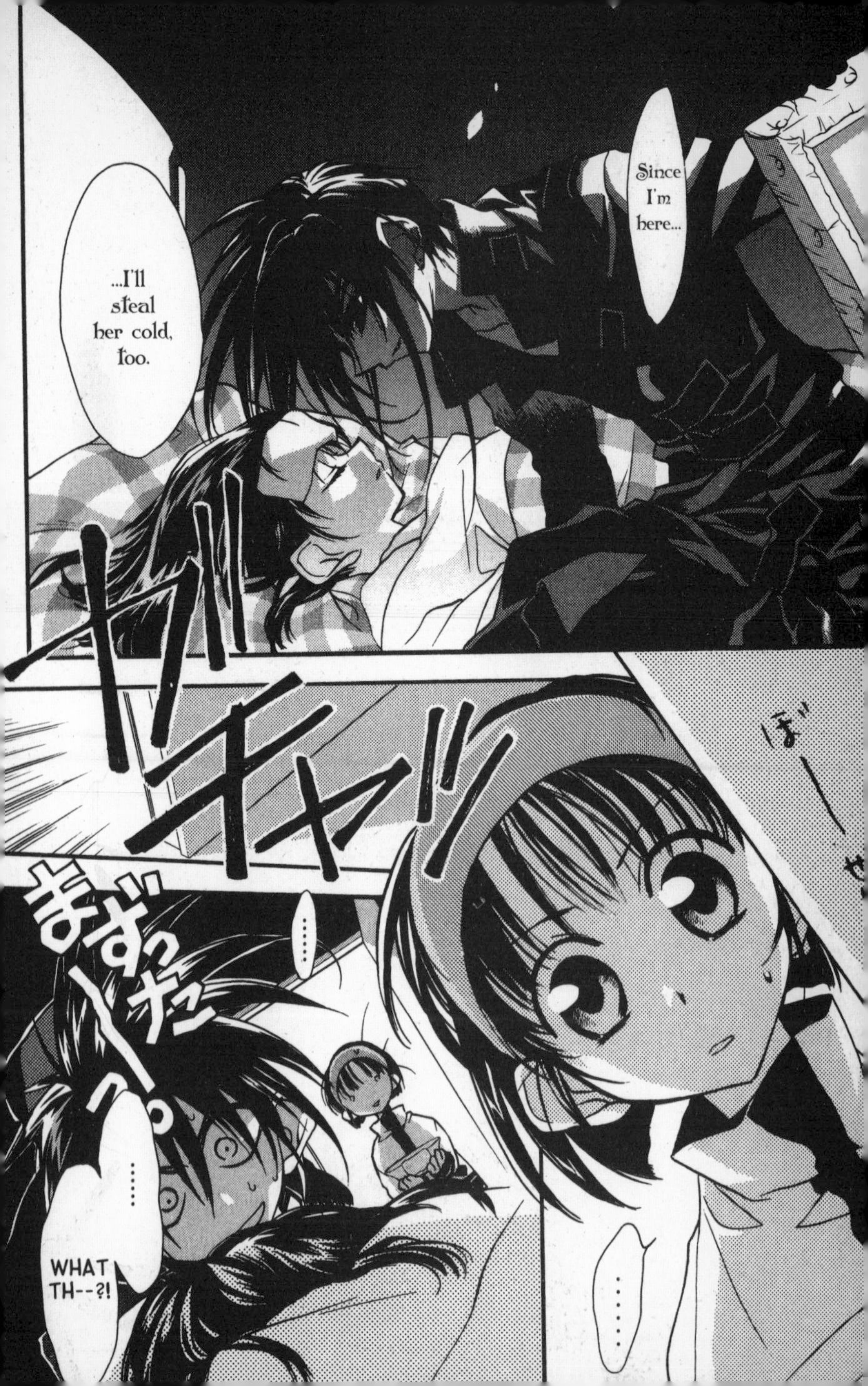
Since I'm here...
...I'll steal her cold, too.
......
......!
......
WHAT TH--?!

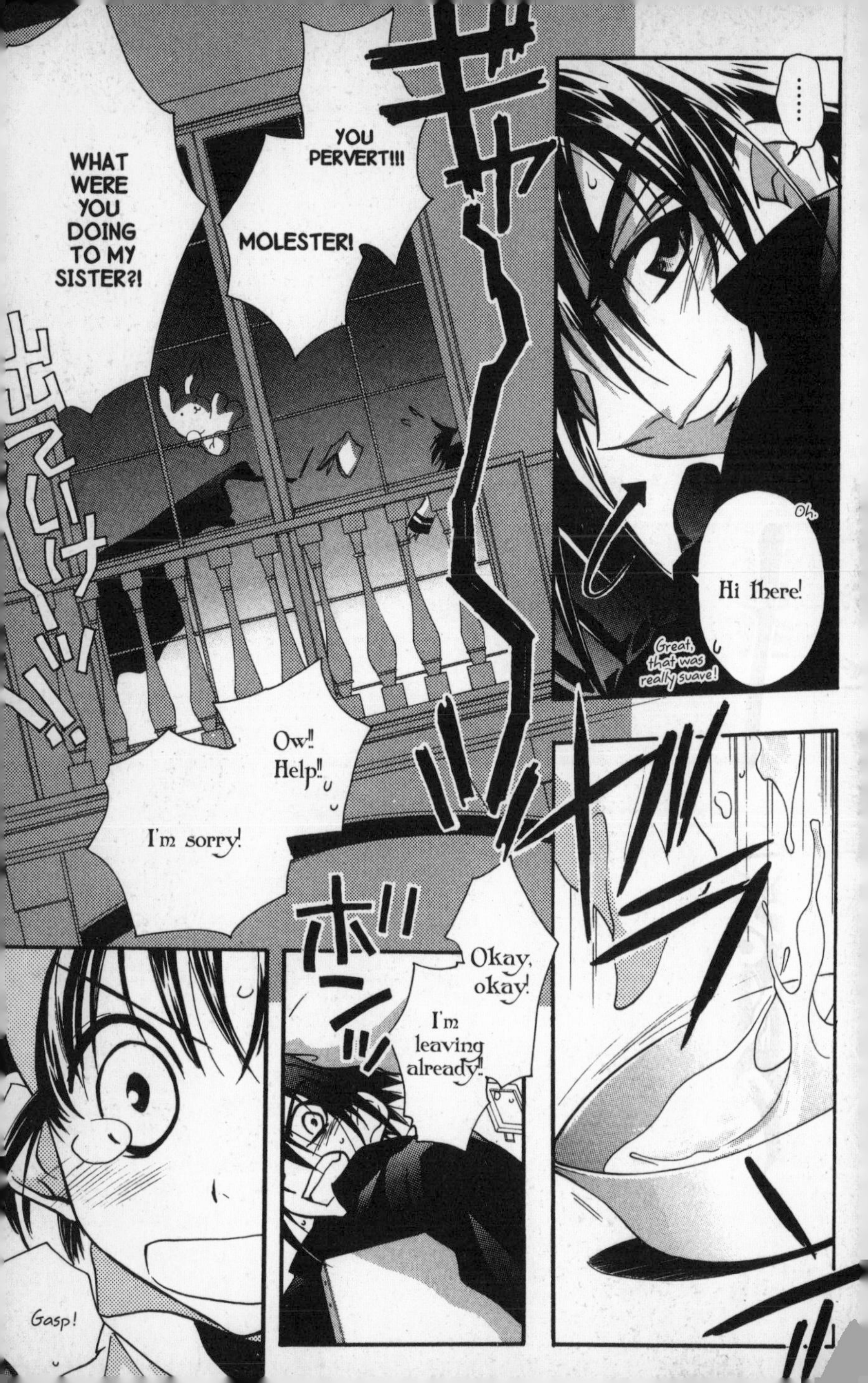
......
Oh.
Hi there!
Great, that was really suave!
YOU PERVERT!!!
MOLESTER!
WHAT WERE YOU DOING TO MY SISTER?!
Ow!! Help!!
I'm sorry!
Okay, okay! I'm leaving already!!
Gasp!

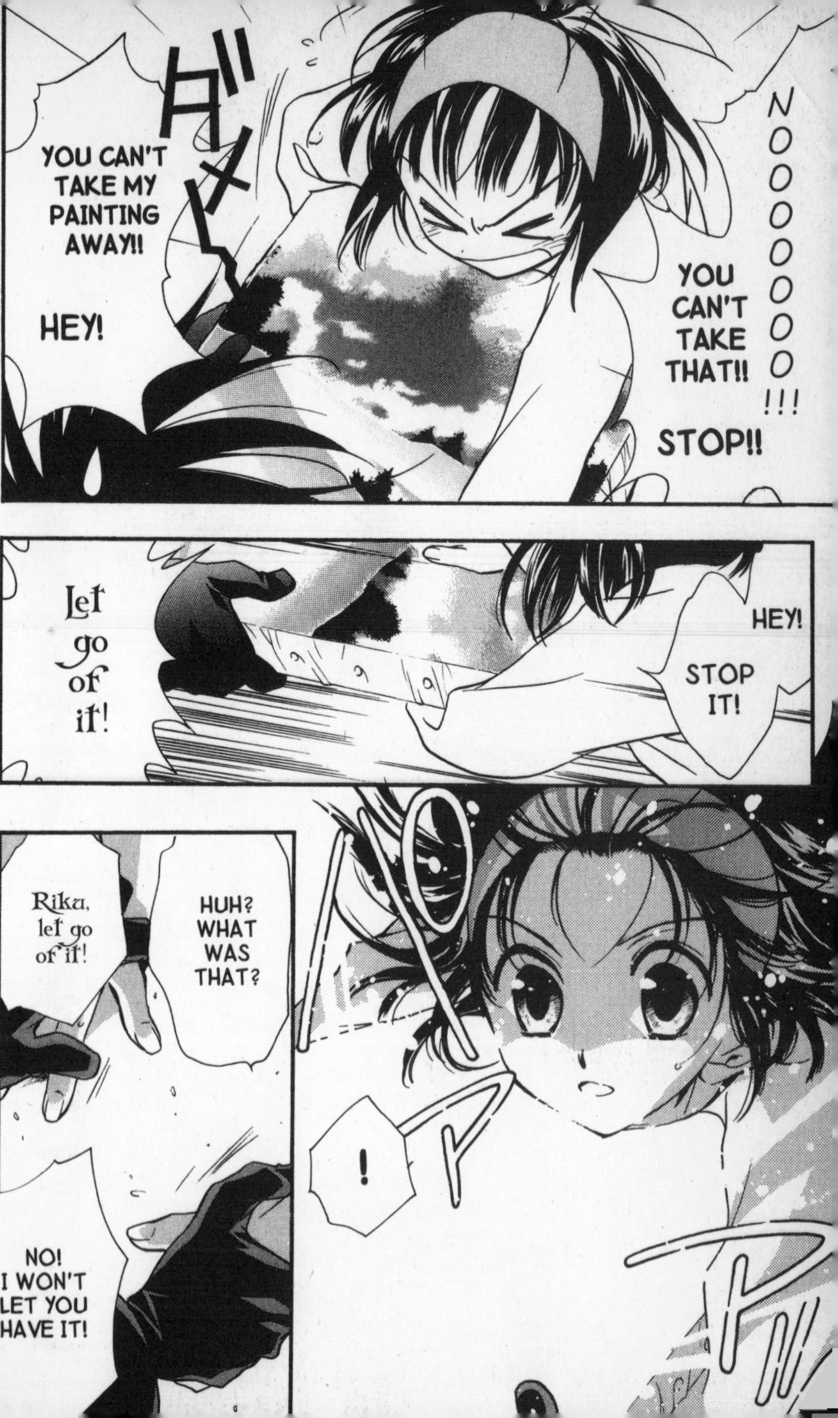
NOOOOOOOO!!!
YOU CAN'T TAKE THAT!!
STOP!!
YOU CAN'T TAKE MY PAINTING AWAY!!
HEY!
HEY!
STOP IT!
Let go of it!
HUH? WHAT WAS THAT?
Riku, let go of it!
!
NO! I WON'T LET YOU HAVE IT!

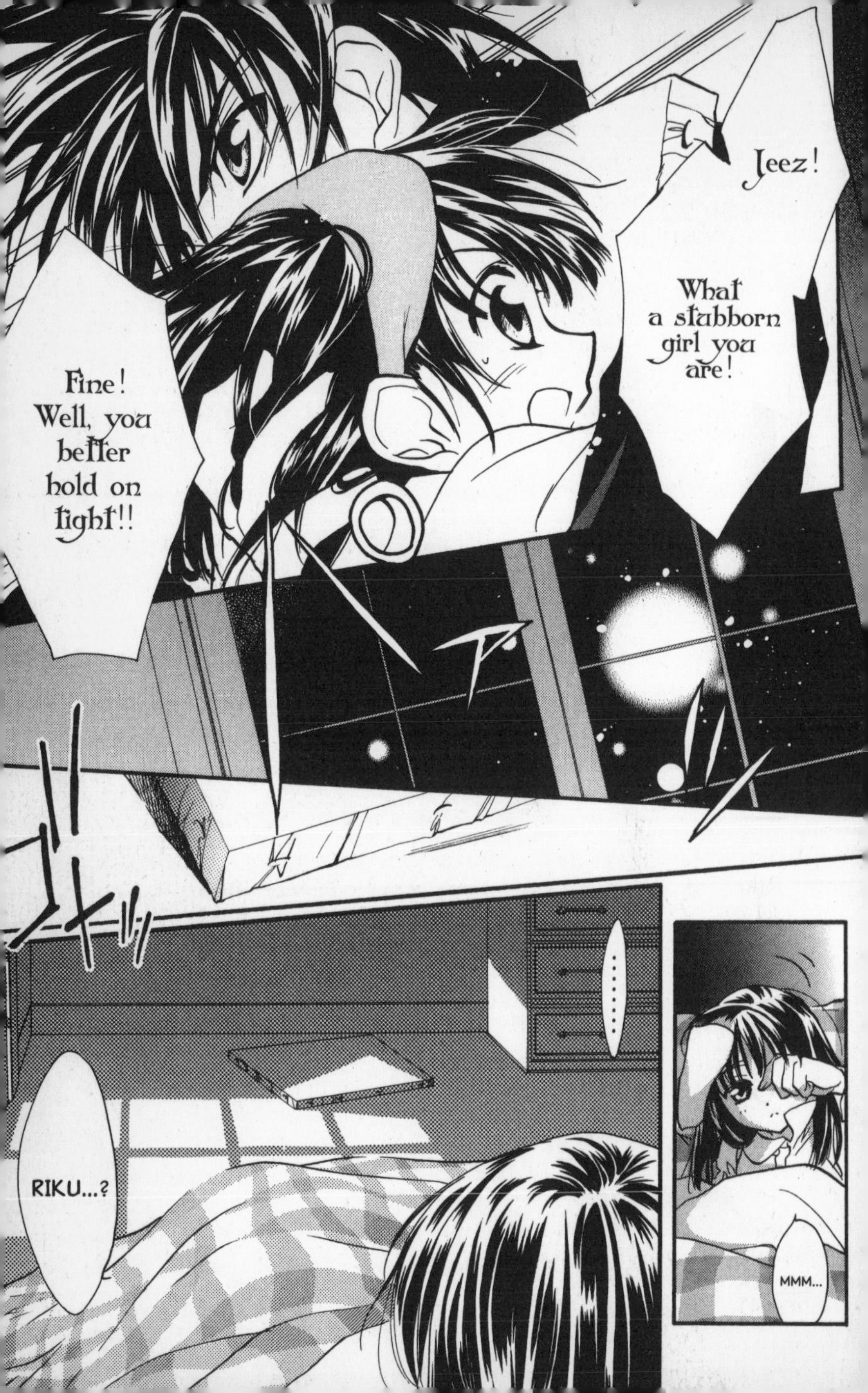
Jeez!
What a stubborn girl you are!
Fine! Well, you better hold on tight!!
MMM...
......
RIKU...?

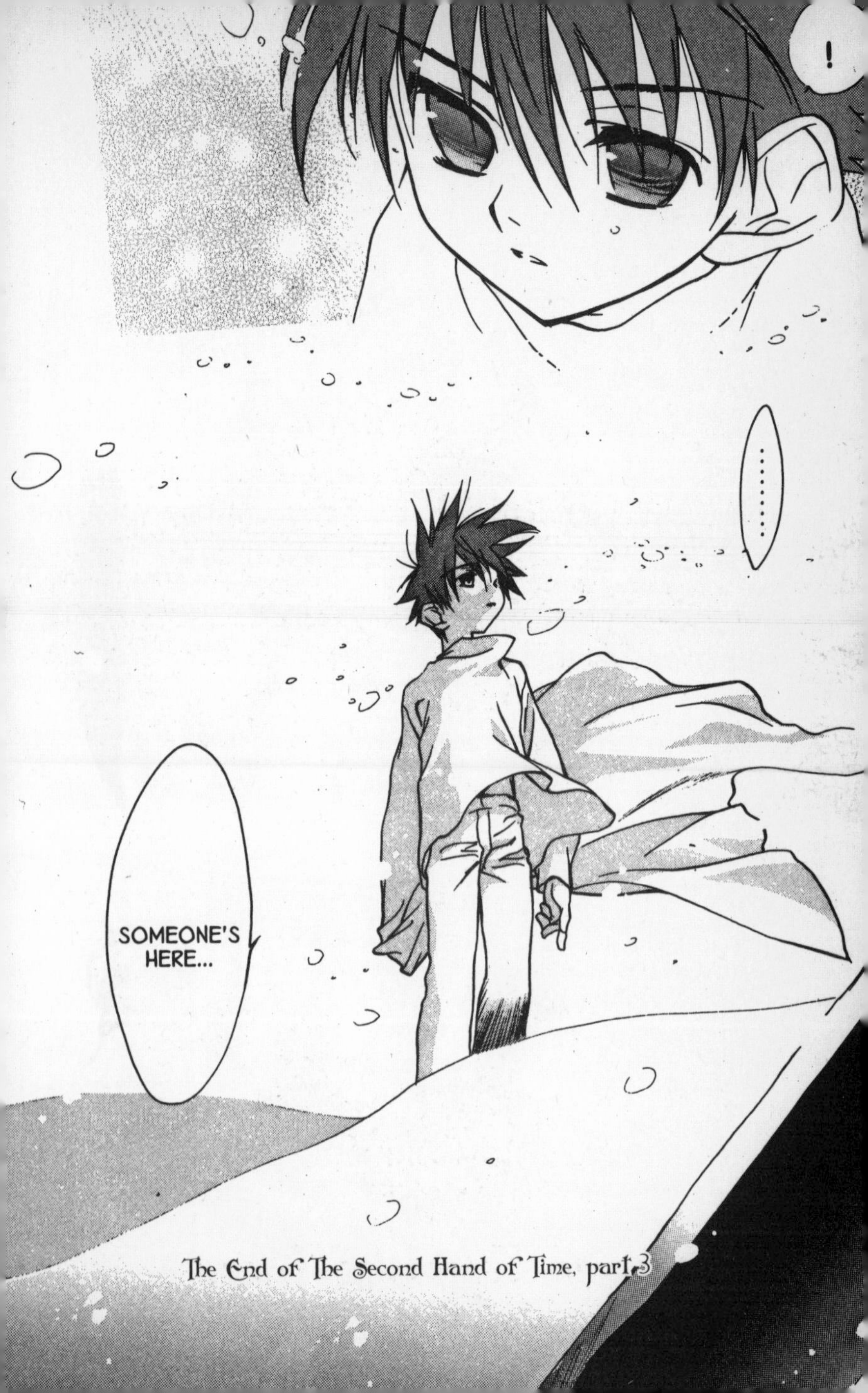
!
......
SOMEONE'S HERE...
The End of The Second Hand of Time, part 3

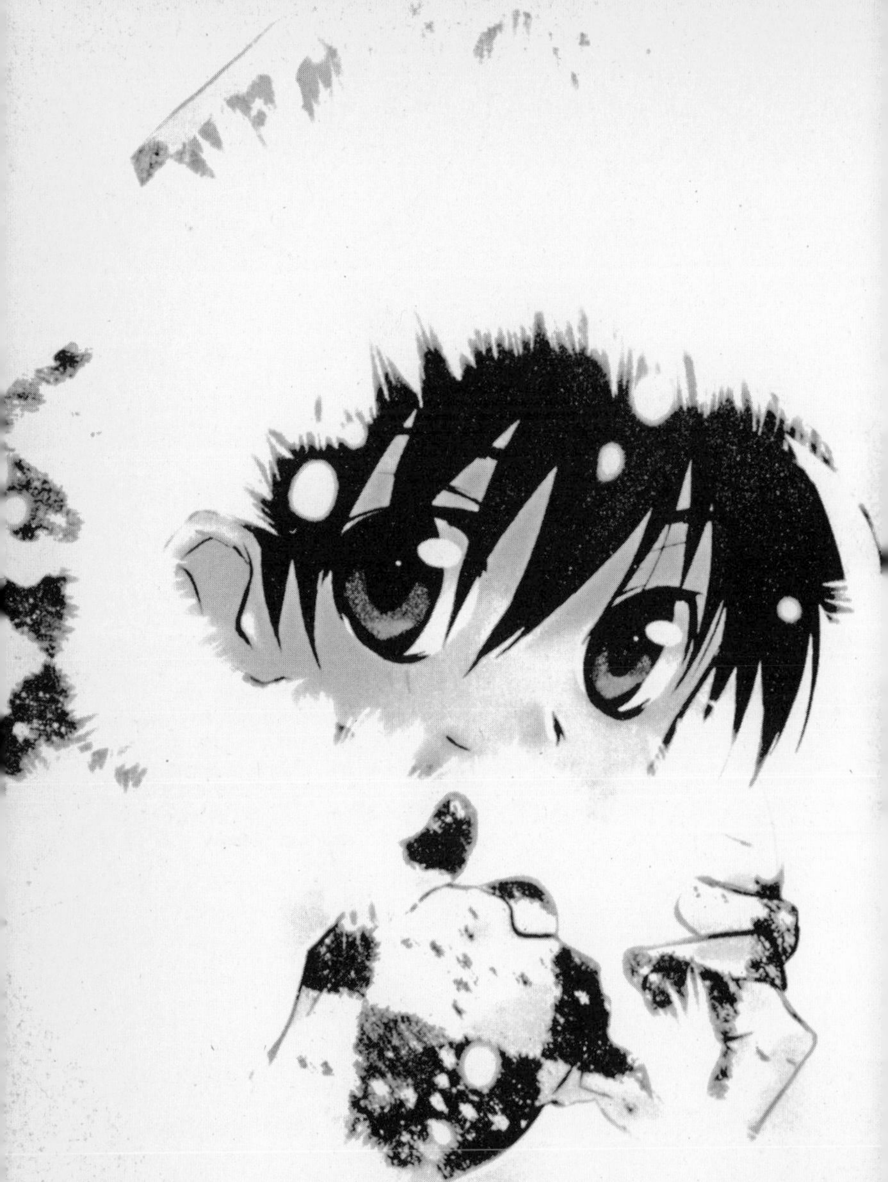

The Second Hand of Time, part 4

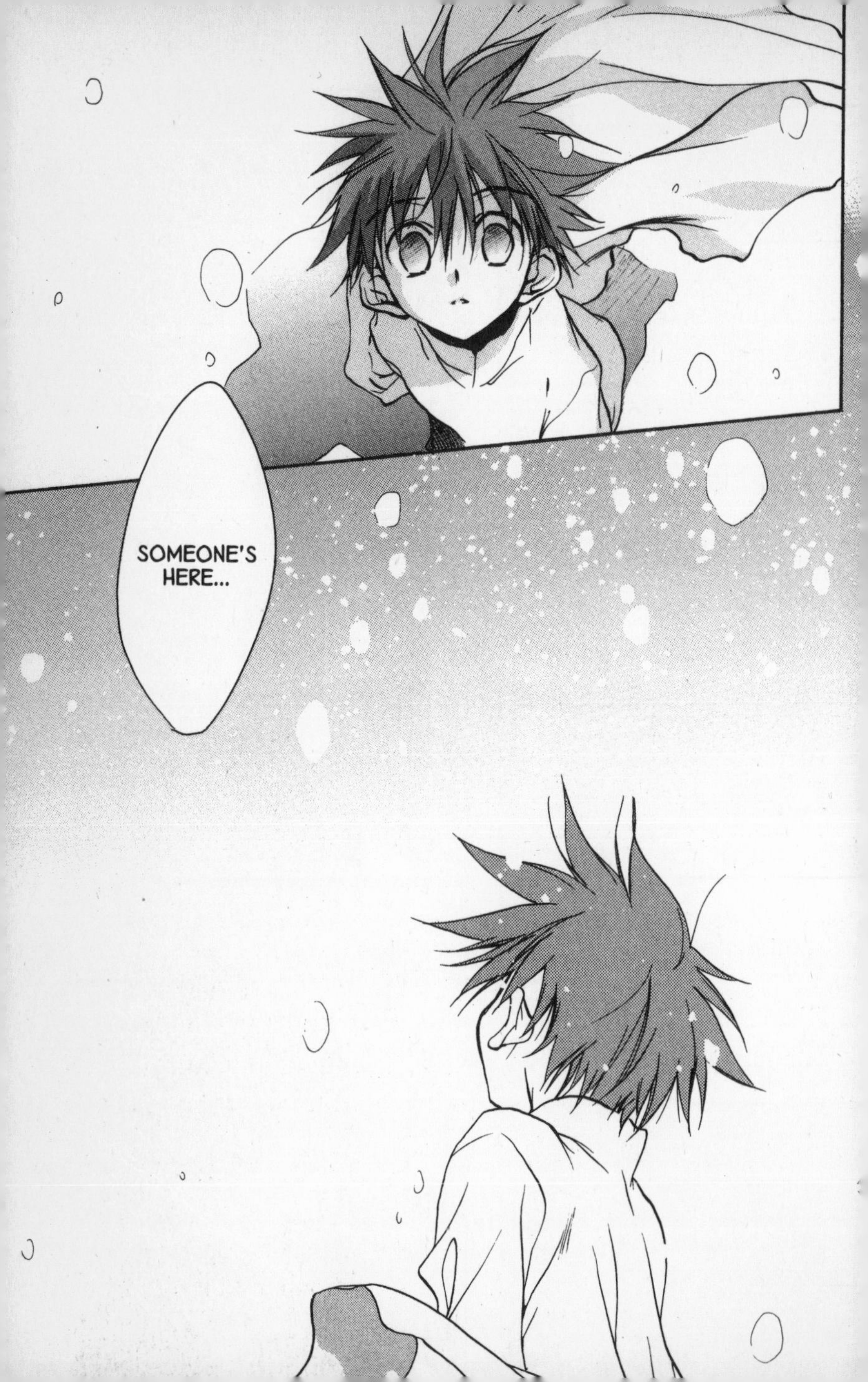
SOMEONE'S HERE...

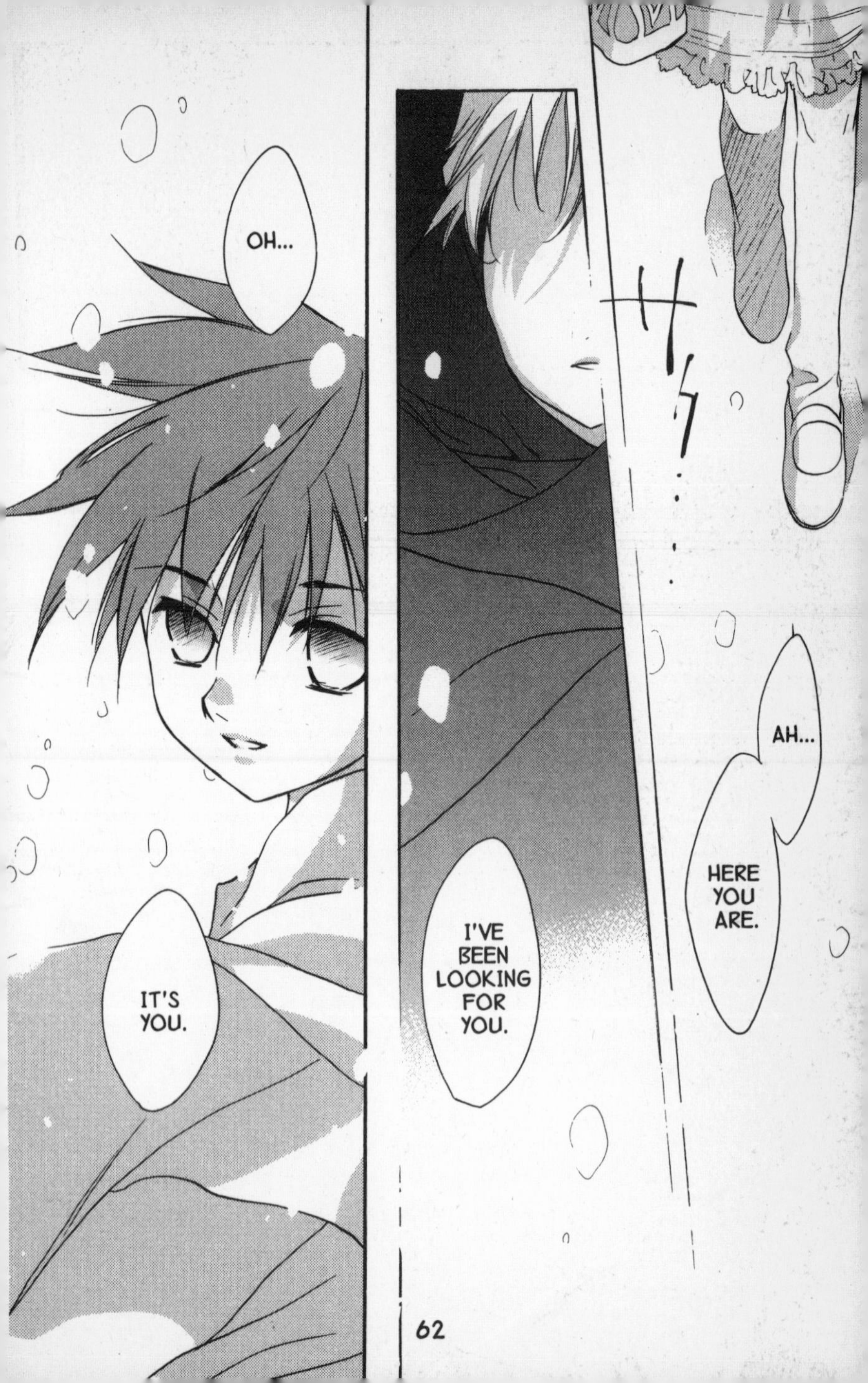
AH...
HERE YOU ARE.
I'VE BEEN LOOKING FOR YOU.
OH...
IT'S YOU.

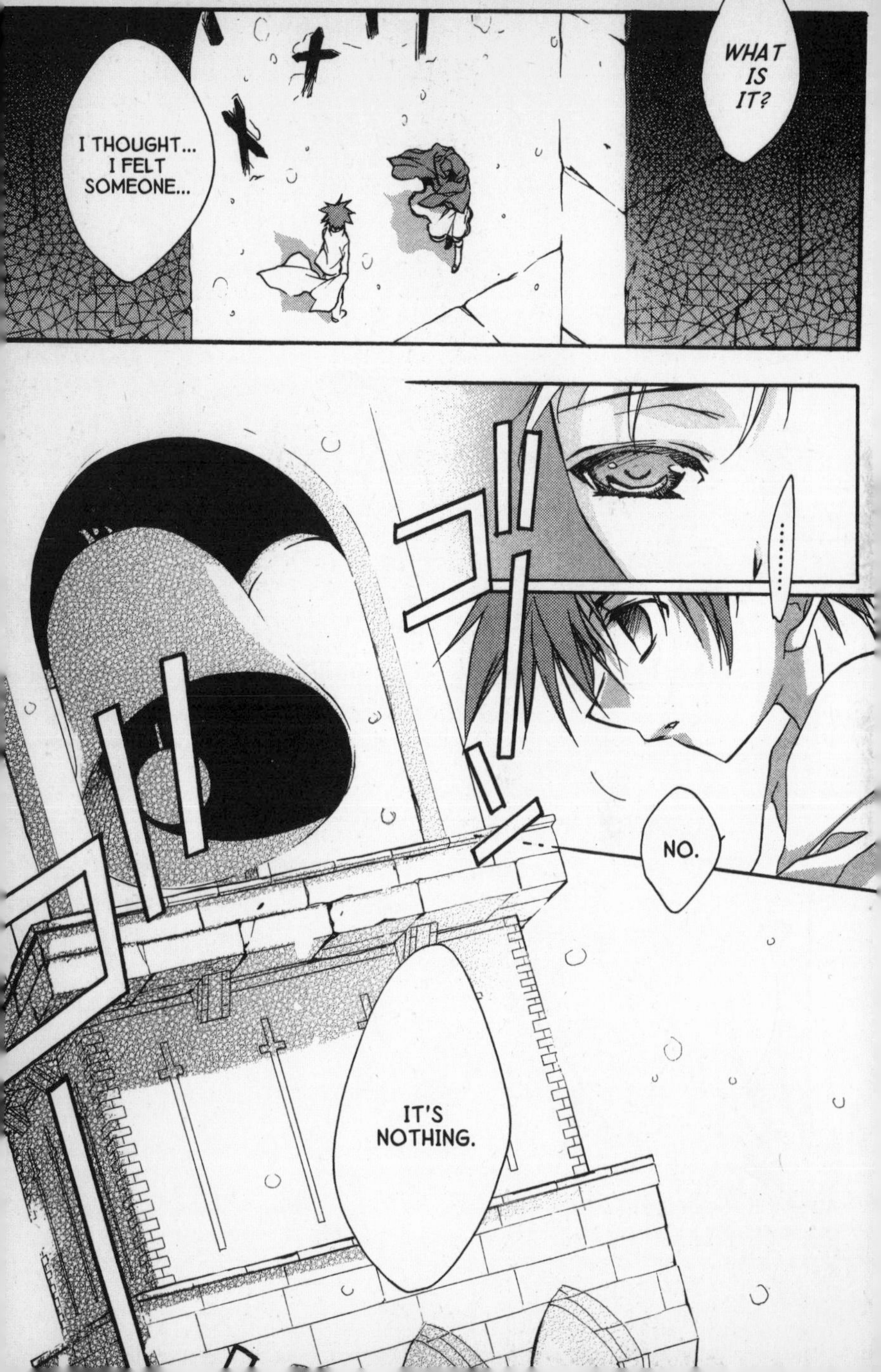
WHAT IS IT?
I THOUGHT... I FELT SOMEONE...
......
NO.
IT'S NOTHING.

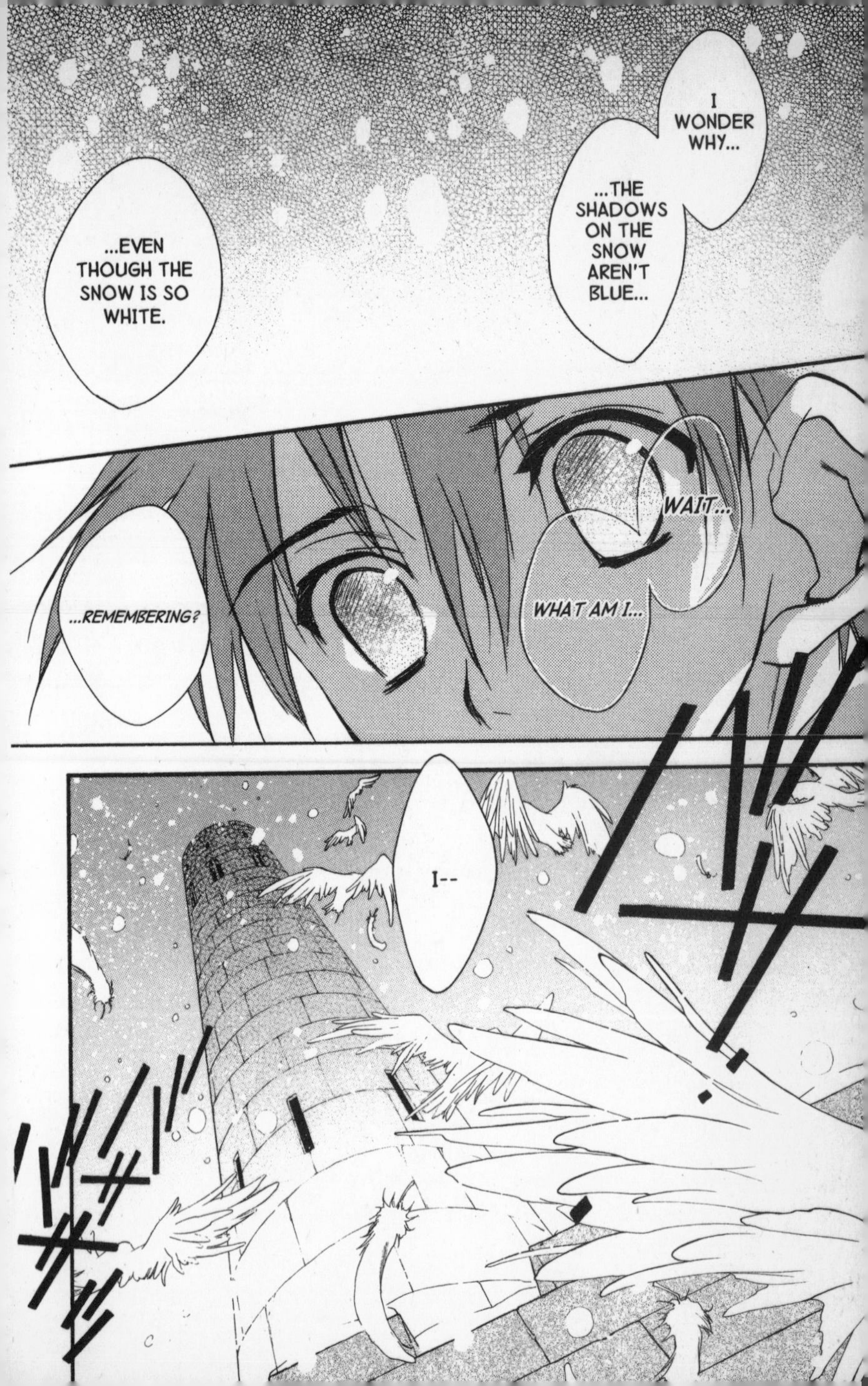
I WONDER WHY...
...THE SHADOWS ON THE SNOW AREN'T BLUE...
...EVEN THOUGH THE SNOW IS SO WHITE.
WAIT...
WHAT AM I...
...REMEMBERING?
I--

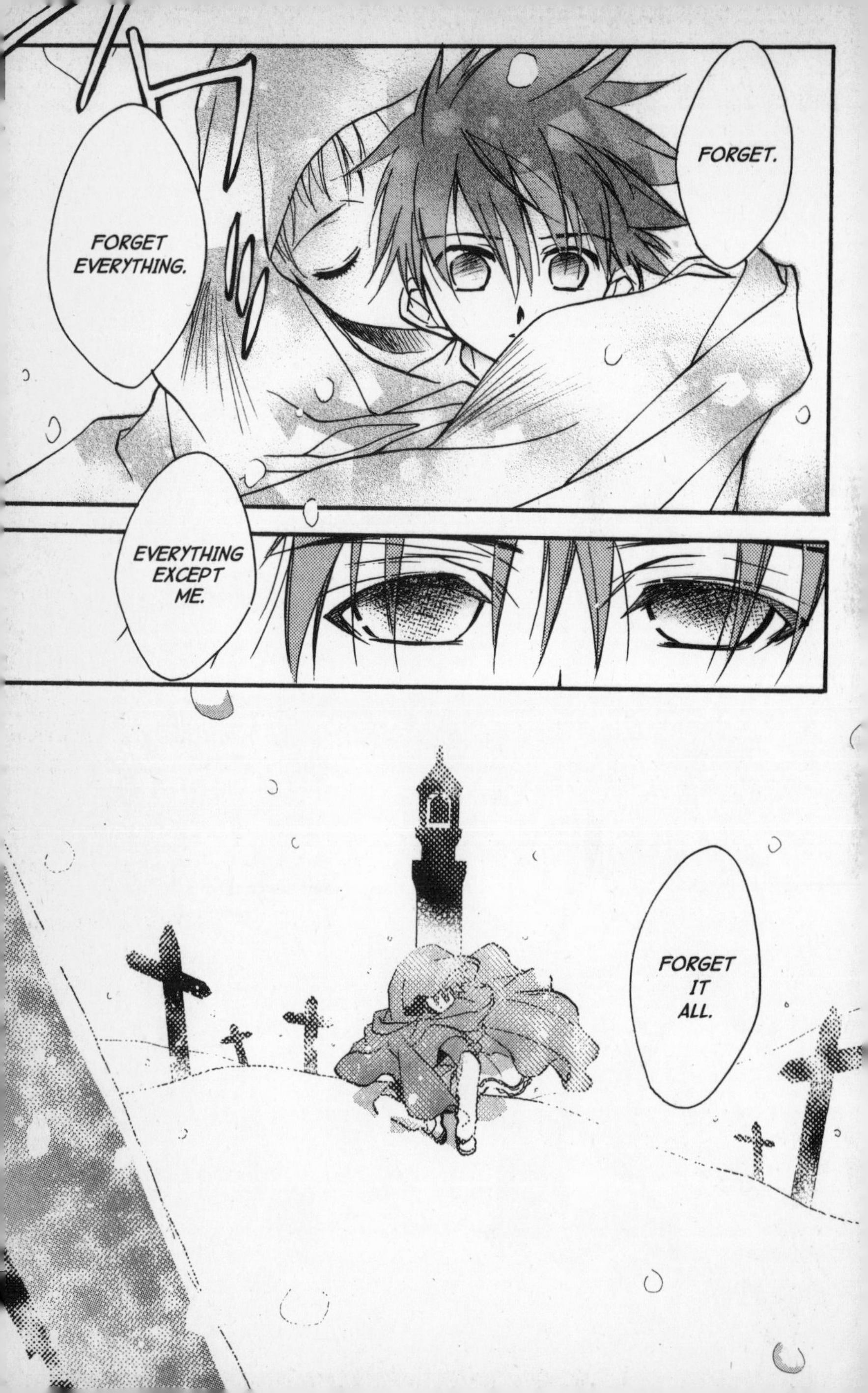
FORGET.
FORGET EVERYTHING.
EVERYTHING EXCEPT ME.
FORGET IT ALL.

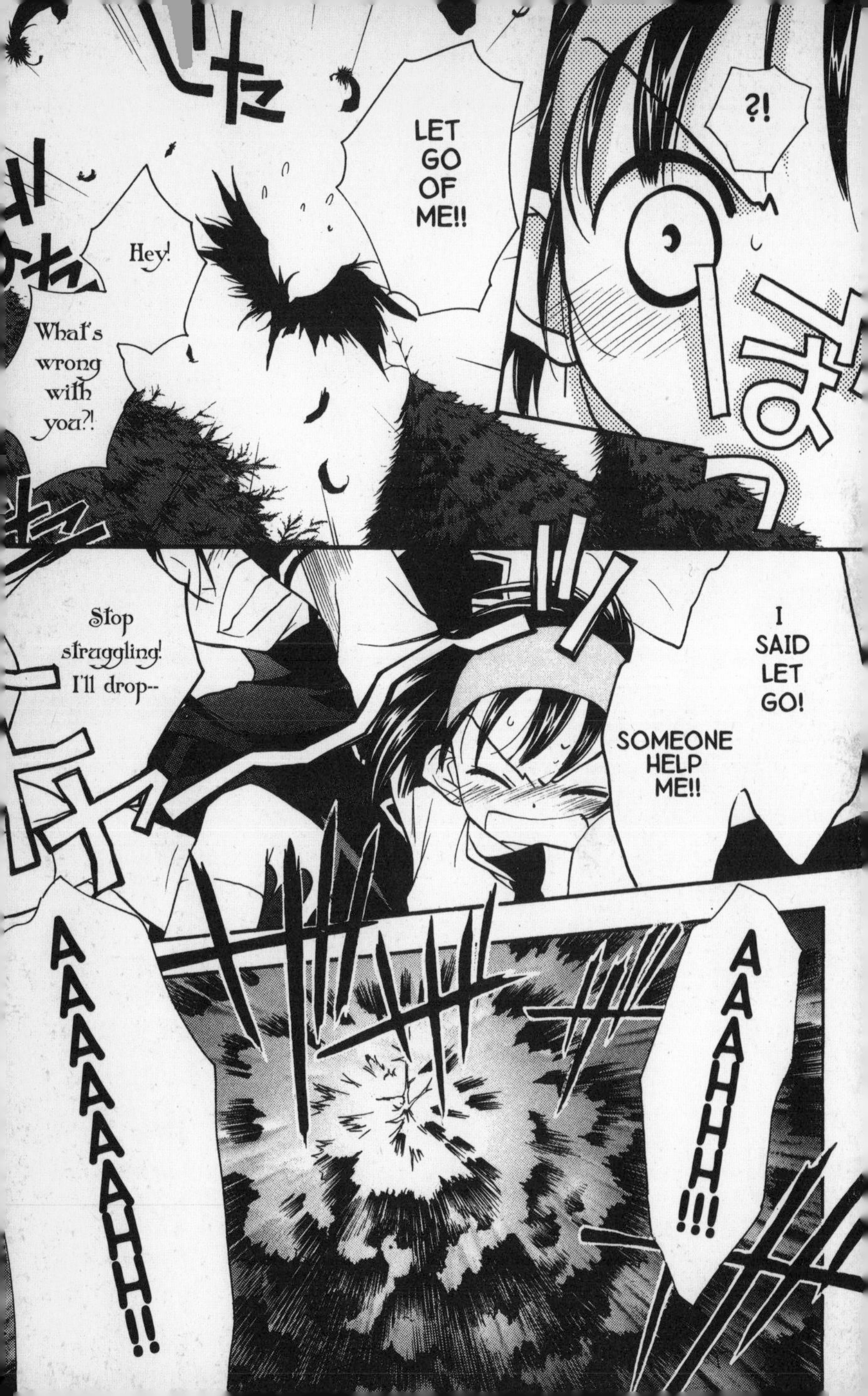
?!
LET GO OF ME!!
Hey!
What's wrong with you?!
I SAID LET GO!
SOMEONE HELP ME!!
Stop struggling! I'll drop--
AAAHHH!!!
AAAAAAHH!!

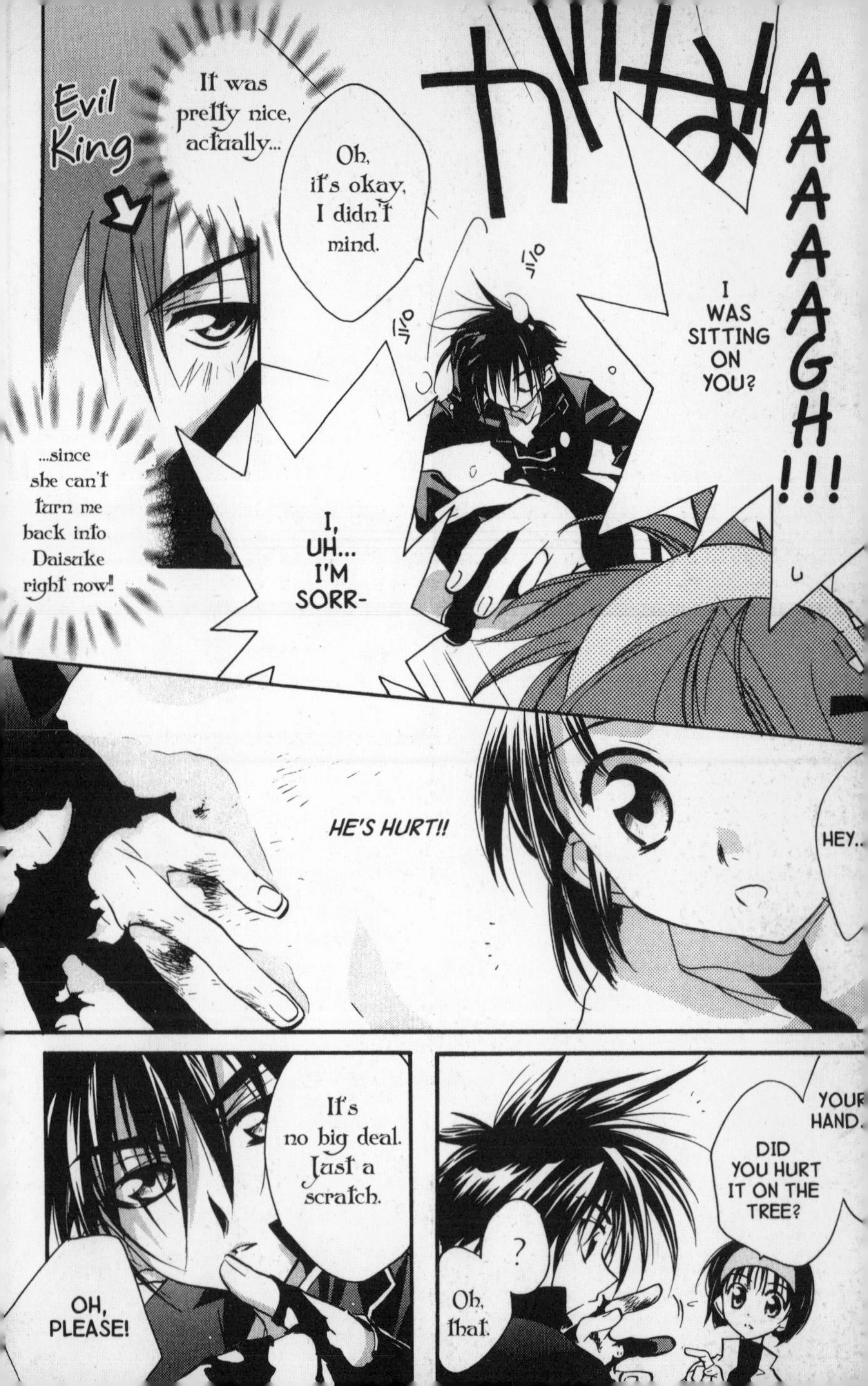

AAAAAAGH!!!
I WAS SITTING ON YOU?
I, UH... I'M SORR-
Oh, it's okay, I didn't mind.
It was pretty nice, actually...
Evil King
...since she can't turn me back into Daisuke right now!!
HEY..
HE'S HURT!!
YOUR HAND.
DID YOU HURT IT ON THE TREE?
?
Oh, that.
It's no big deal. Just a scratch.
OH, PLEASE!

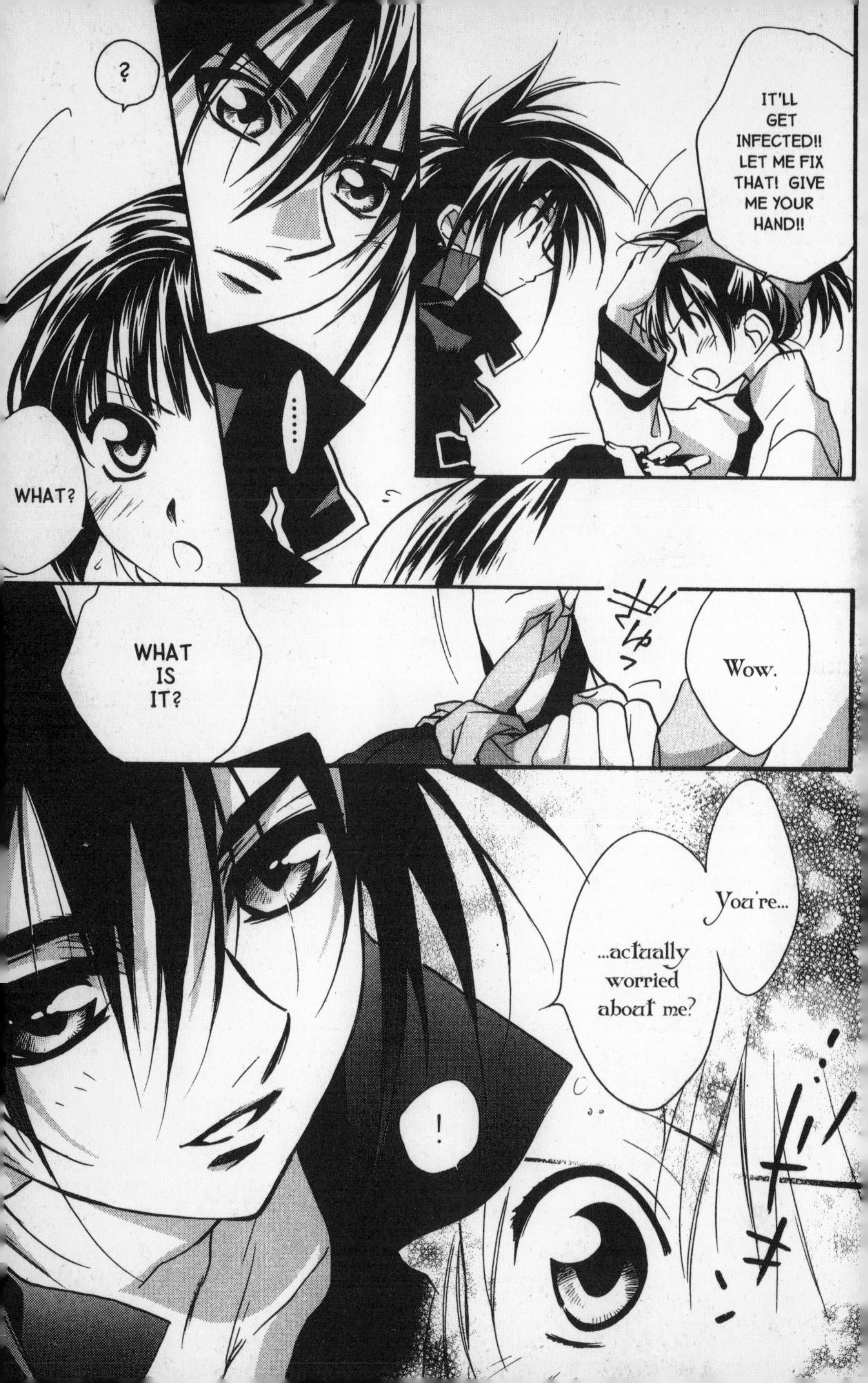
IT'LL GET INFECTED!! LET ME FIX THAT! GIVE ME YOUR HAND!!
......
?
WHAT?
Wow.
WHAT IS IT?
You're...
...actually worried about me?
!

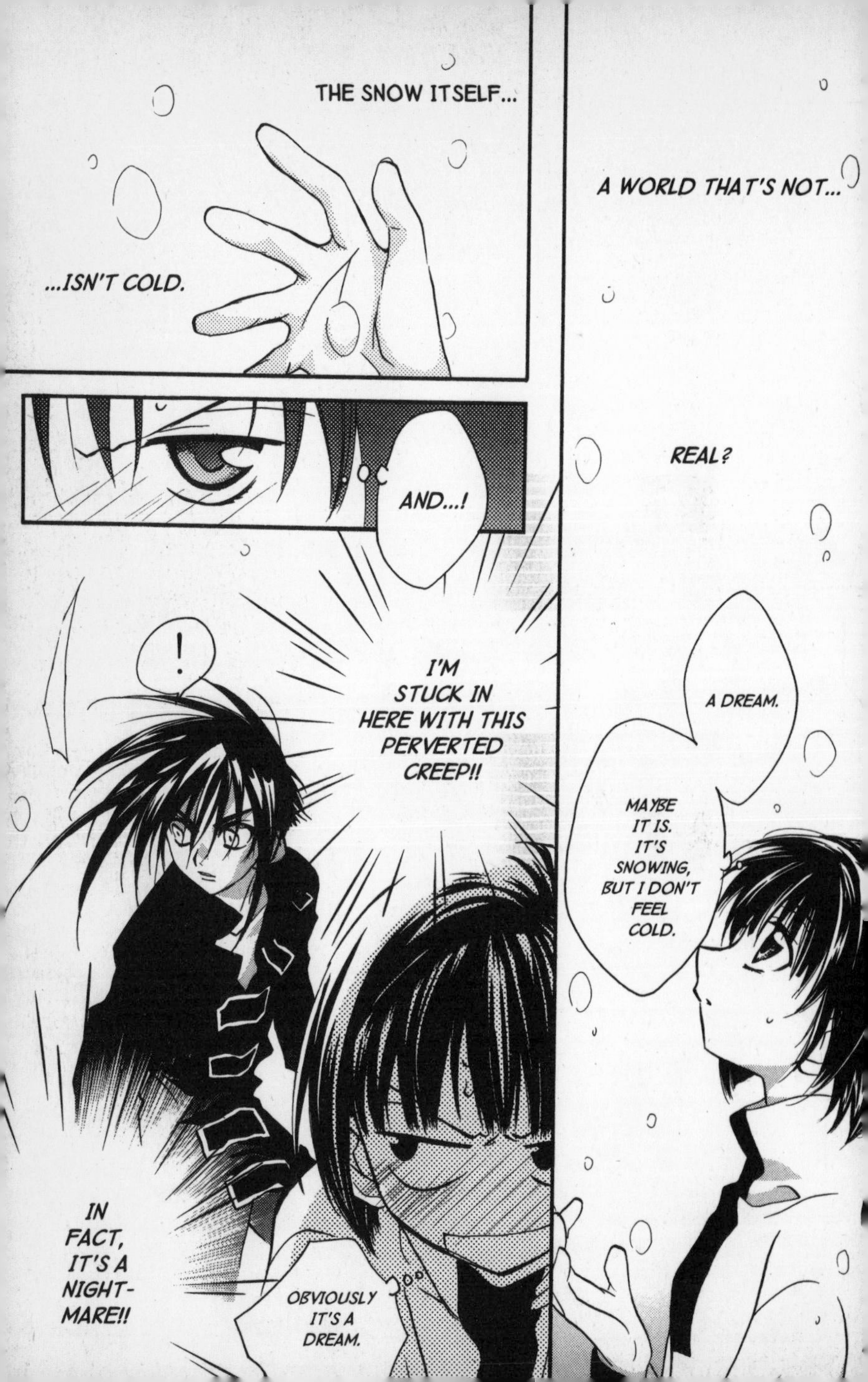

A WORLD THAT'S NOT...
REAL?
THE SNOW ITSELF...
...ISN'T COLD.
AND...!
A DREAM.
MAYBE IT IS. IT'S SNOWING, BUT I DON'T FEEL COLD.
!
I'M STUCK IN HERE WITH THIS PERVERTED CREEP!!
OBVIOUSLY IT'S A DREAM.
IN FACT, IT'S A NIGHT-MARE!!

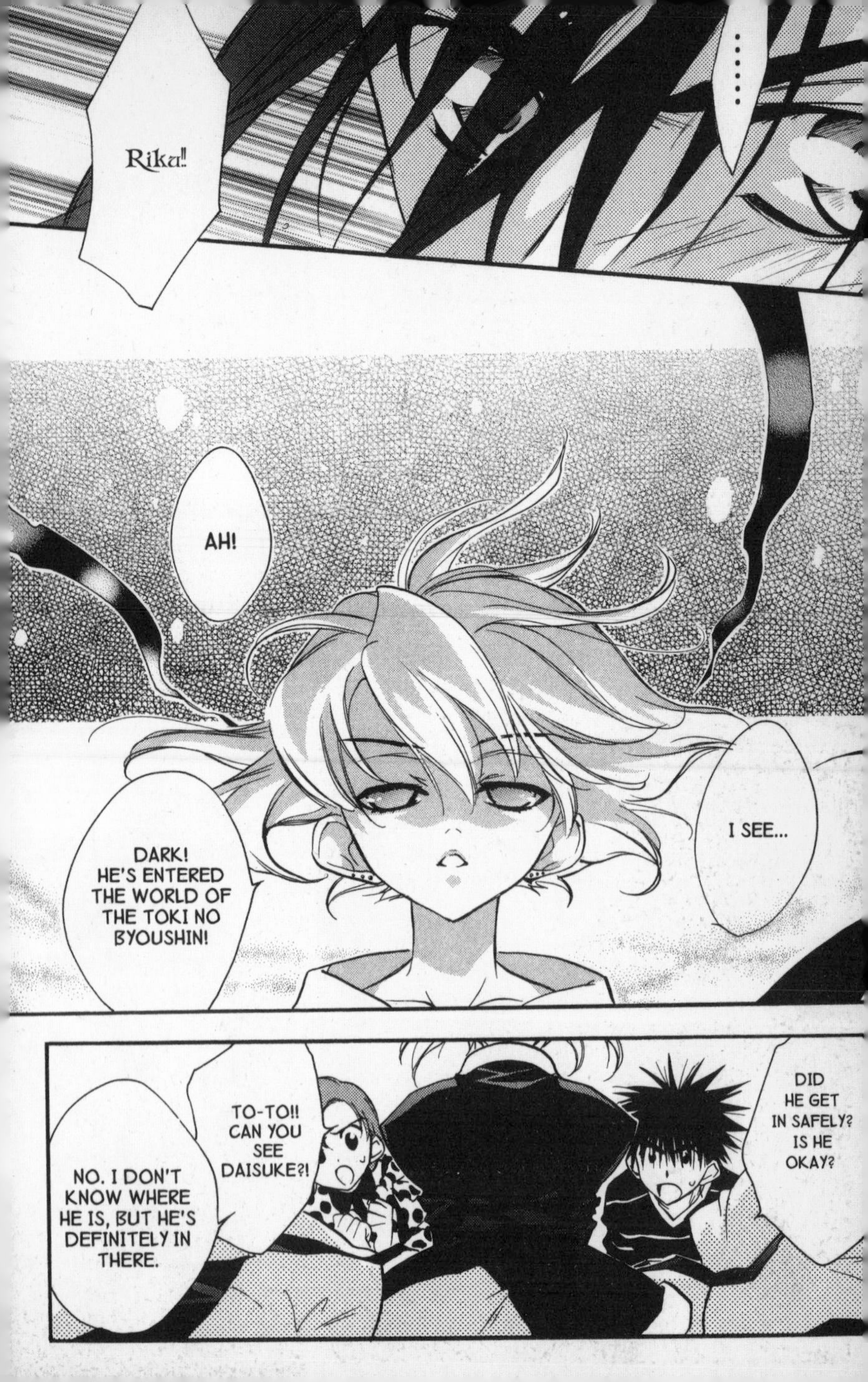

.....
Riku!!
AH!
DARK! HE'S ENTERED THE WORLD OF THE TOKI NO BYOUSHIN!
I SEE...
DID HE GET IN SAFELY? IS HE OKAY?
TO-TO!! CAN YOU SEE DAISUKE?!
NO. I DON'T KNOW WHERE HE IS, BUT HE'S DEFINITELY IN THERE.

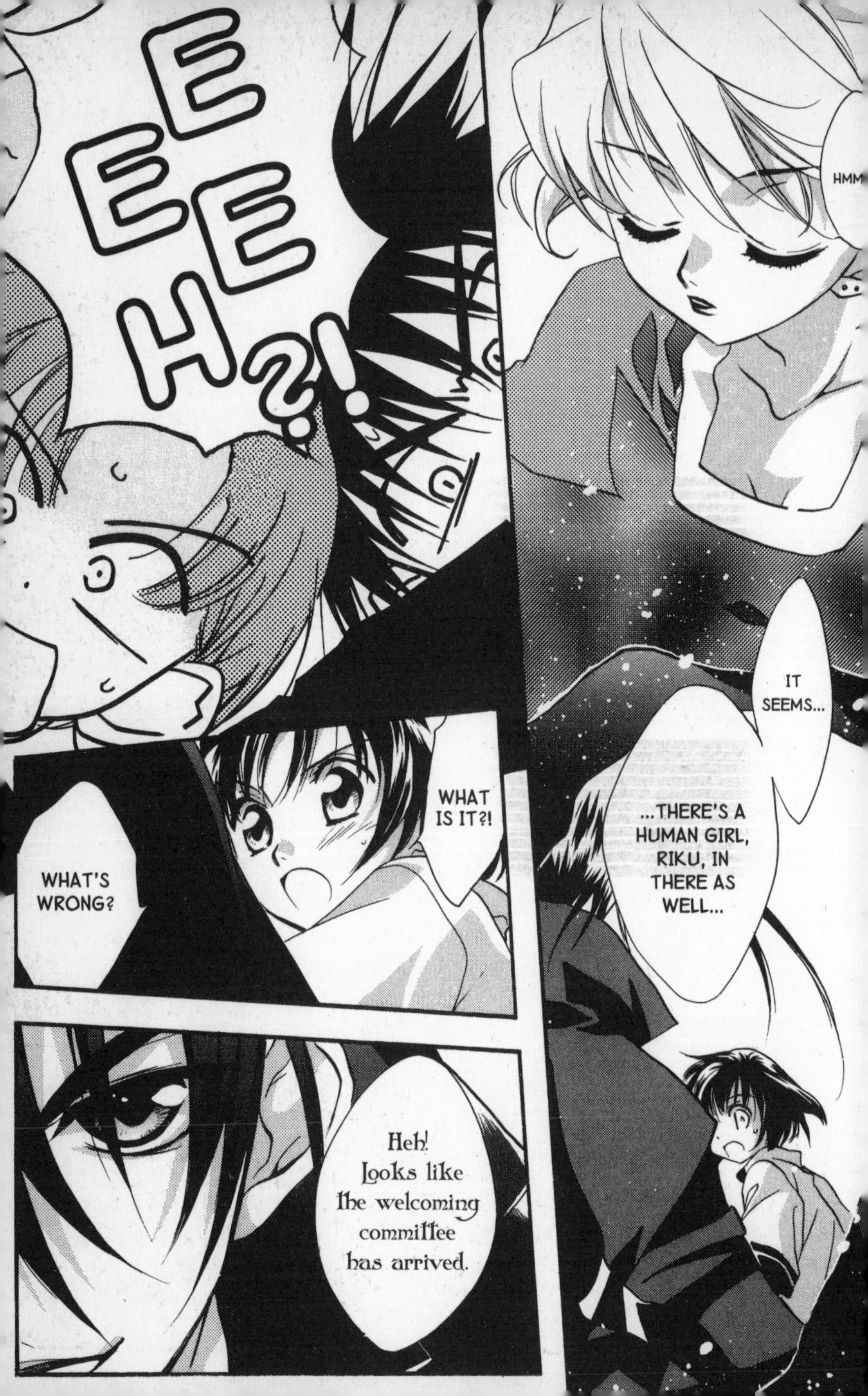
HMM
IT SEEMS...
...THERE'S A HUMAN GIRL, RIKU, IN THERE AS WELL...
EEEEH?!
WHAT IS IT?!
WHAT'S WRONG?
Heh! Looks like the welcoming committee has arrived.

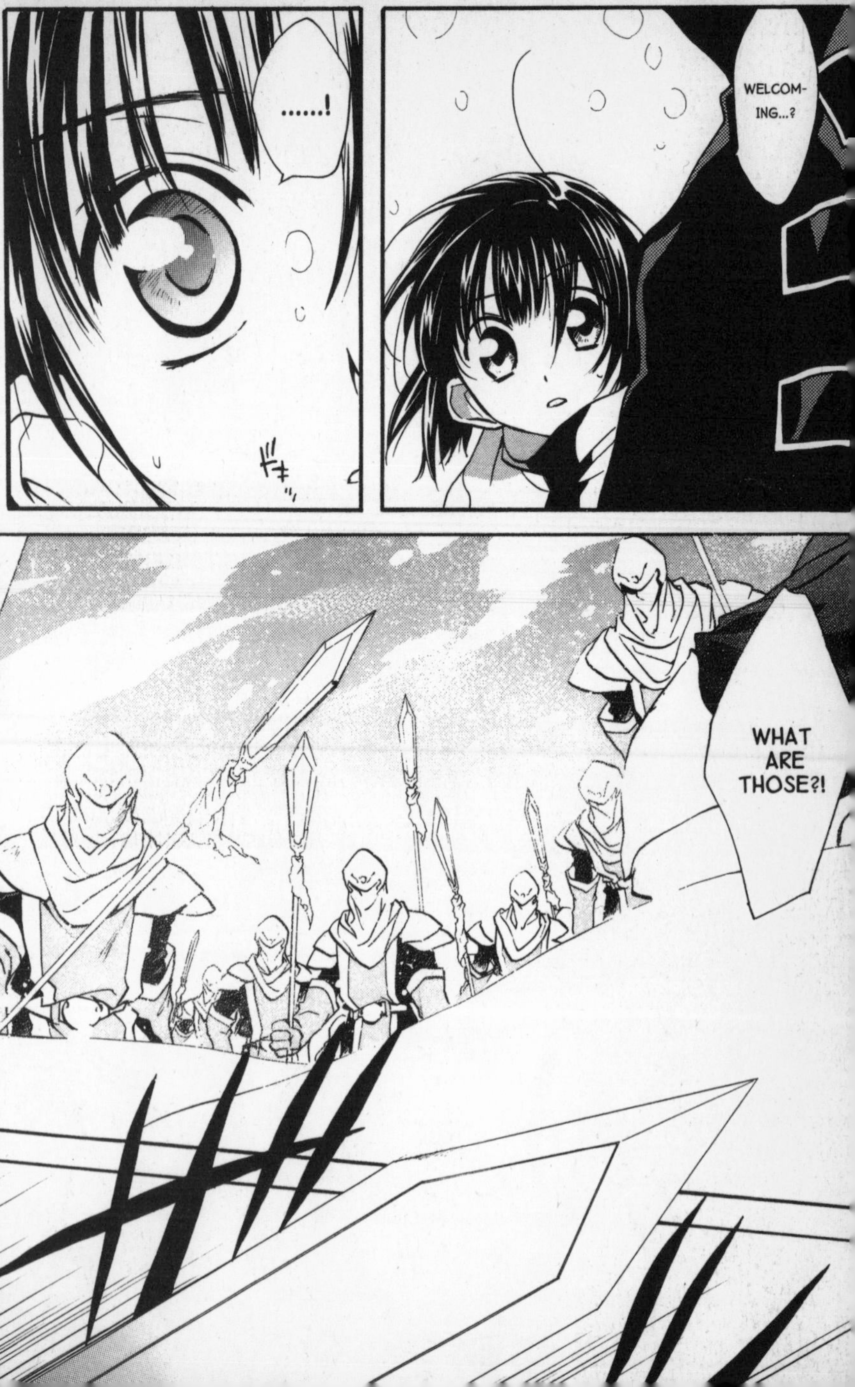
WELCOM-
ING...?
......!
WHAT
ARE
THOSE?!

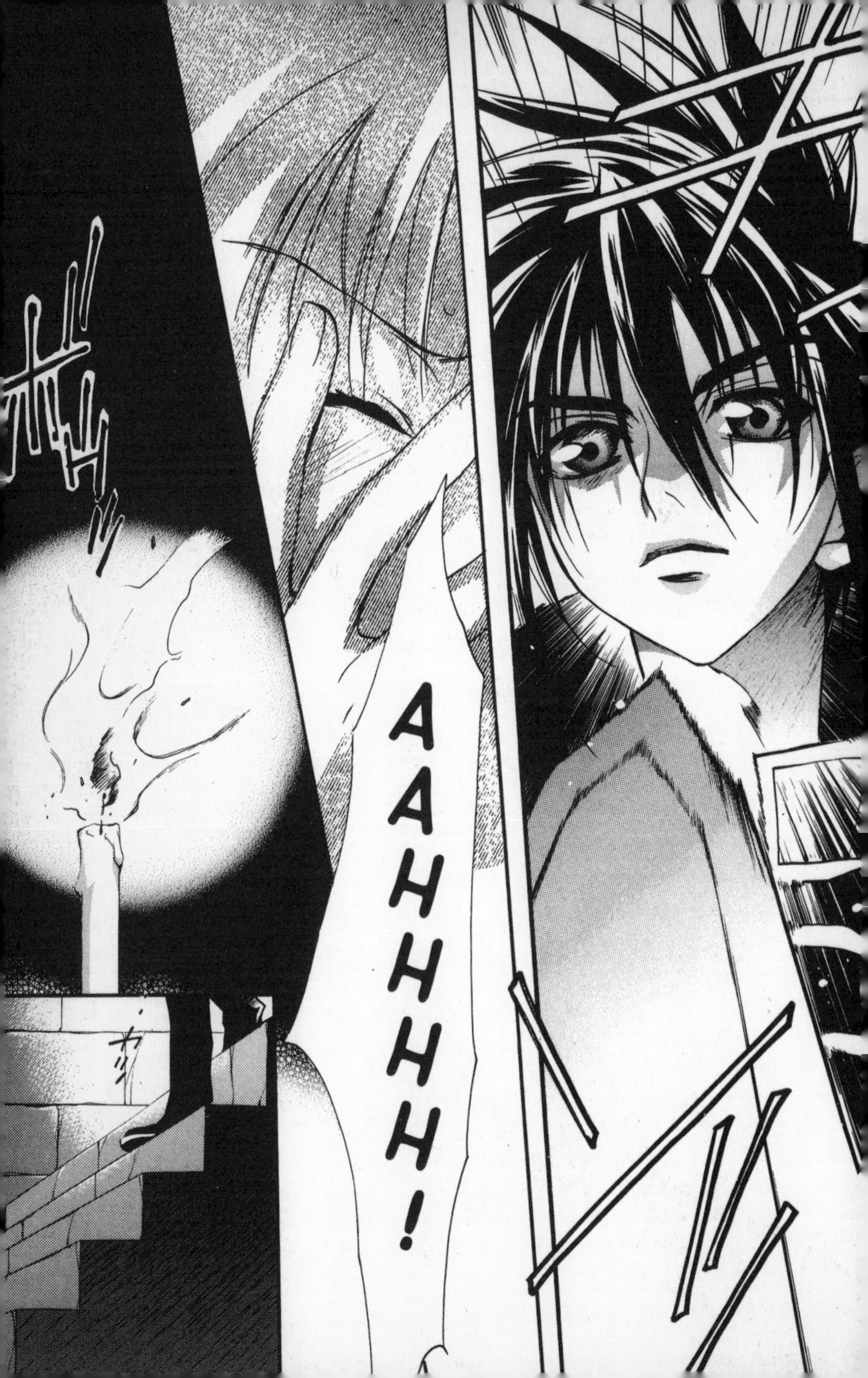
AAHHHH!

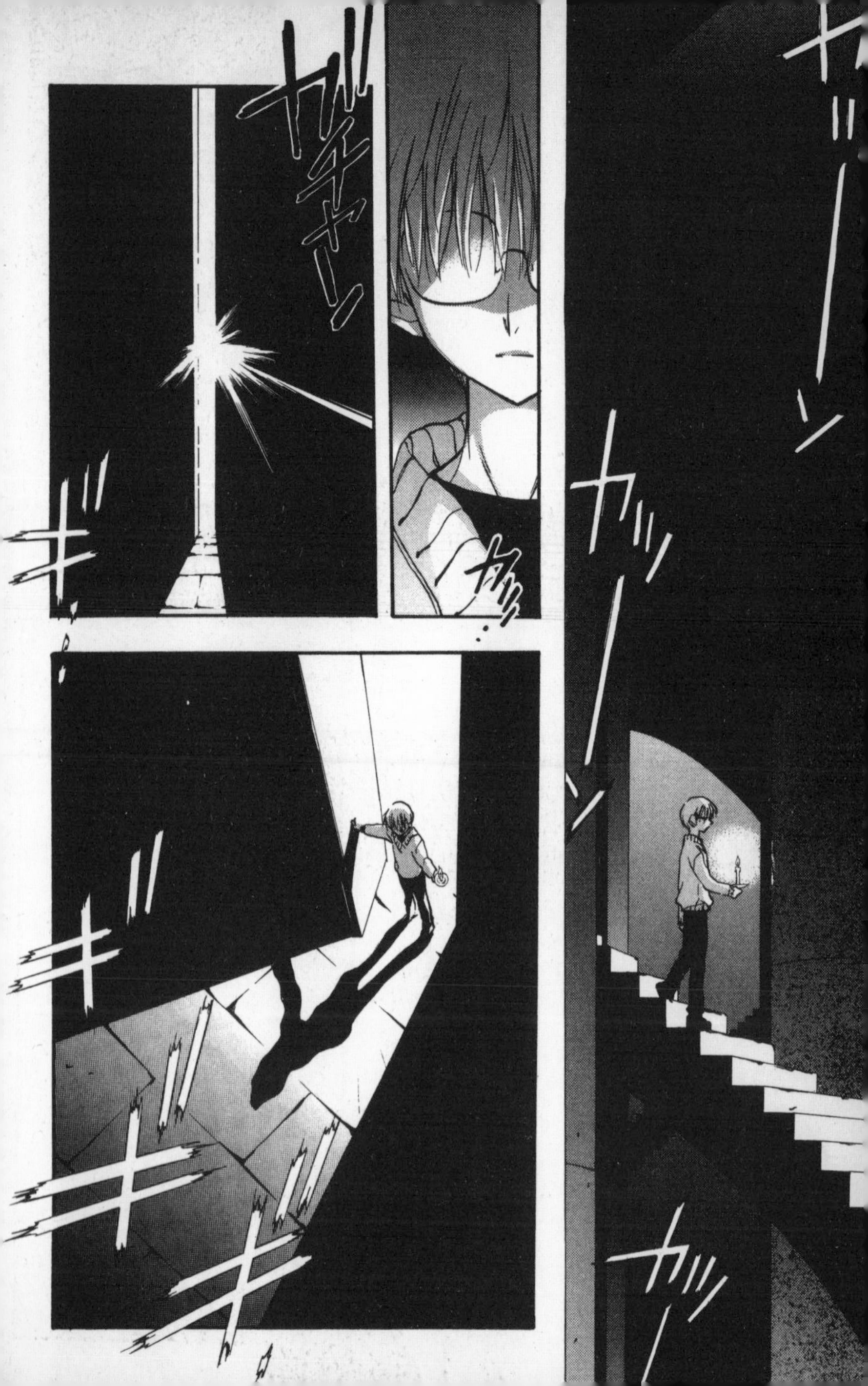

ギーーン
カツーン
カツ
ガチャーン
ギ
ギギギ

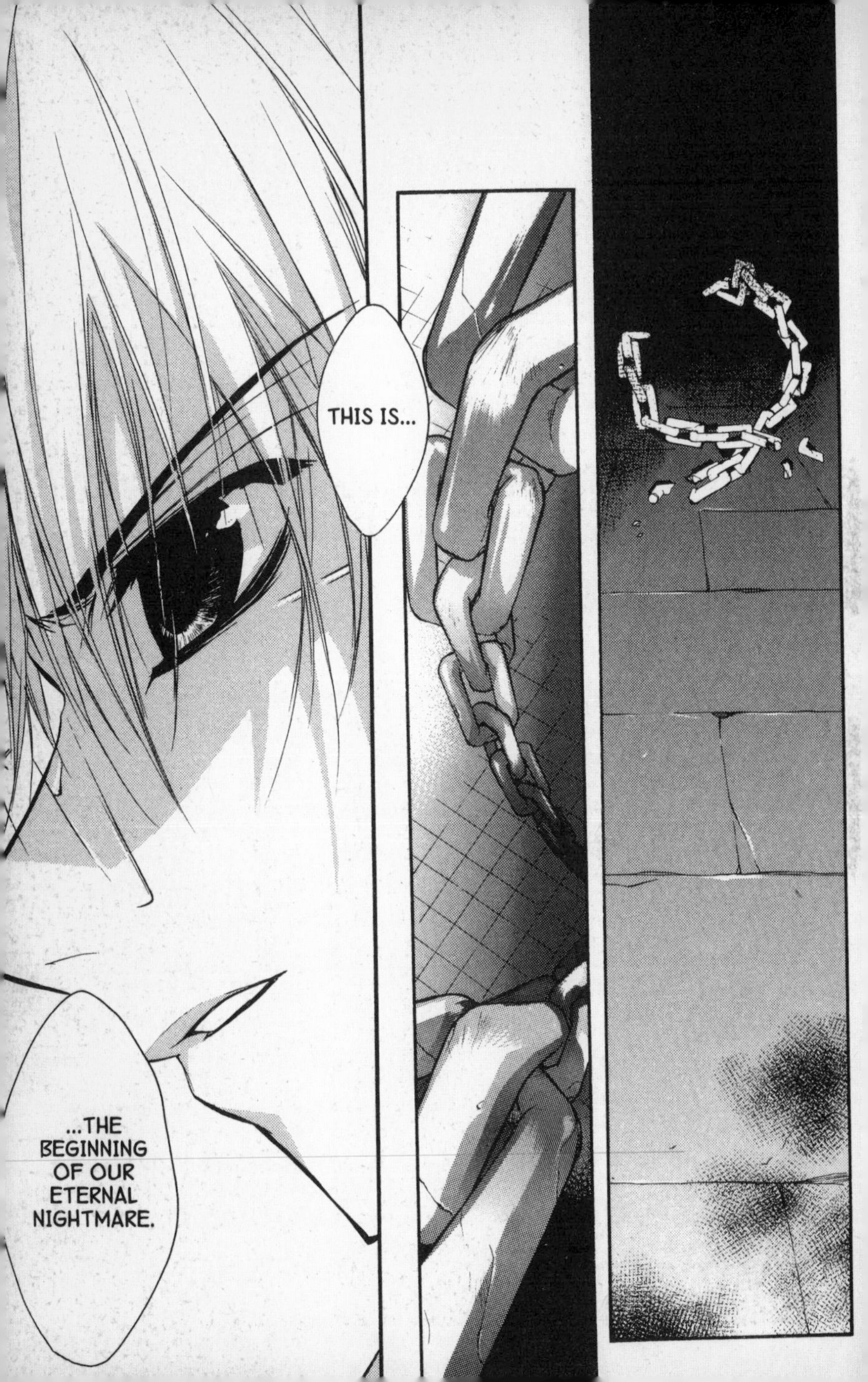
THIS IS...
...THE BEGINNING OF OUR ETERNAL NIGHTMARE.

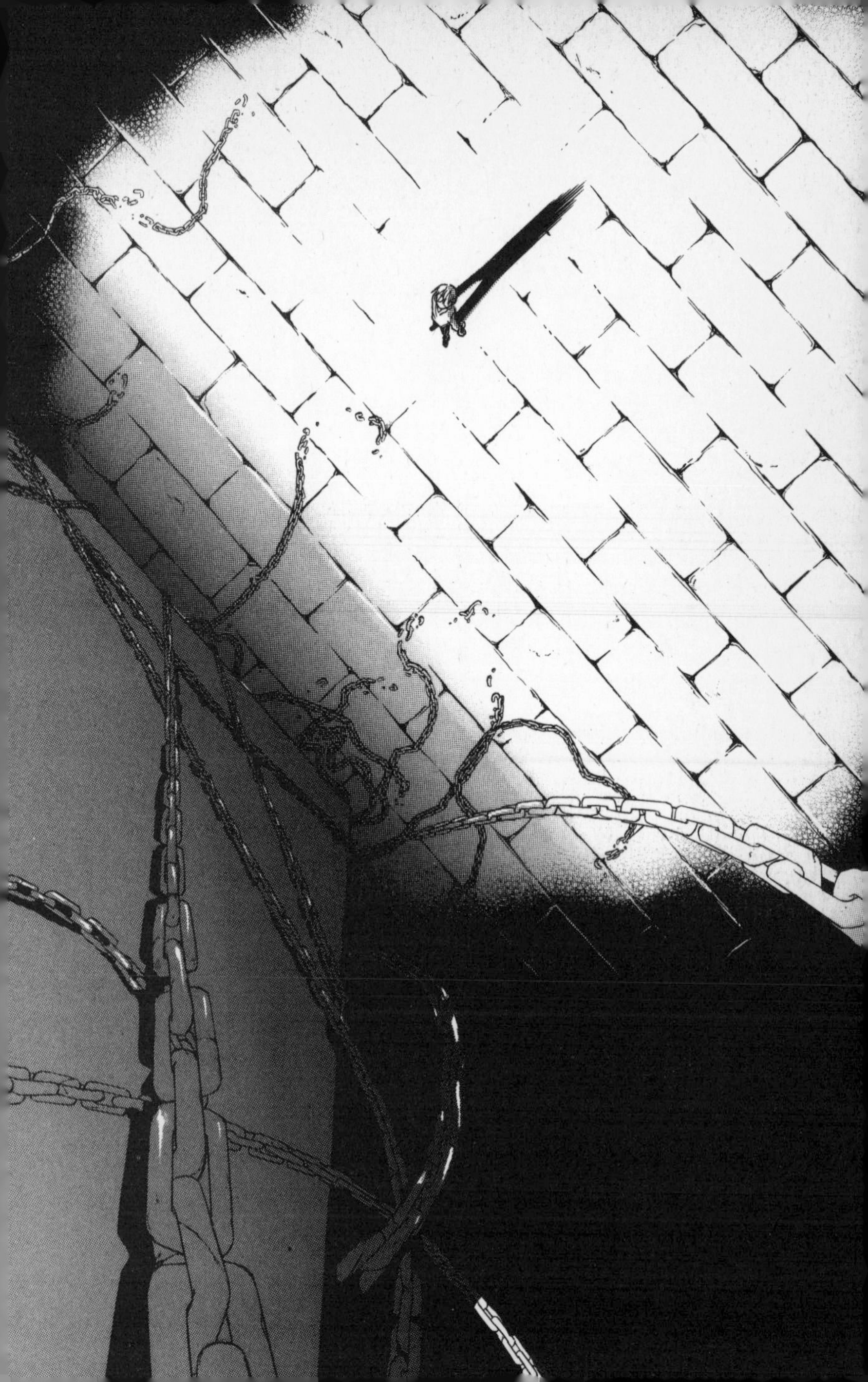

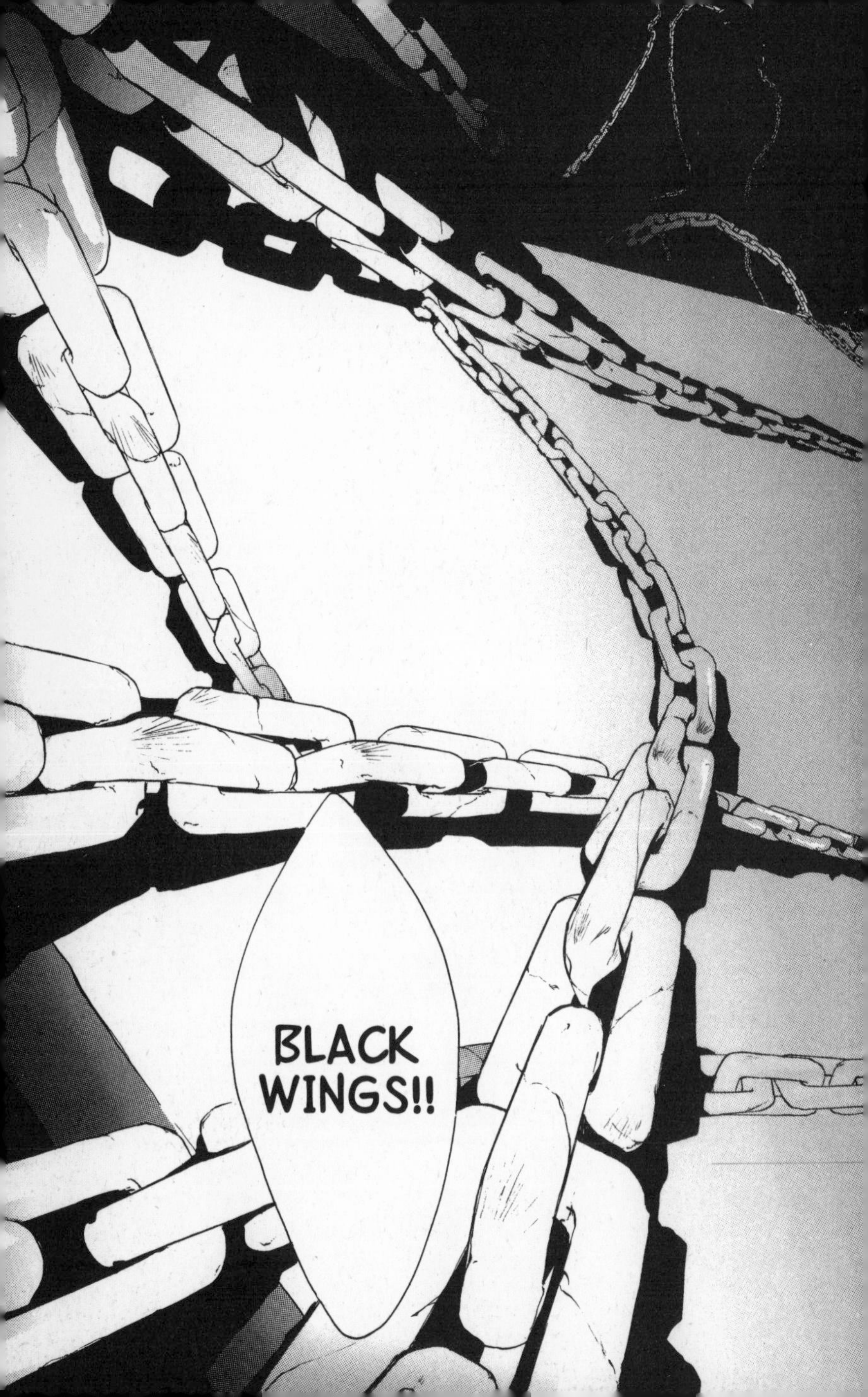
BLACK WINGS!!

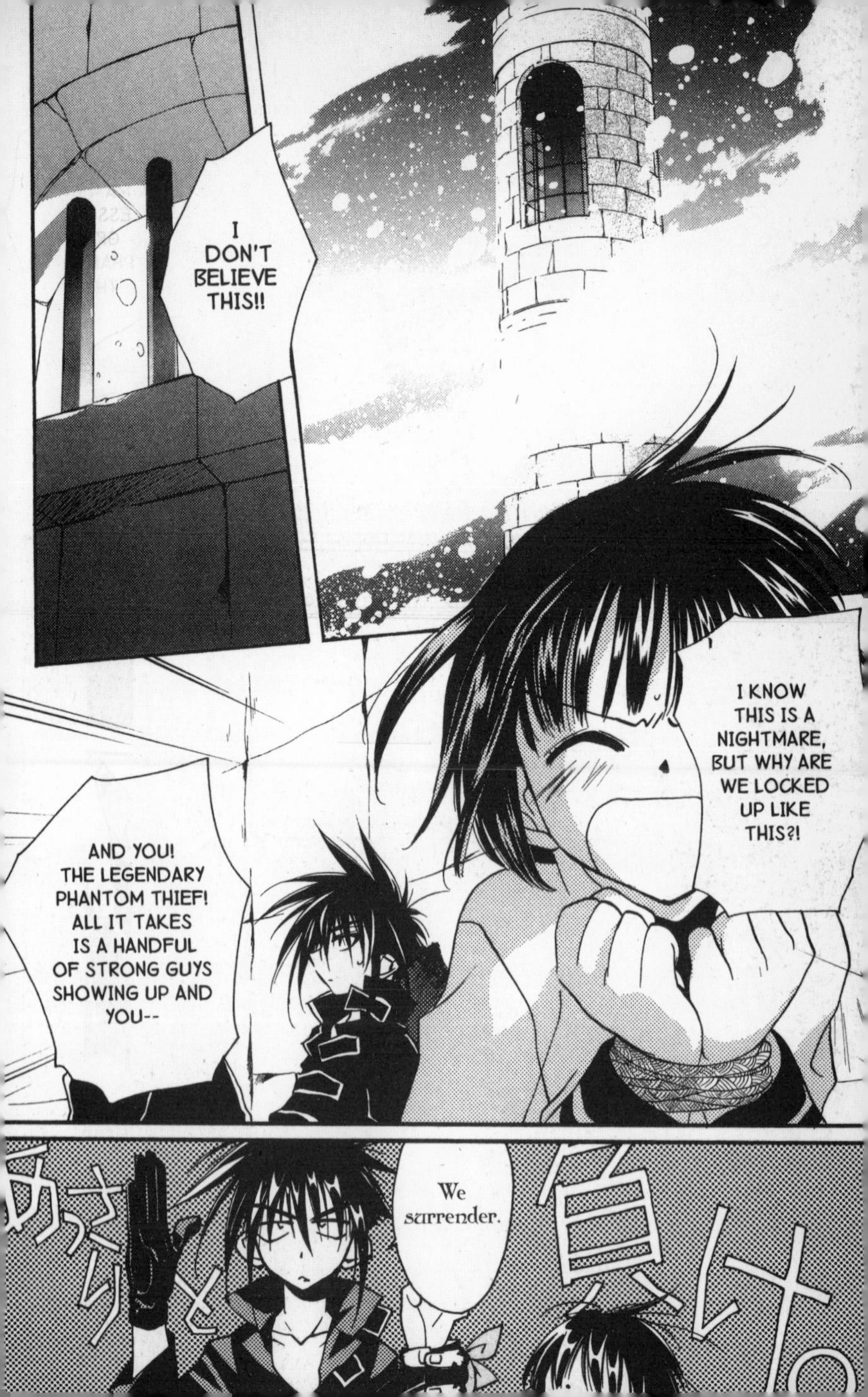
I DON'T BELIEVE THIS!!
I KNOW THIS IS A NIGHTMARE, BUT WHY ARE WE LOCKED UP LIKE THIS?!
AND YOU! THE LEGENDARY PHANTOM THIEF! ALL IT TAKES IS A HANDFUL OF STRONG GUYS SHOWING UP AND YOU--
We surrender.
あっさりと
負け

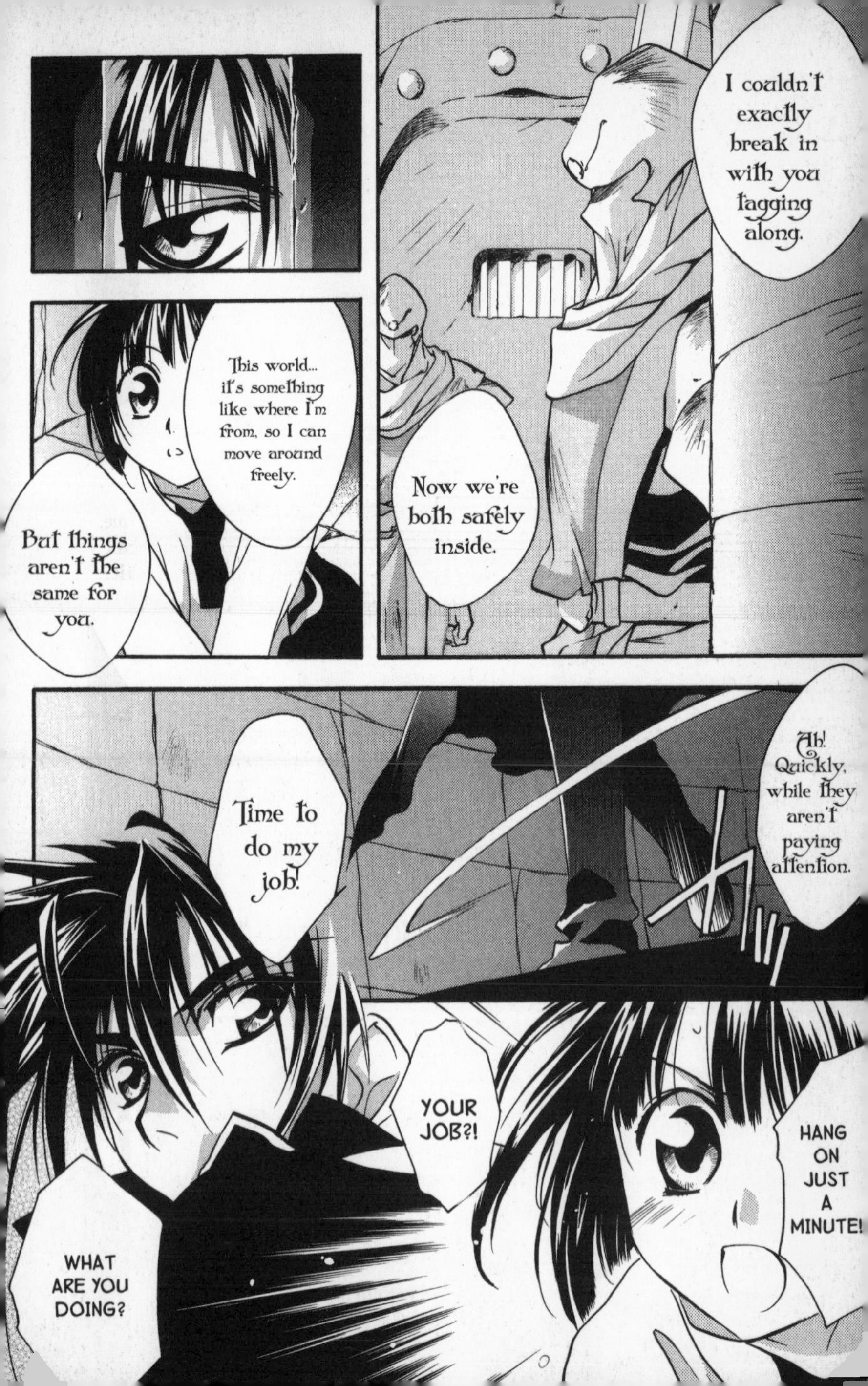
I couldn't exactly break in with you tagging along.
Now we're both safely inside.
This world... it's something like where I'm from, so I can move around freely.
But things aren't the same for you.
Ah! Quickly, while they aren't paying attention.
Time to do my job!
HANG ON JUST A MINUTE!
YOUR JOB?!
WHAT ARE YOU DOING?

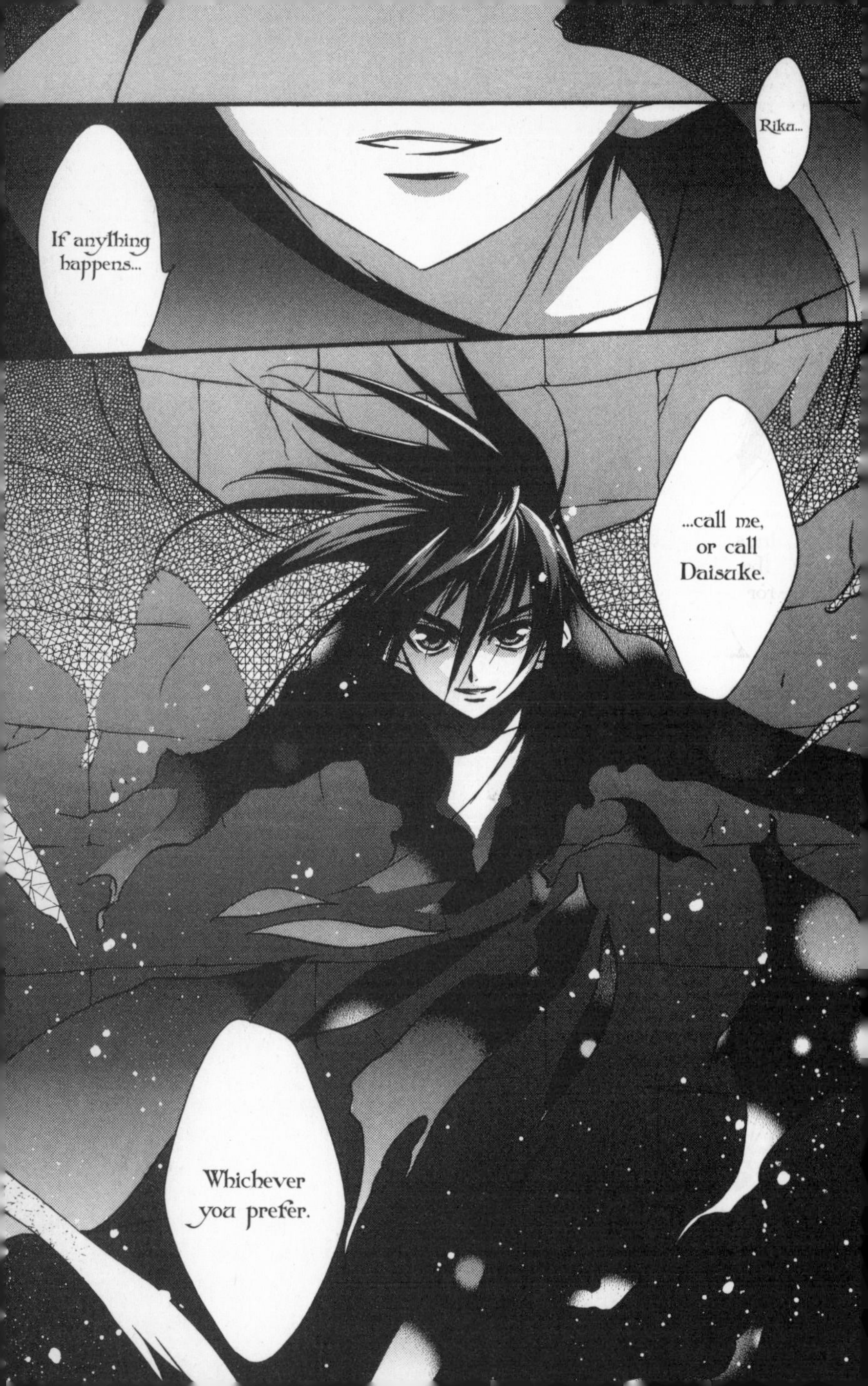
Riku...
If anything happens...
...call me, or call Daisuke.
Whichever you prefer.

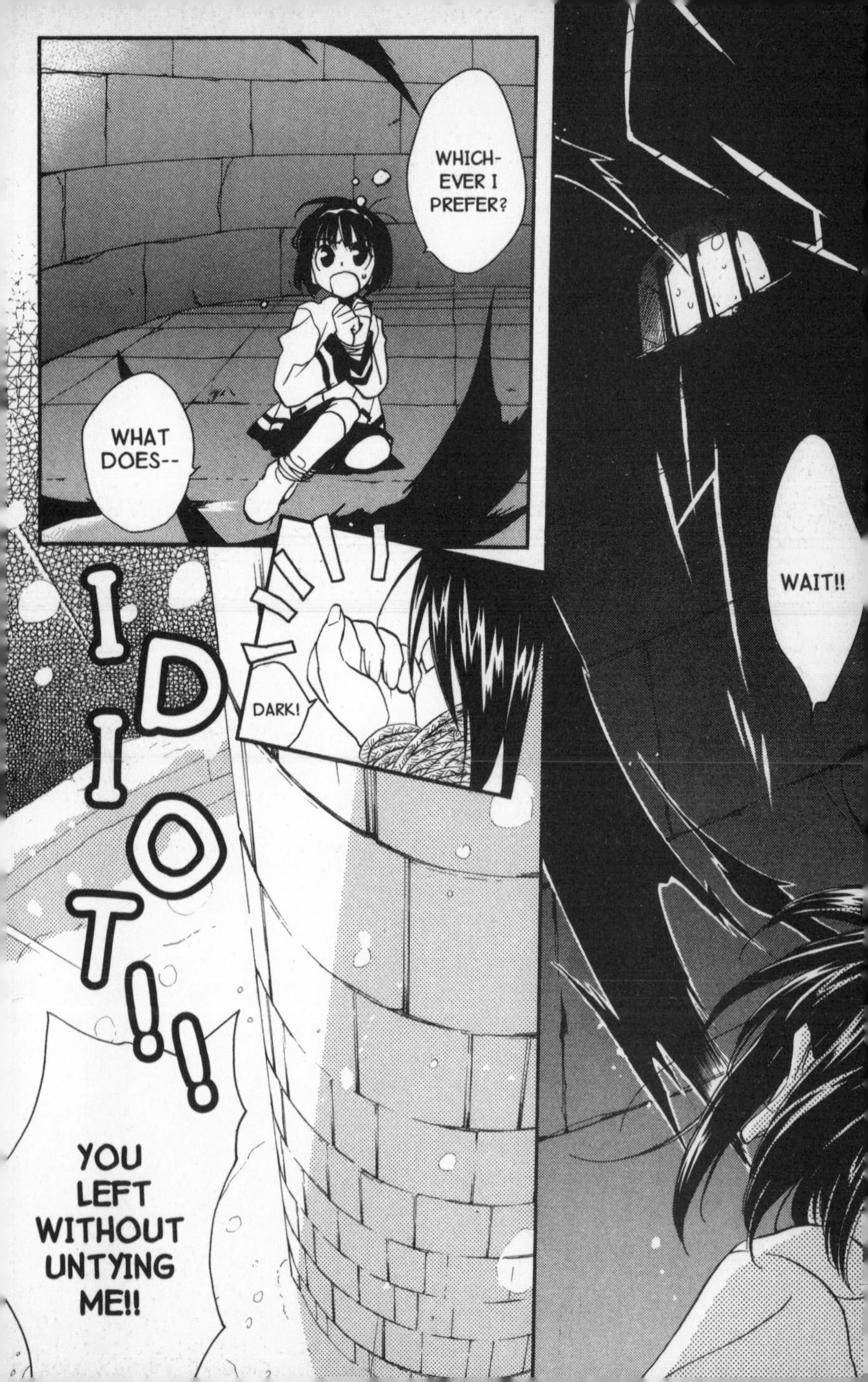
WHICH-EVER I PREFER?
WHAT DOES--
WAIT!!
DARK!
IDIOT!!!
YOU LEFT WITHOUT UNTYING ME!!

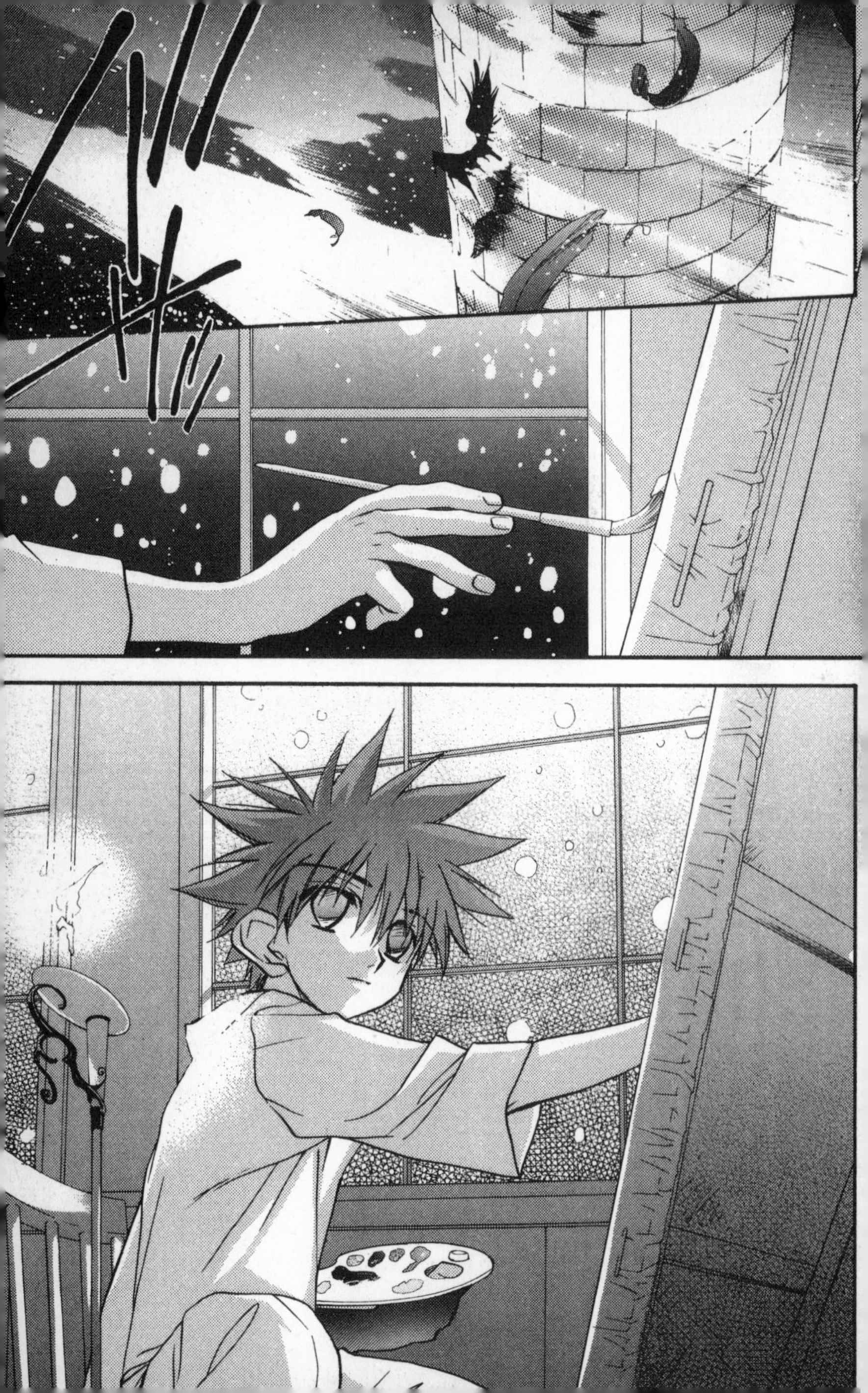

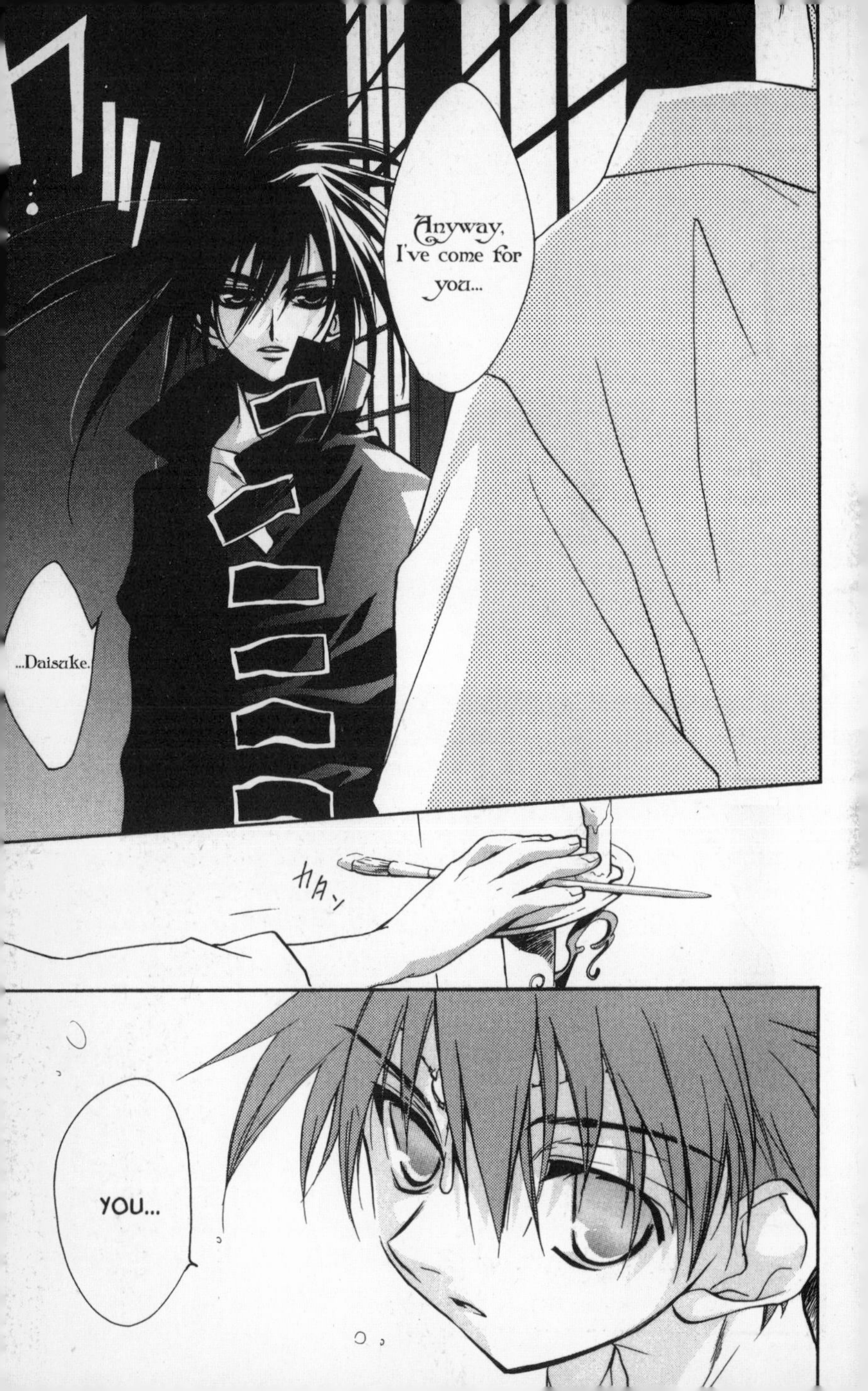
Anyway, I've come for you...
...Daisuke.
カタン
YOU...

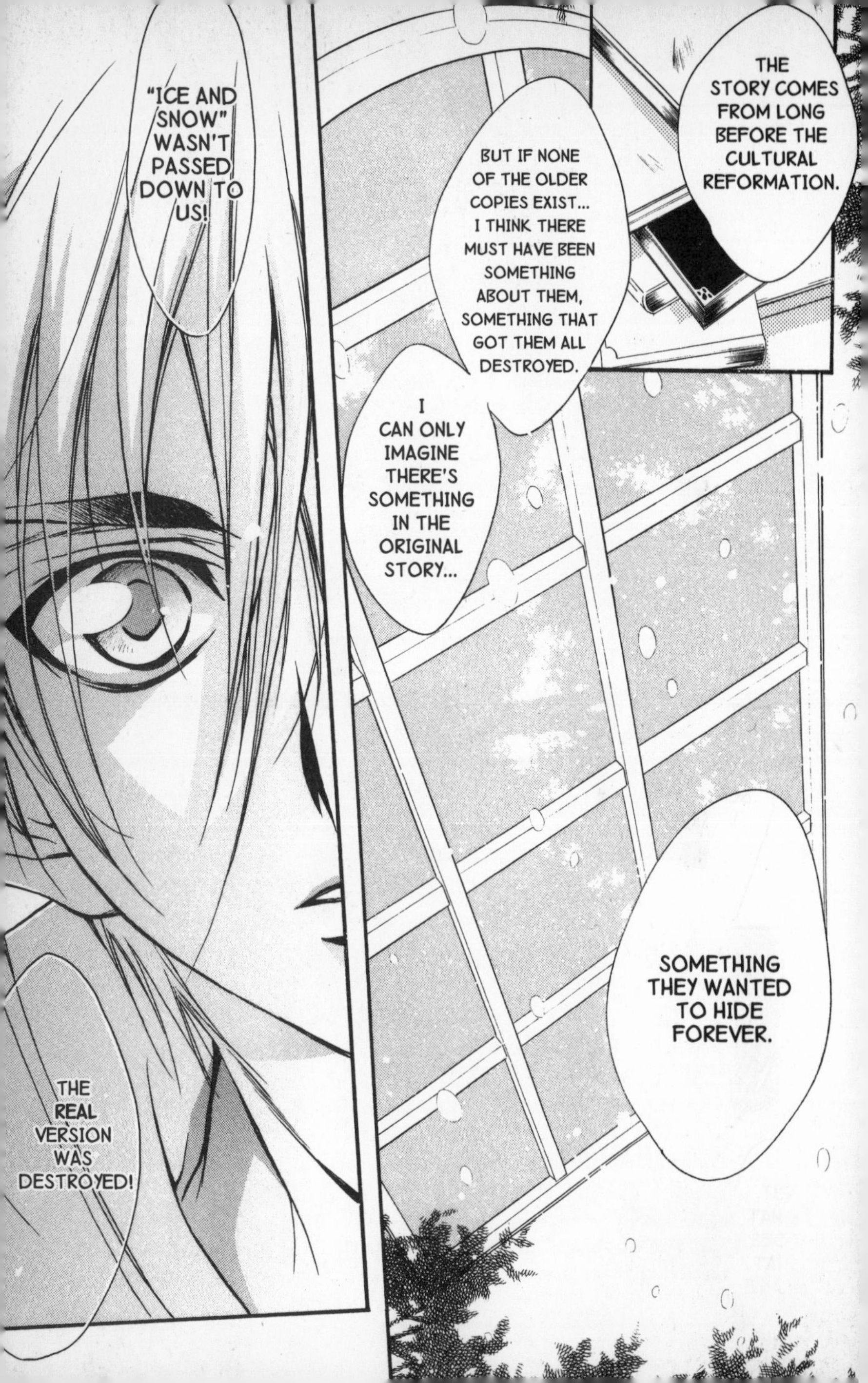
THE STORY COMES FROM LONG BEFORE THE CULTURAL REFORMATION.
BUT IF NONE OF THE OLDER COPIES EXIST... I THINK THERE MUST HAVE BEEN SOMETHING ABOUT THEM, SOMETHING THAT GOT THEM ALL DESTROYED.
I CAN ONLY IMAGINE THERE'S SOMETHING IN THE ORIGINAL STORY...
SOMETHING THEY WANTED TO HIDE FOREVER.
"ICE AND SNOW" WASN'T PASSED DOWN TO US!
THE REAL VERSION WAS DESTROYED!

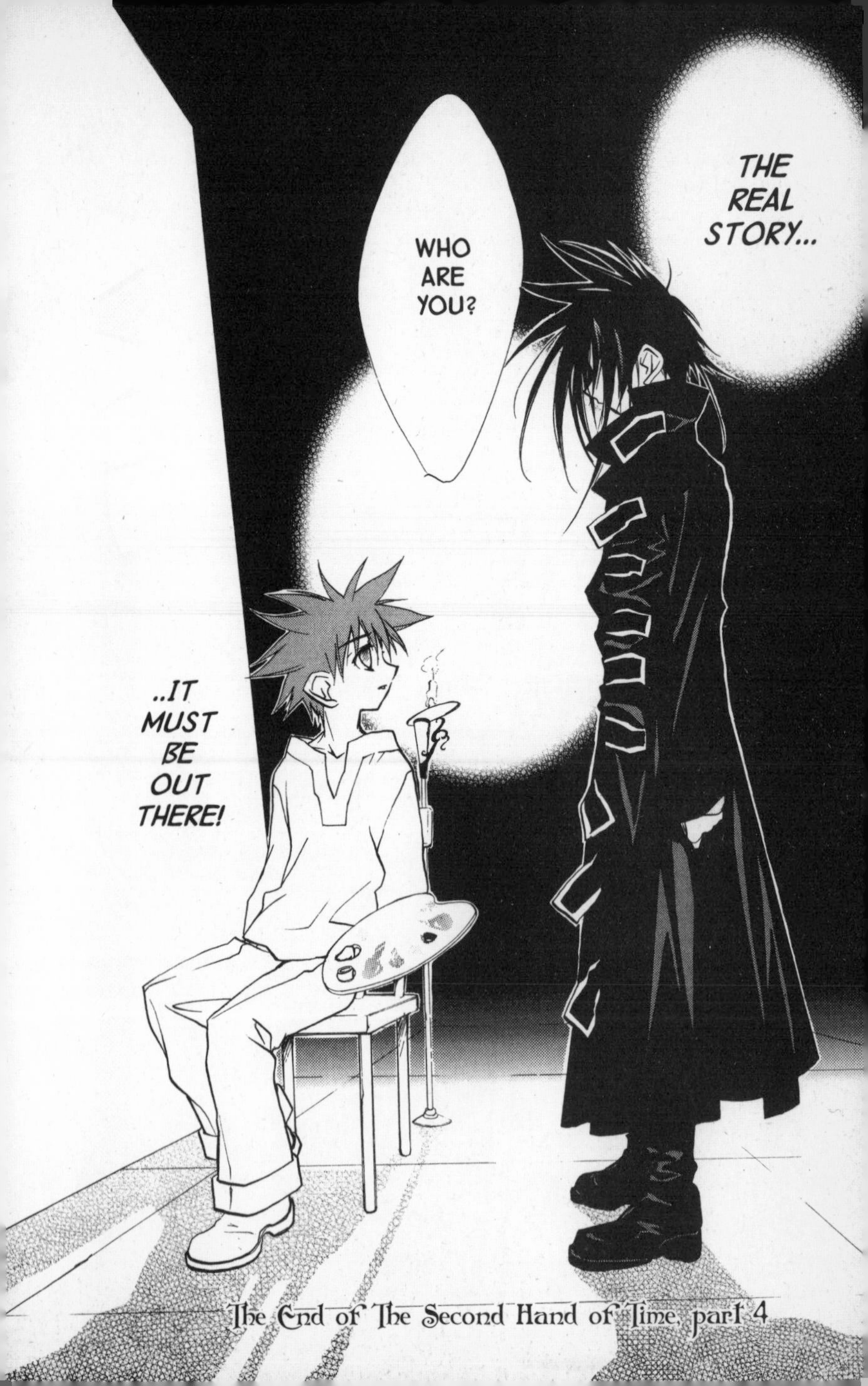
THE REAL STORY...
WHO ARE YOU?
..IT MUST BE OUT THERE!
The End of The Second Hand of Time, part 4

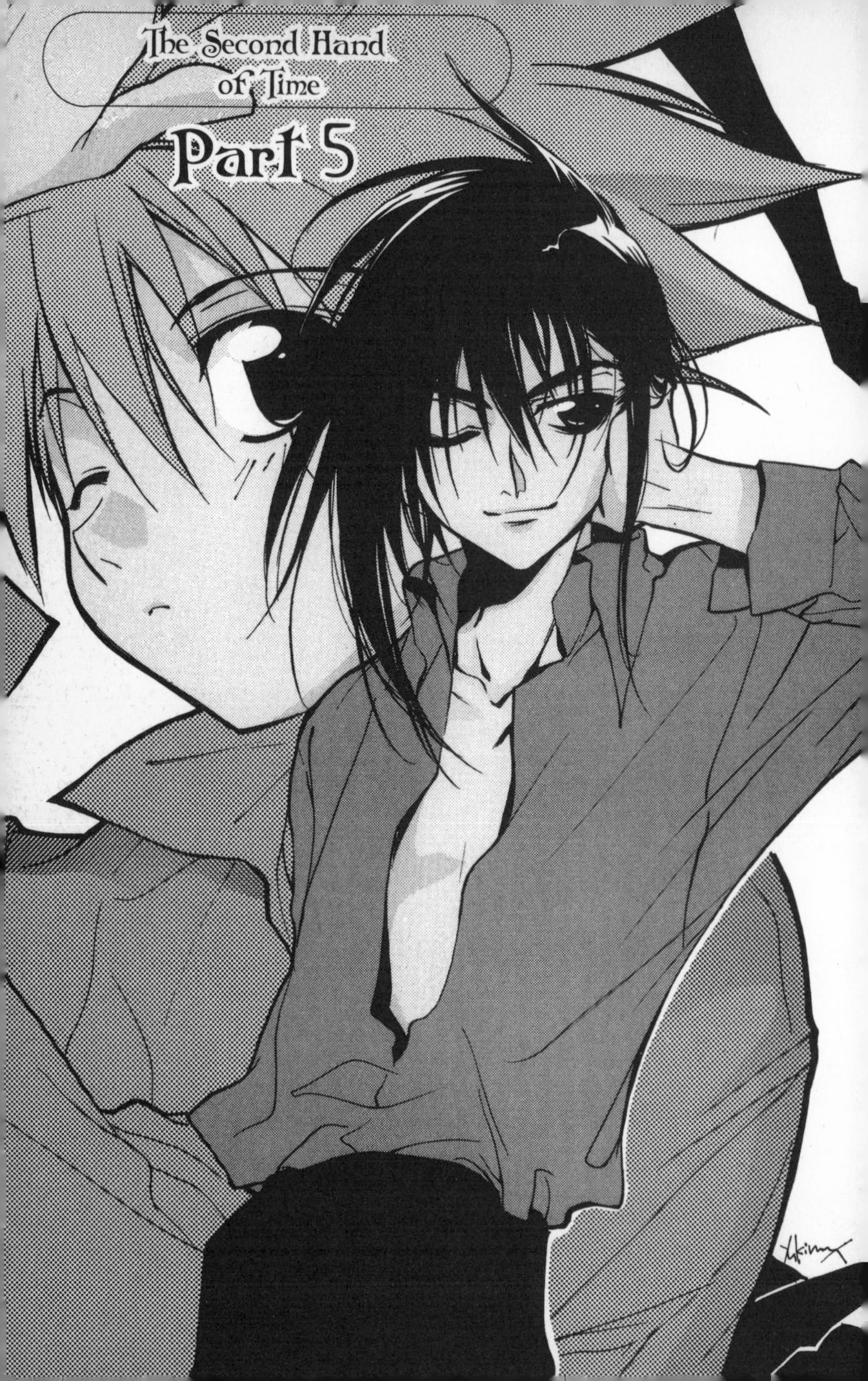
The Second Hand of Time
Part 5

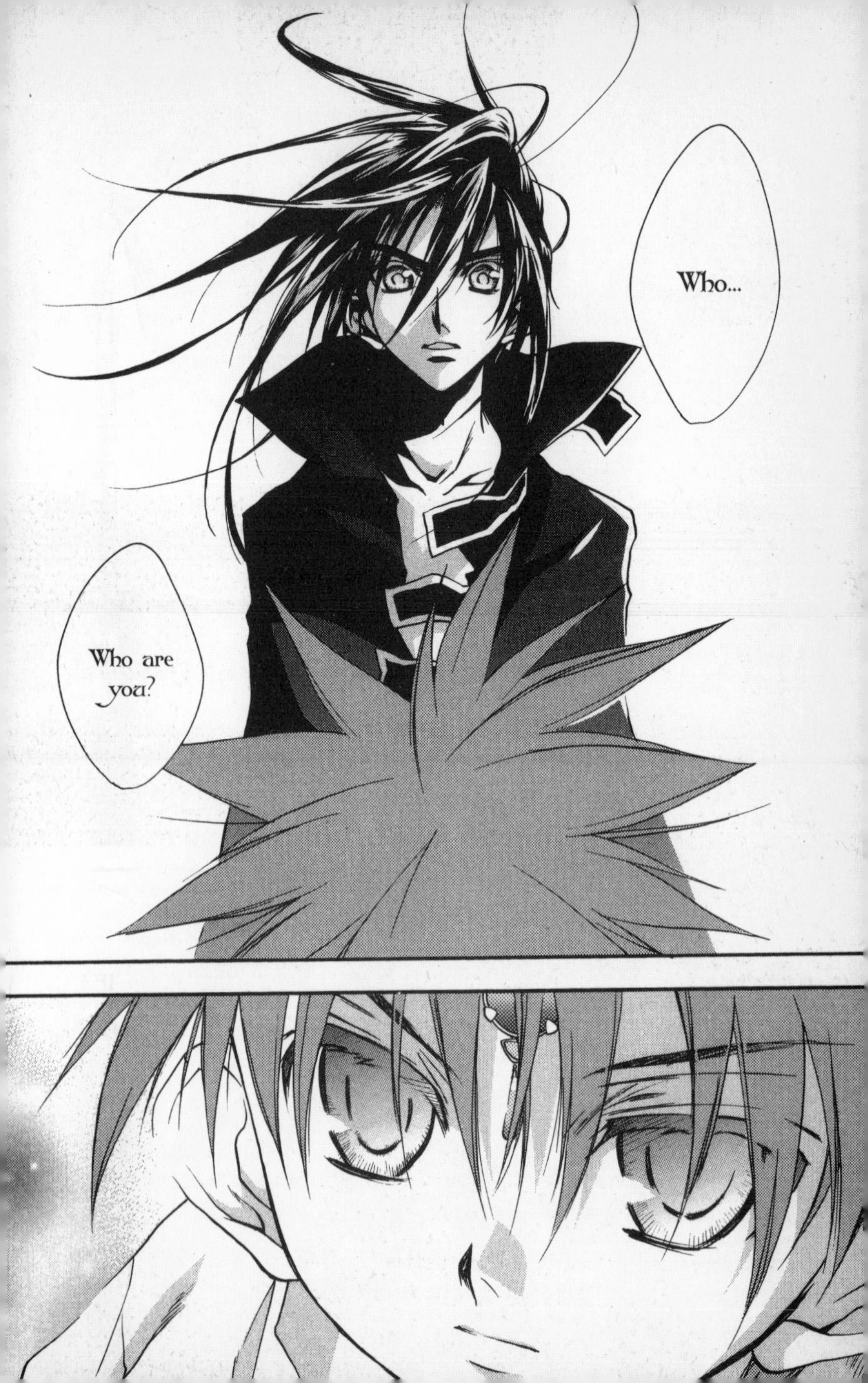
Who...
Who are you?

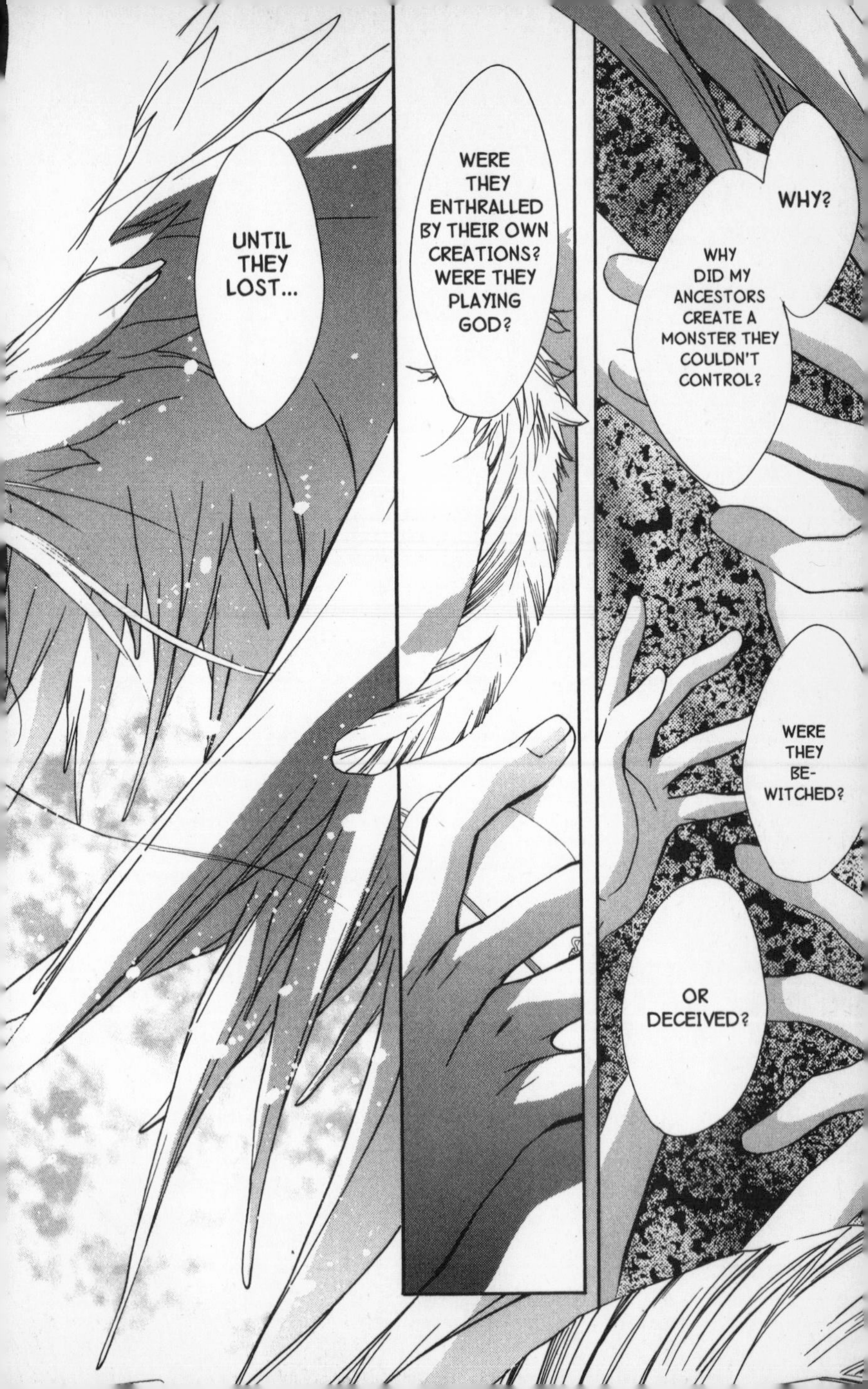
WHY?
WHY DID MY ANCESTORS CREATE A MONSTER THEY COULDN'T CONTROL?
WERE THEY BE-WITCHED?
OR DECEIVED?
WERE THEY ENTHRALLED BY THEIR OWN CREATIONS? WERE THEY PLAYING GOD?
UNTIL THEY LOST...

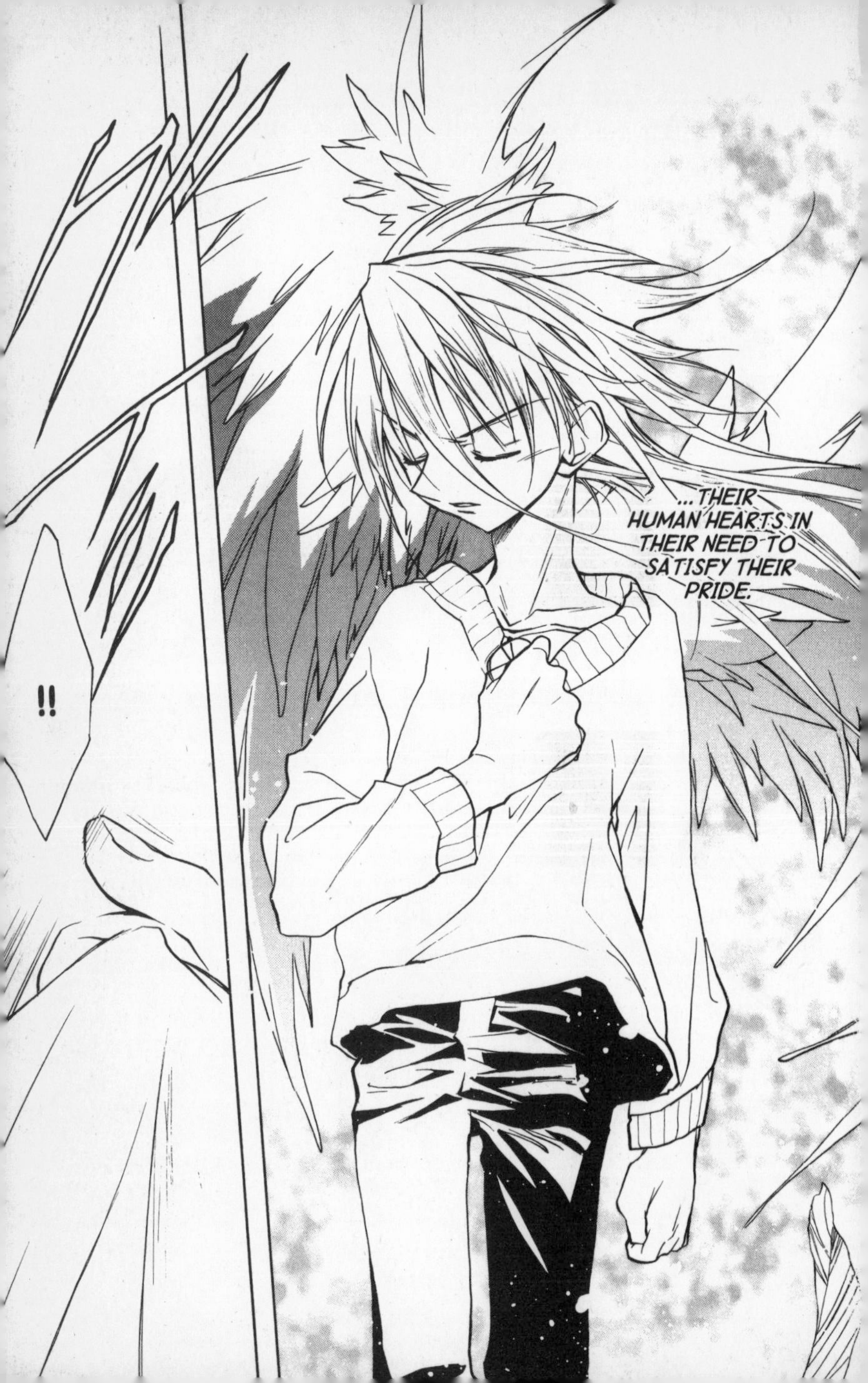
...THEIR HUMAN HEARTS IN THEIR NEED TO SATISFY THEIR PRIDE.
!!

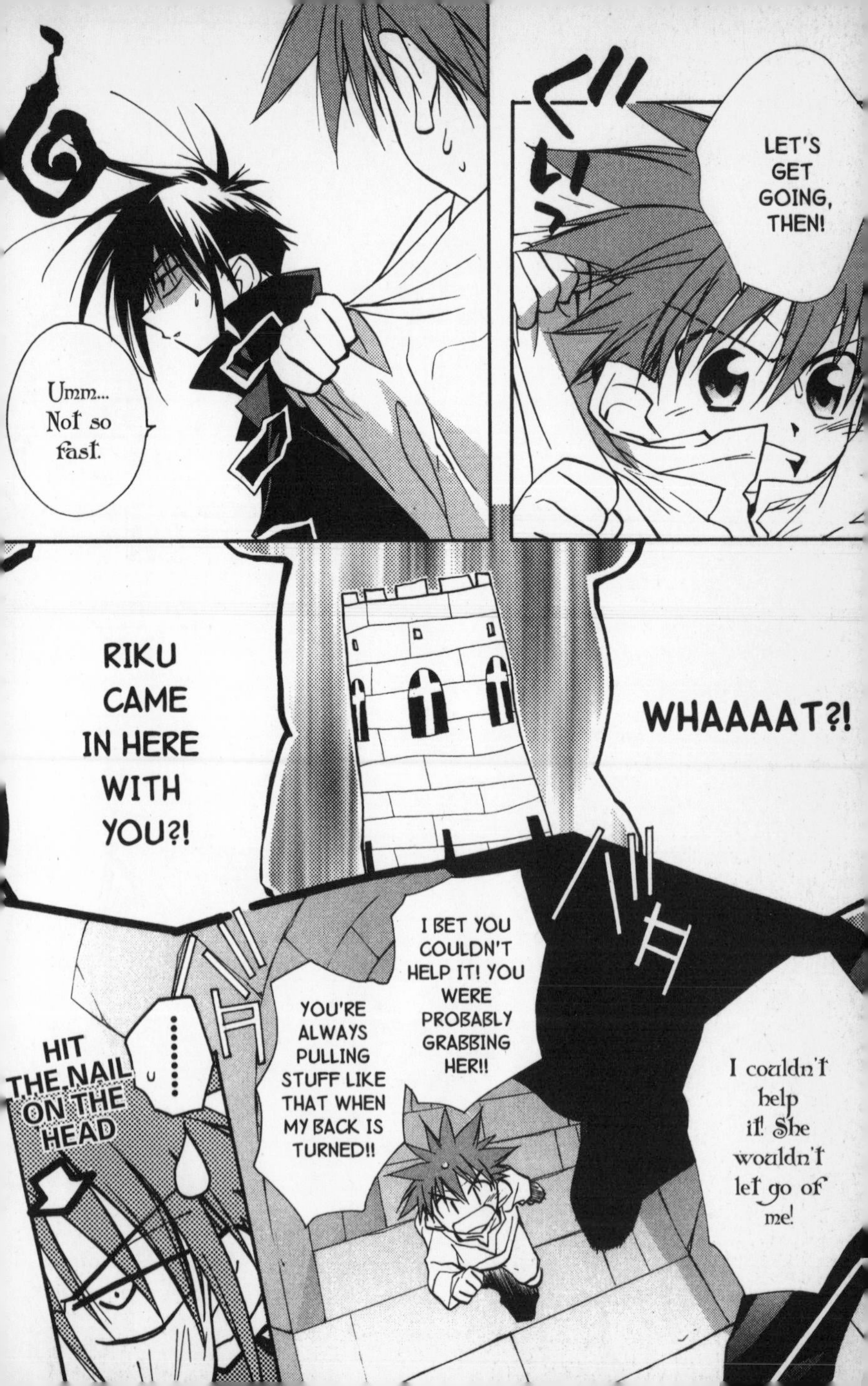
LET'S GET GOING, THEN!
Umm... Not so fast.
WHAAAAT?!
RIKU CAME IN HERE WITH YOU?!
I couldn't help it! She wouldn't let go of me!
I BET YOU COULDN'T HELP IT! YOU WERE PROBABLY GRABBING HER!!
YOU'RE ALWAYS PULLING STUFF LIKE THAT WHEN MY BACK IS TURNED!!
......
HIT THE NAIL ON THE HEAD

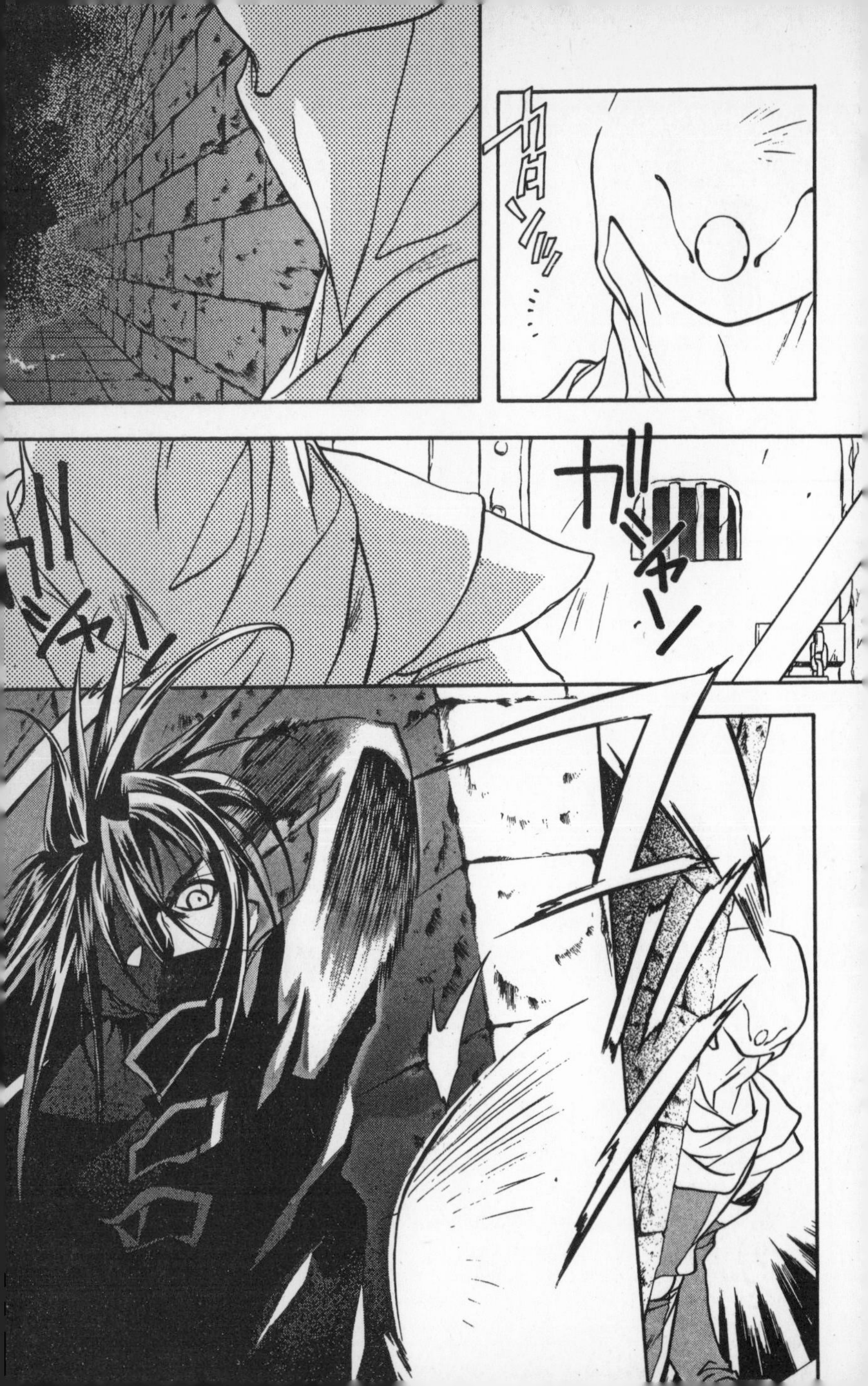
ガシャン
ガシャン

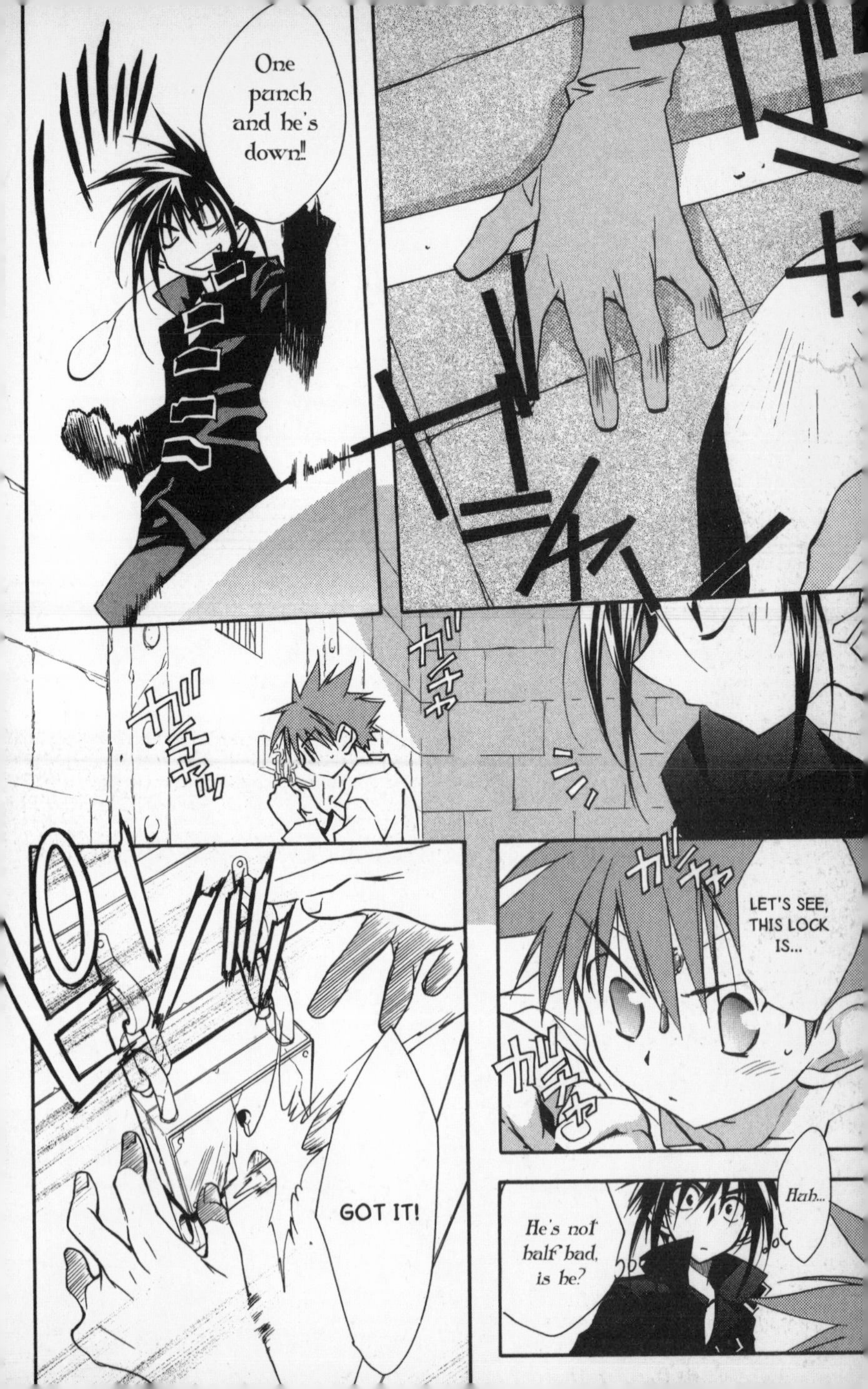
One punch and he's down!!
LET'S SEE, THIS LOCK IS...
GOT IT!
Huh...
He's not half bad, is he?

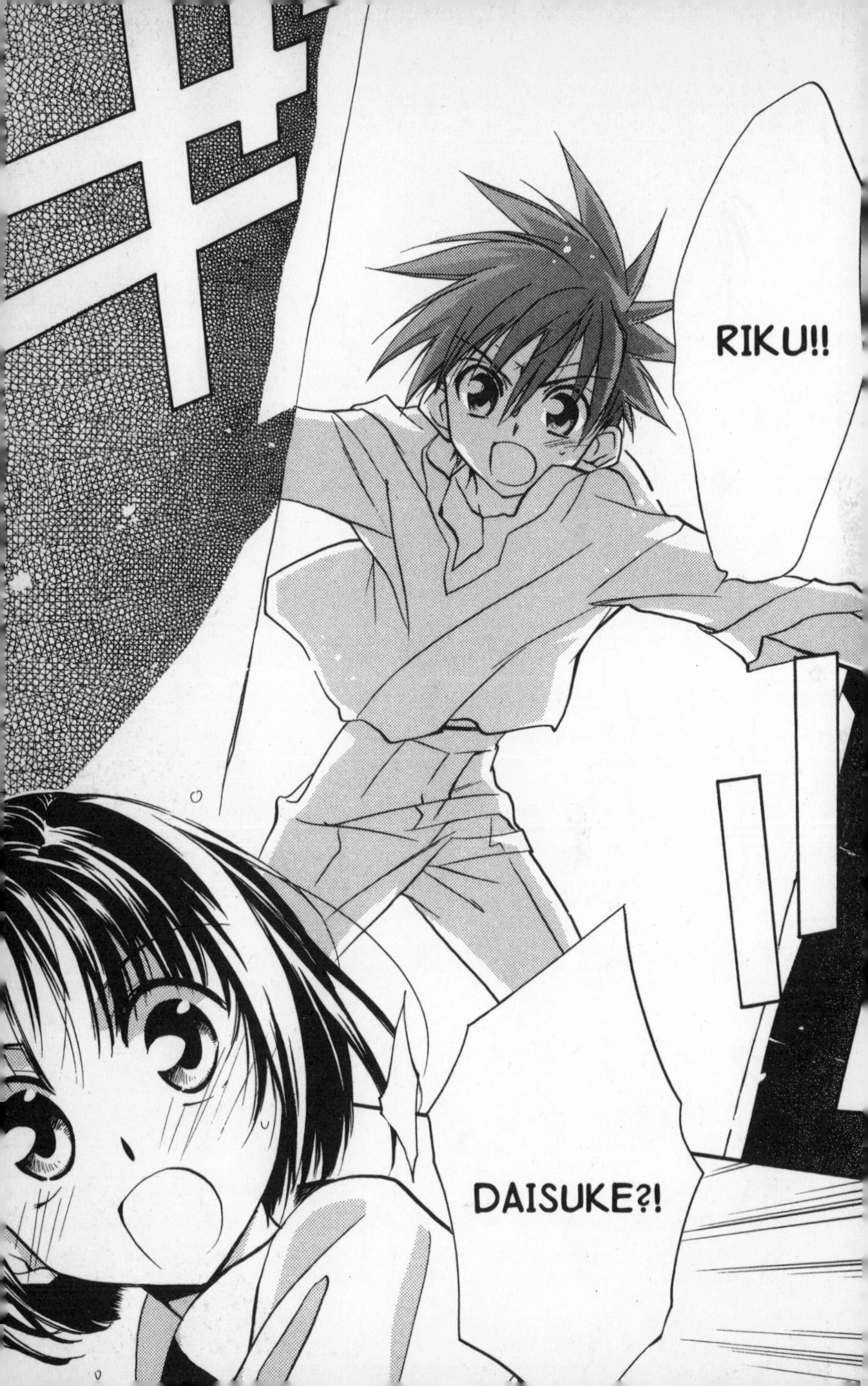
RIKU!!
DAISUKE?!

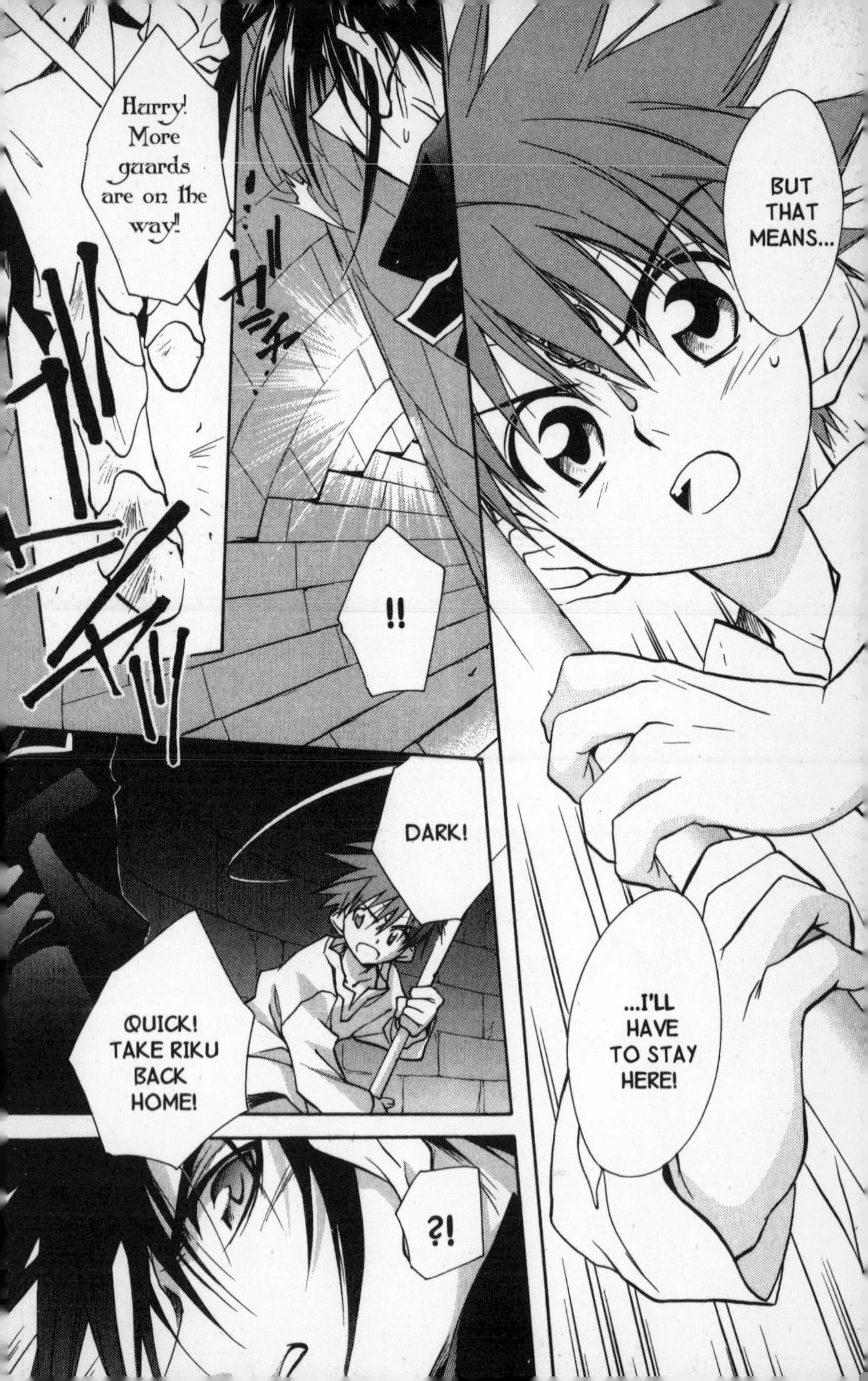
BUT THAT MEANS...
Hurry! More guards are on the way!!
!!
...I'LL HAVE TO STAY HERE!
DARK!
QUICK! TAKE RIKU BACK HOME!
?!

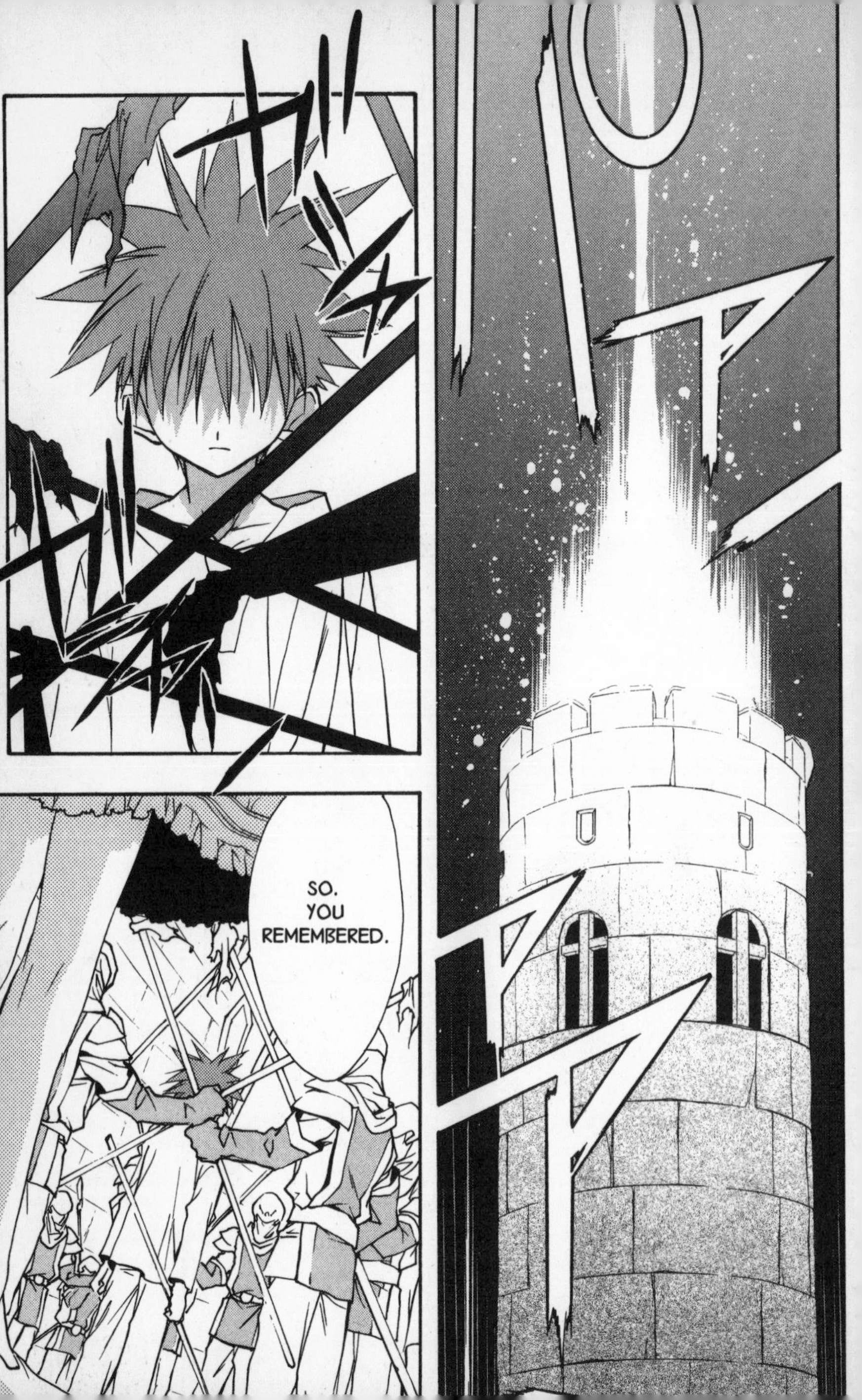
SO. YOU REMEMBERED.

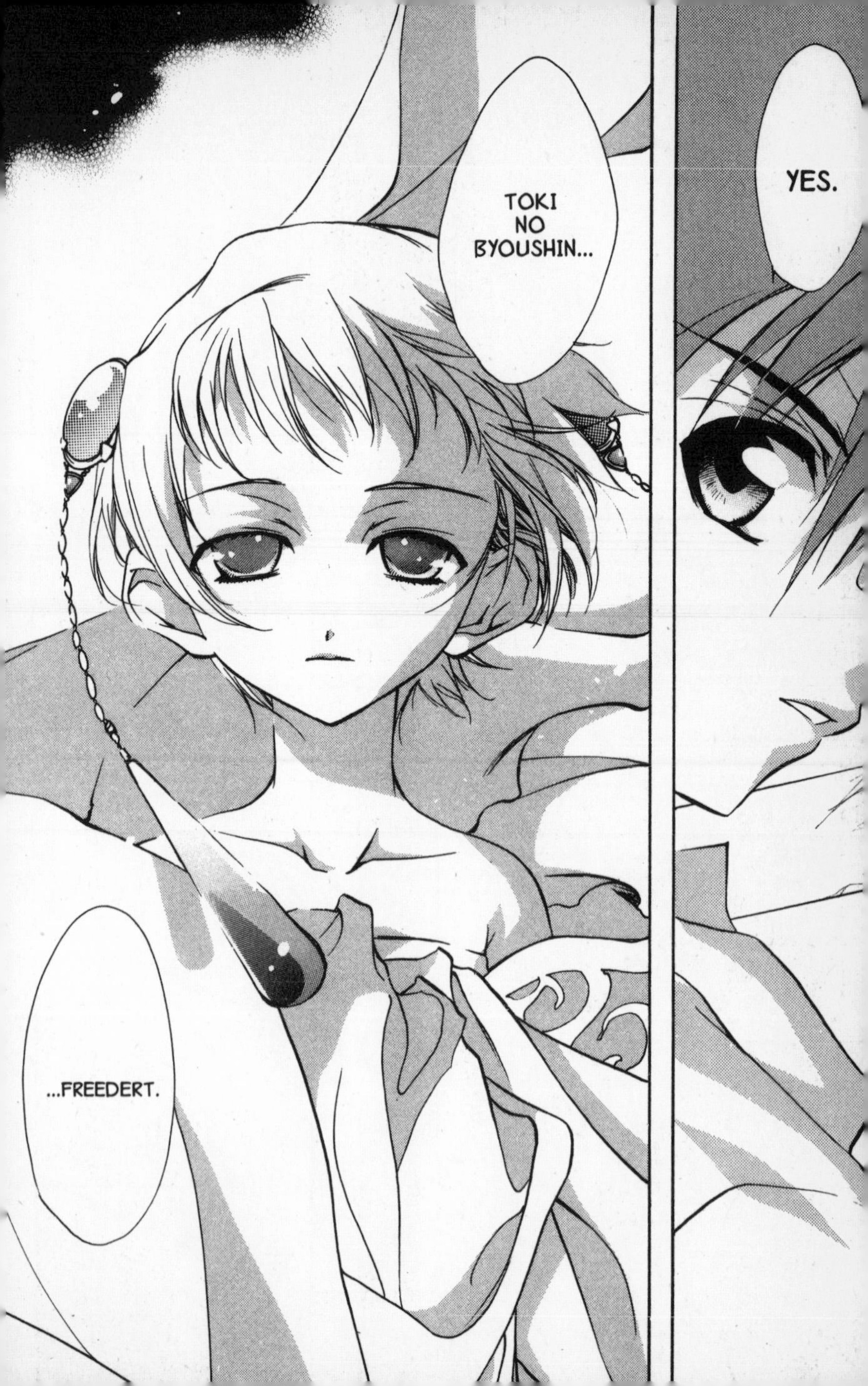
TOKI NO BYOUSHIN...
YES.
...FREEDERT.

The End of The Second Hand of Time, part 5

All the works of art created in this world...

...have a soul.

All the things that people have prayed for...

...have life.

But...

Those souls and lives...

...can't all end up in a beautiful place after their struggles...

As in this story...

The Second Hand
of Time

Part 6

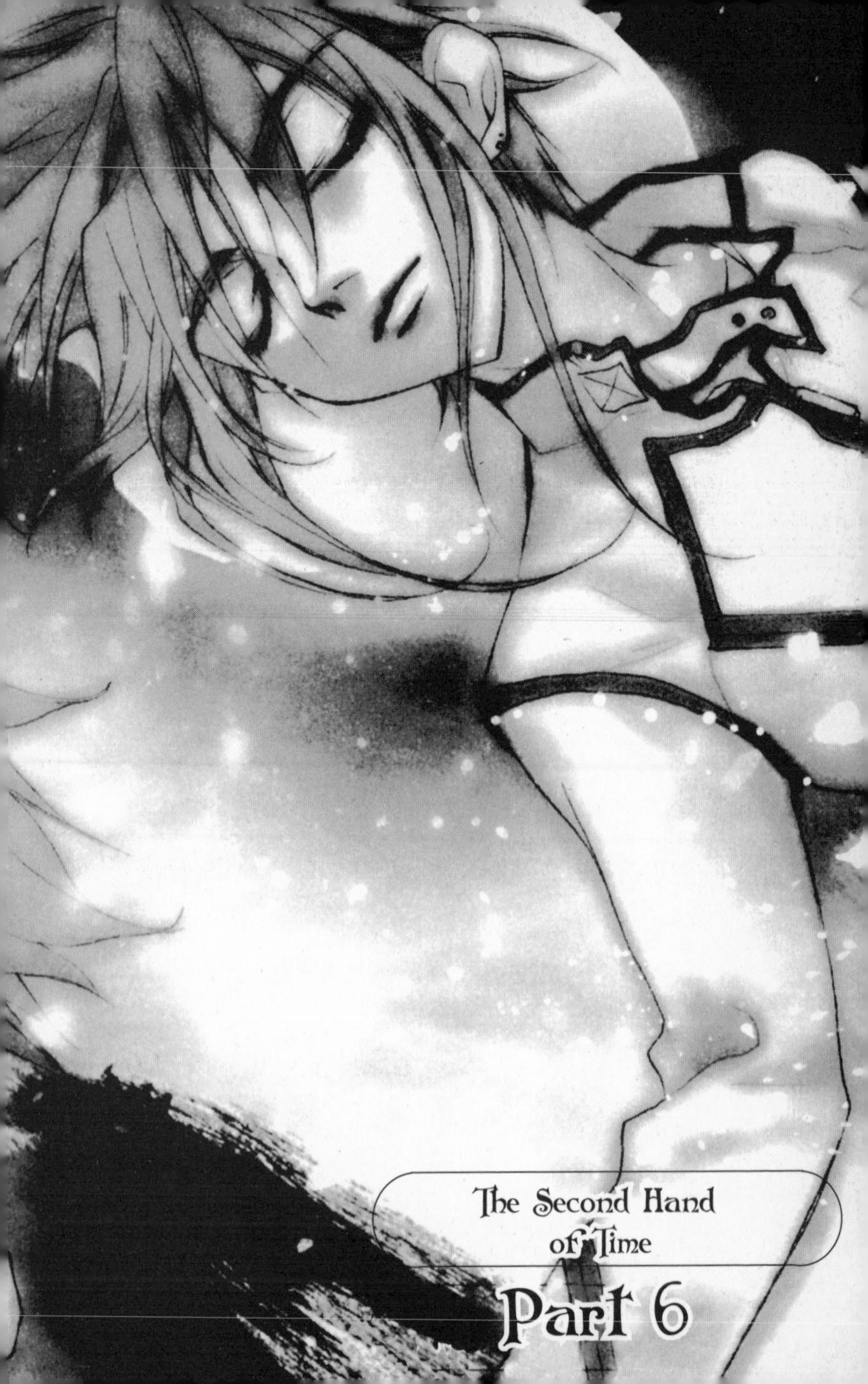
The Second Hand of Time
Part 6

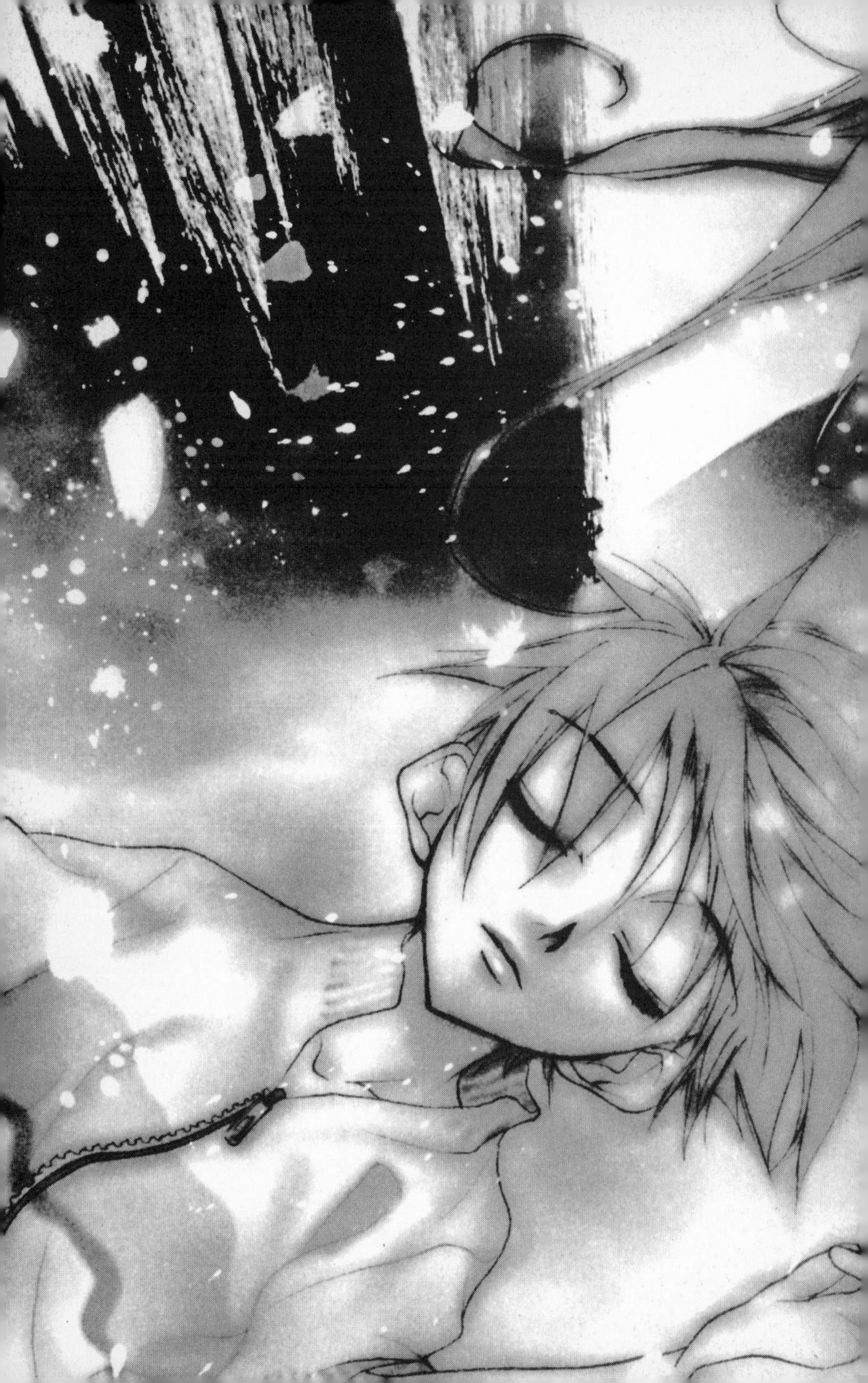

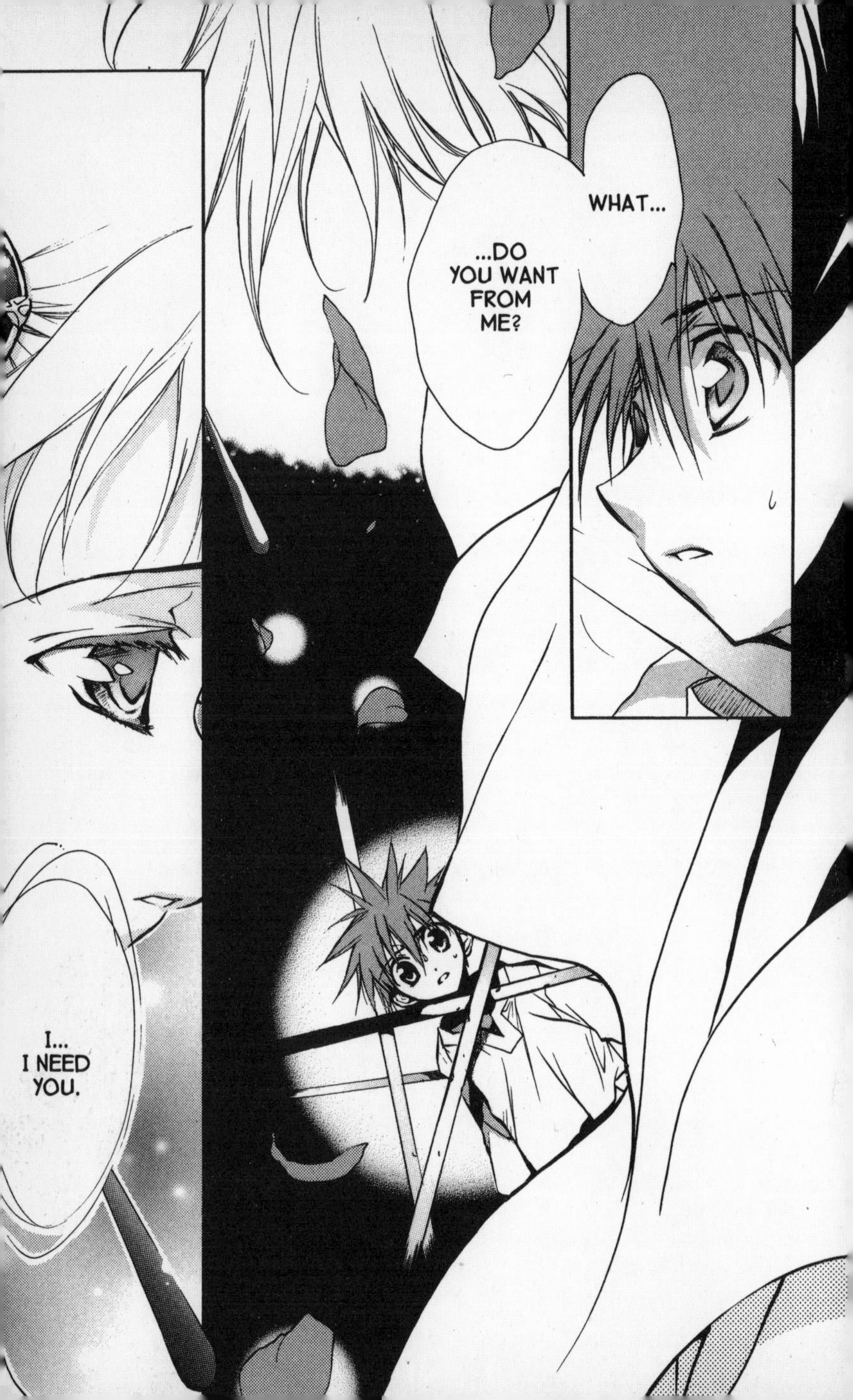
WHAT...
...DO YOU WANT FROM ME?
I... I NEED YOU.

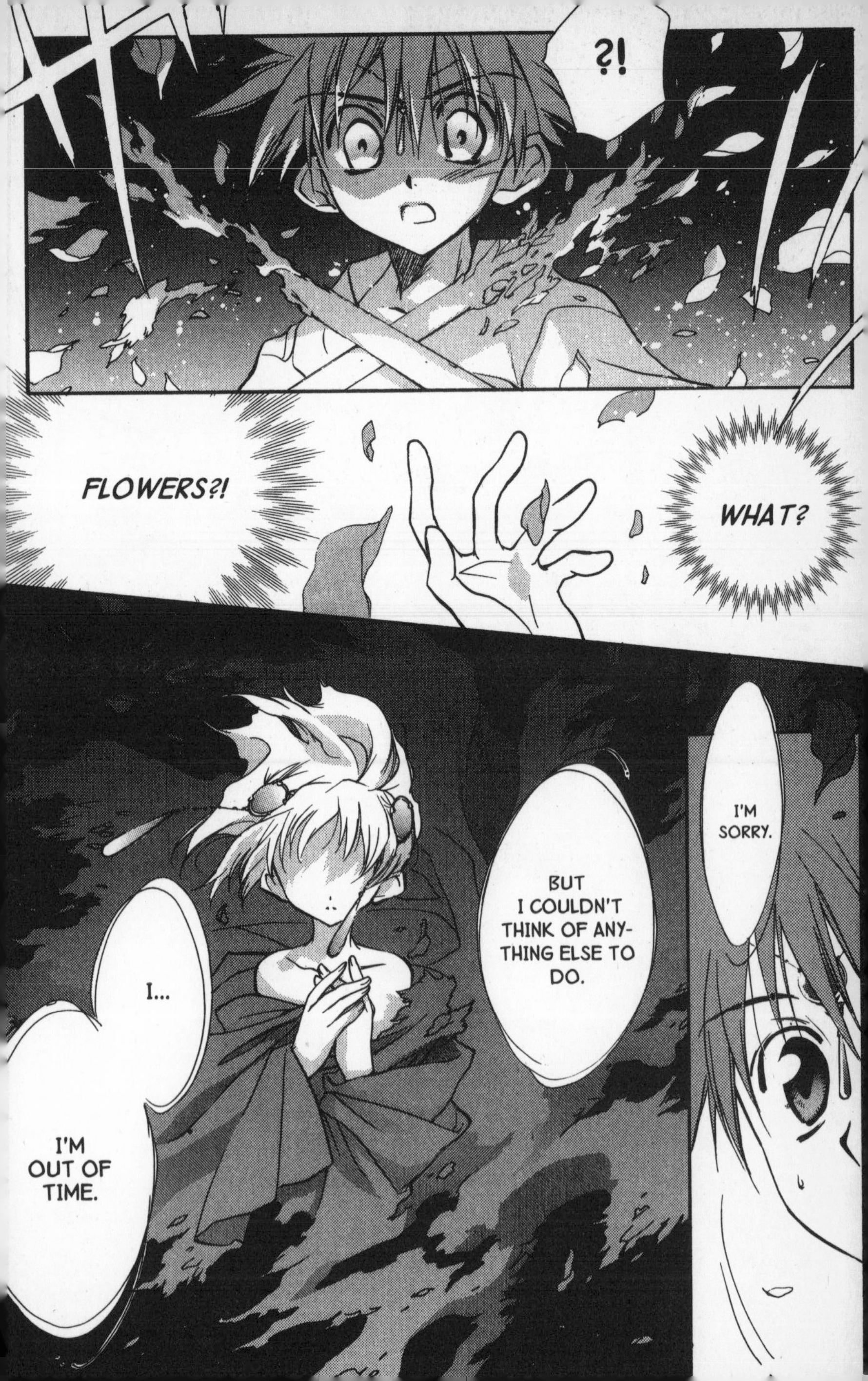
?!
WHAT?
FLOWERS?!
I'M SORRY.
BUT I COULDN'T THINK OF ANYTHING ELSE TO DO.
I...
I'M OUT OF TIME.

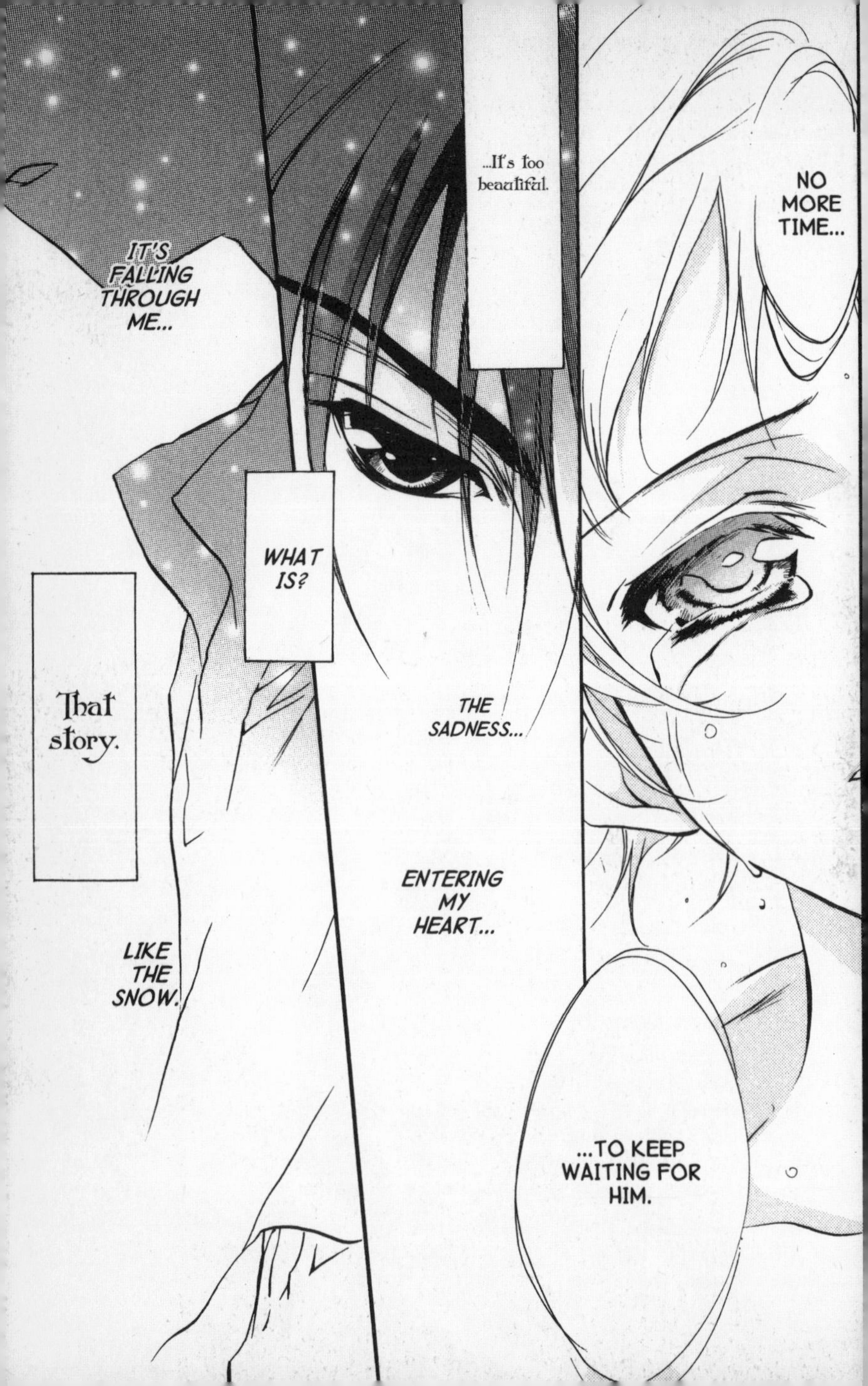
NO MORE TIME...
...TO KEEP WAITING FOR HIM.
...It's too beautiful.
WHAT IS?
THE SADNESS...
ENTERING MY HEART...
IT'S FALLING THROUGH ME...
That story.
LIKE THE SNOW.

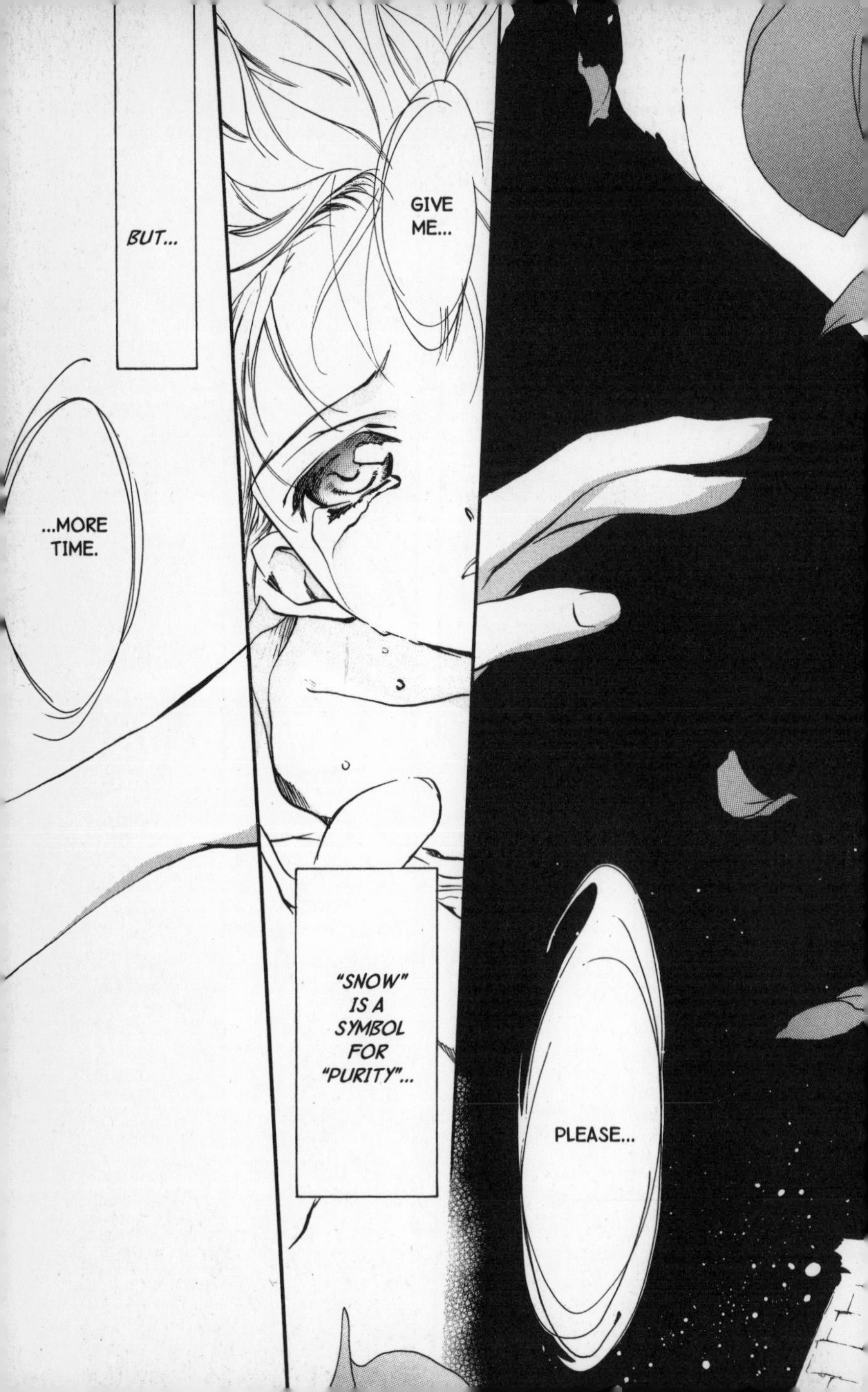
PLEASE...
GIVE ME...
"SNOW" IS A SYMBOL FOR "PURITY"...
BUT...
...MORE TIME.

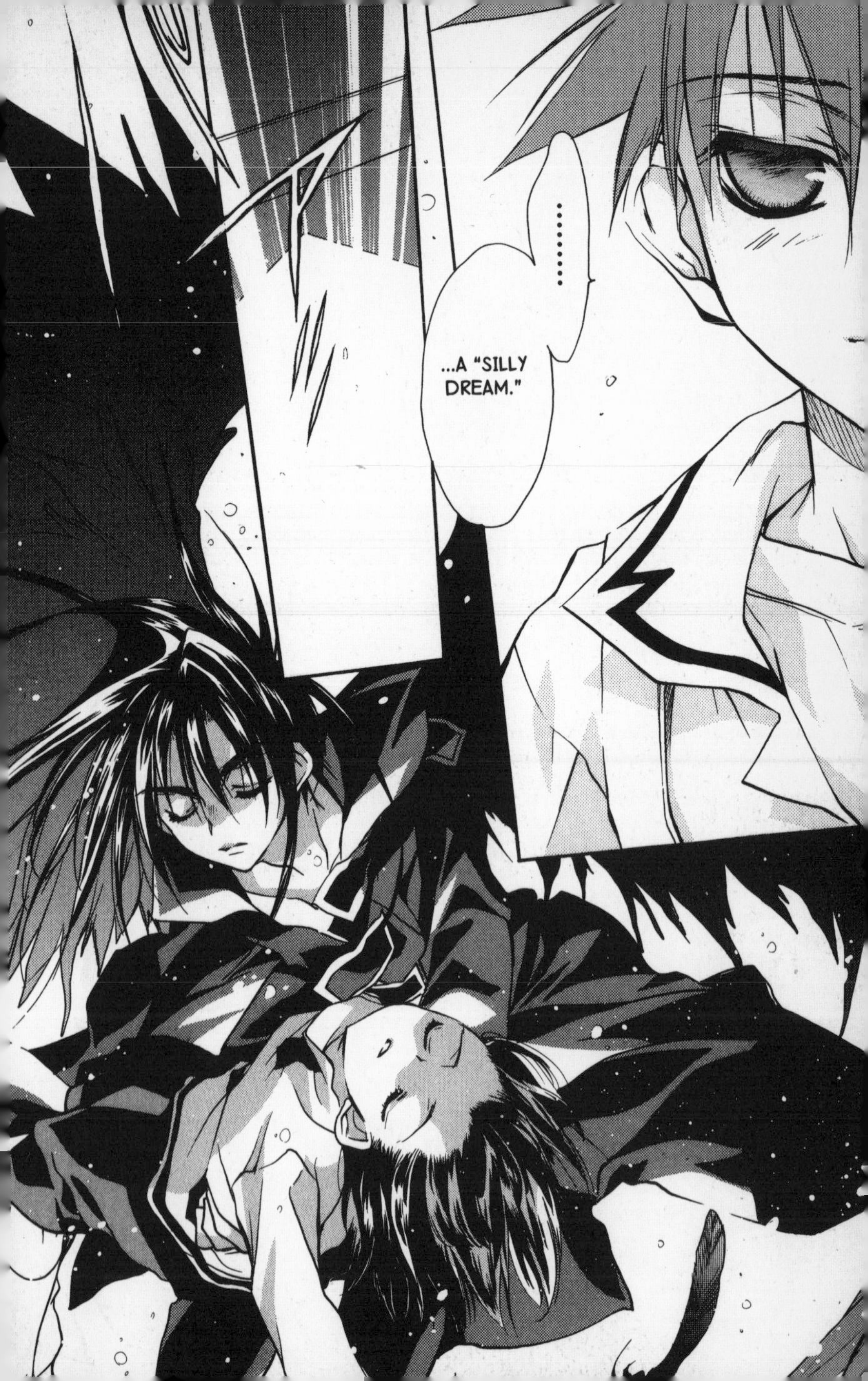
......
...A "SILLY DREAM."

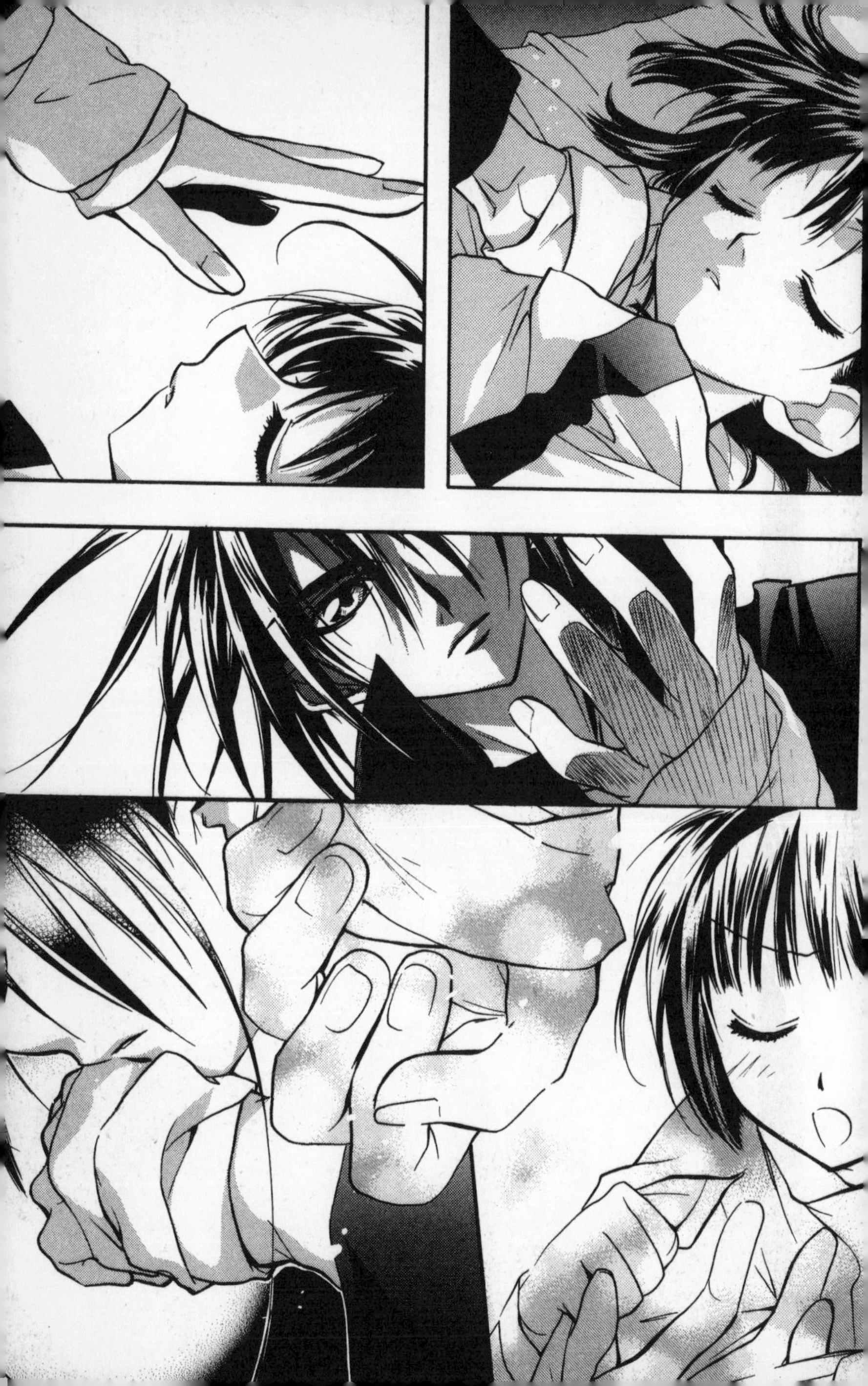

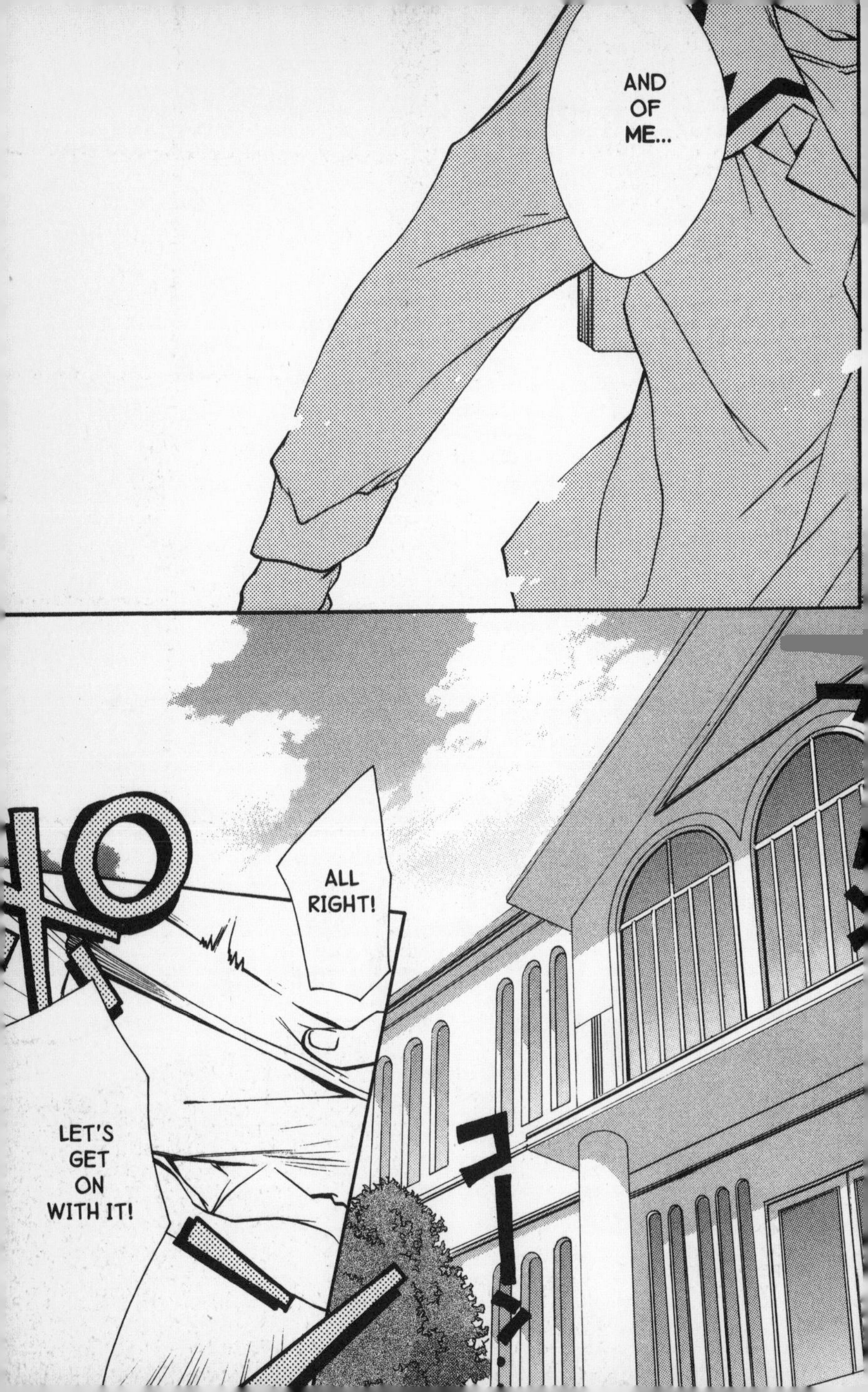
AND OF ME...
ALL RIGHT!
LET'S GET ON WITH IT!

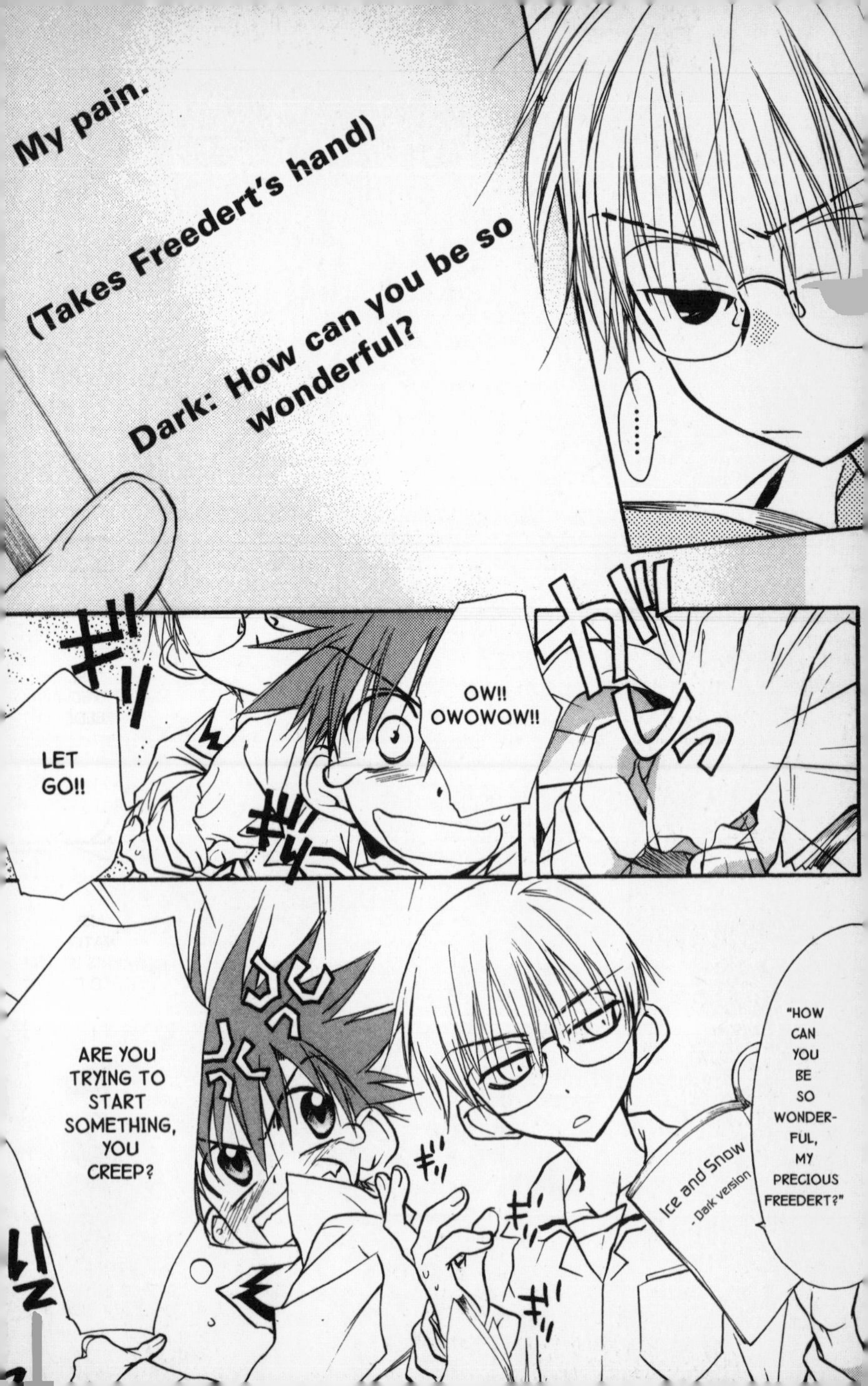
......
My pain.
(Takes Freedert's hand)
Dark: How can you be so wonderful?
OW!! OWOWOW!!
LET GO!!
"HOW CAN YOU BE SO WONDER-FUL, MY PRECIOUS FREEDERT?"
Ice and Snow
- Dark version
ARE YOU TRYING TO START SOMETHING, YOU CREEP?

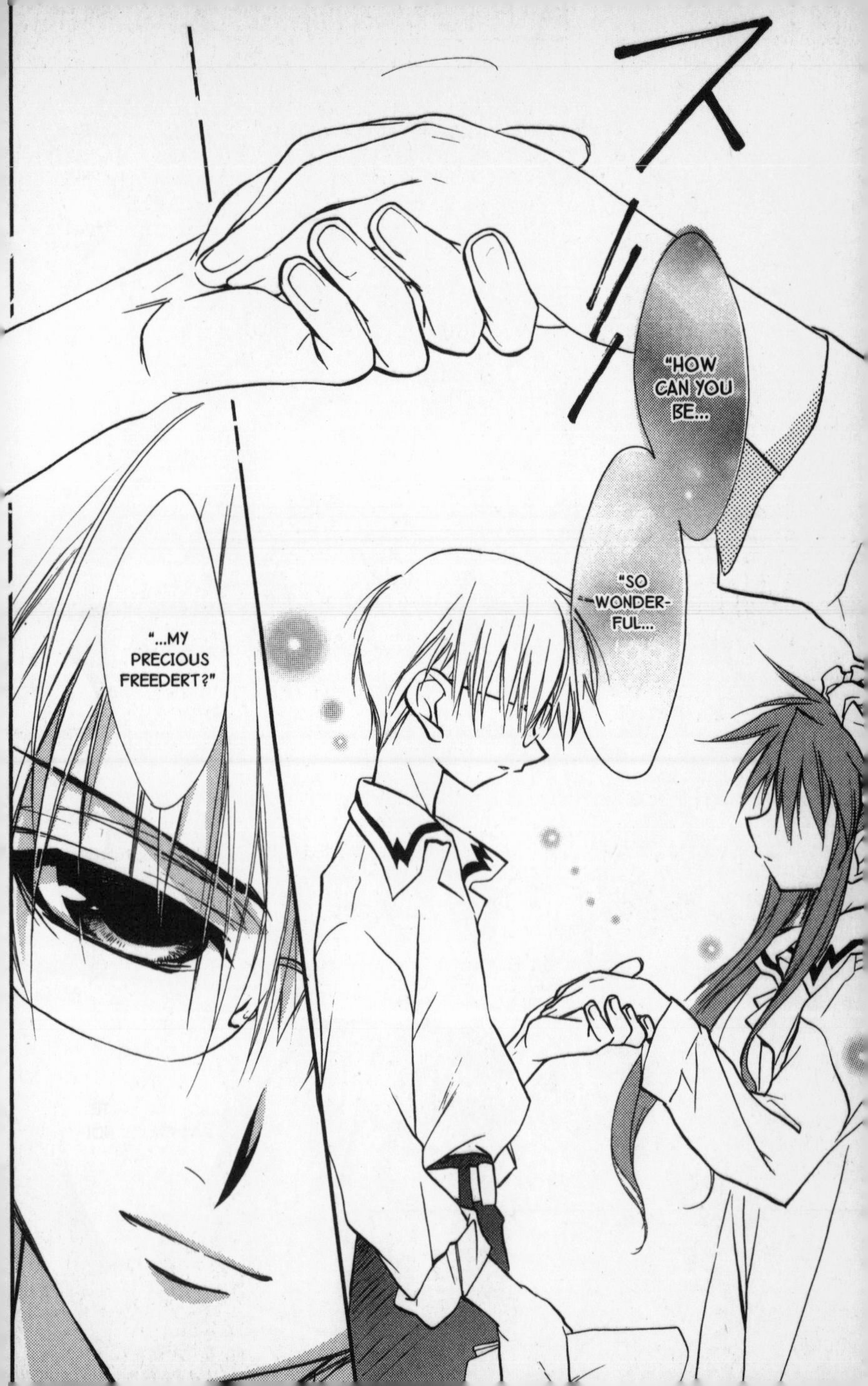
"HOW CAN YOU BE...
"SO WONDERFUL...
"...MY PRECIOUS FREEDERT?"

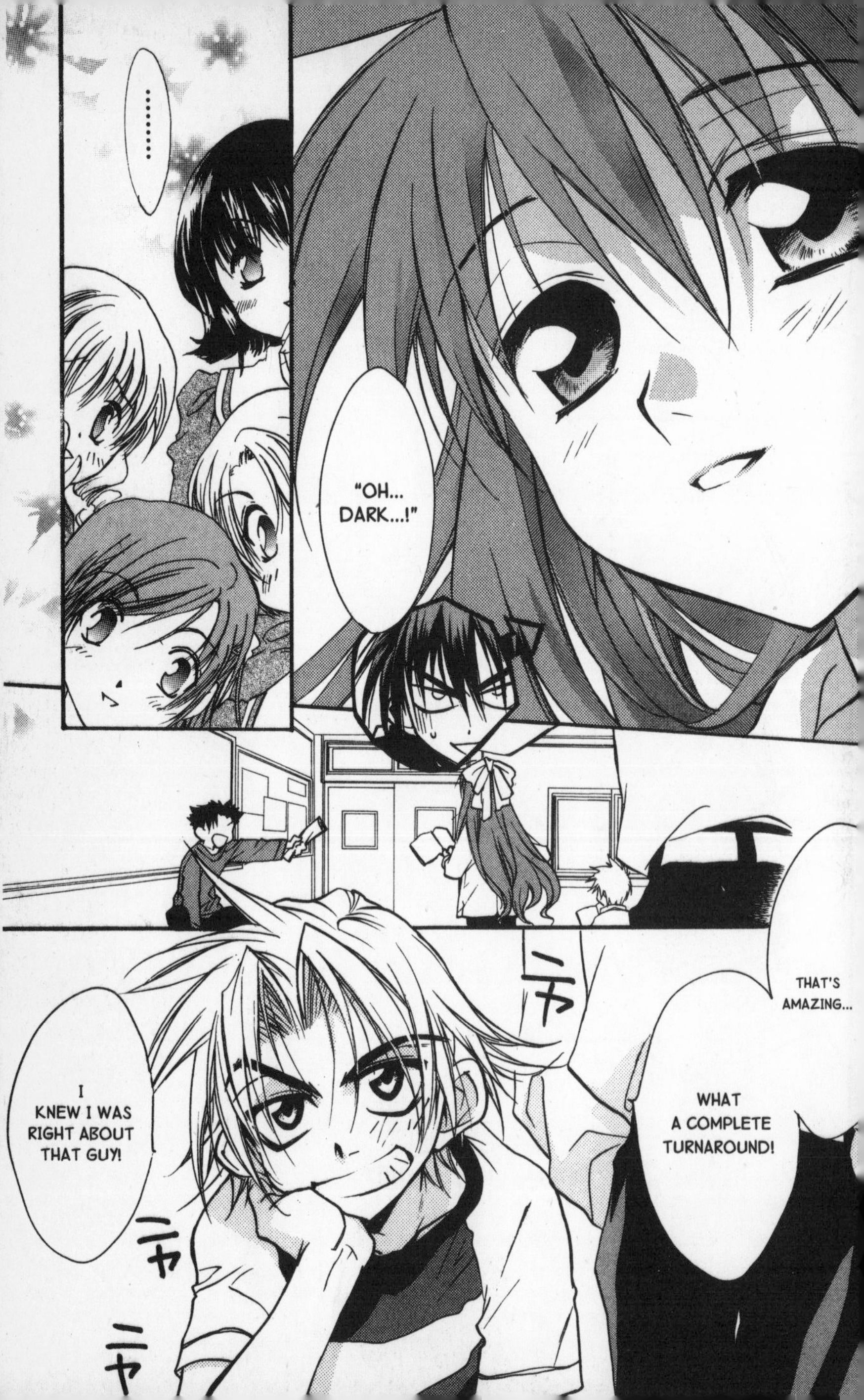
"OH... DARK...!"
......
THAT'S AMAZING...
WHAT A COMPLETE TURNAROUND!
ニヤ
I KNEW I WAS RIGHT ABOUT THAT GUY!
ニヤ
ニヤ

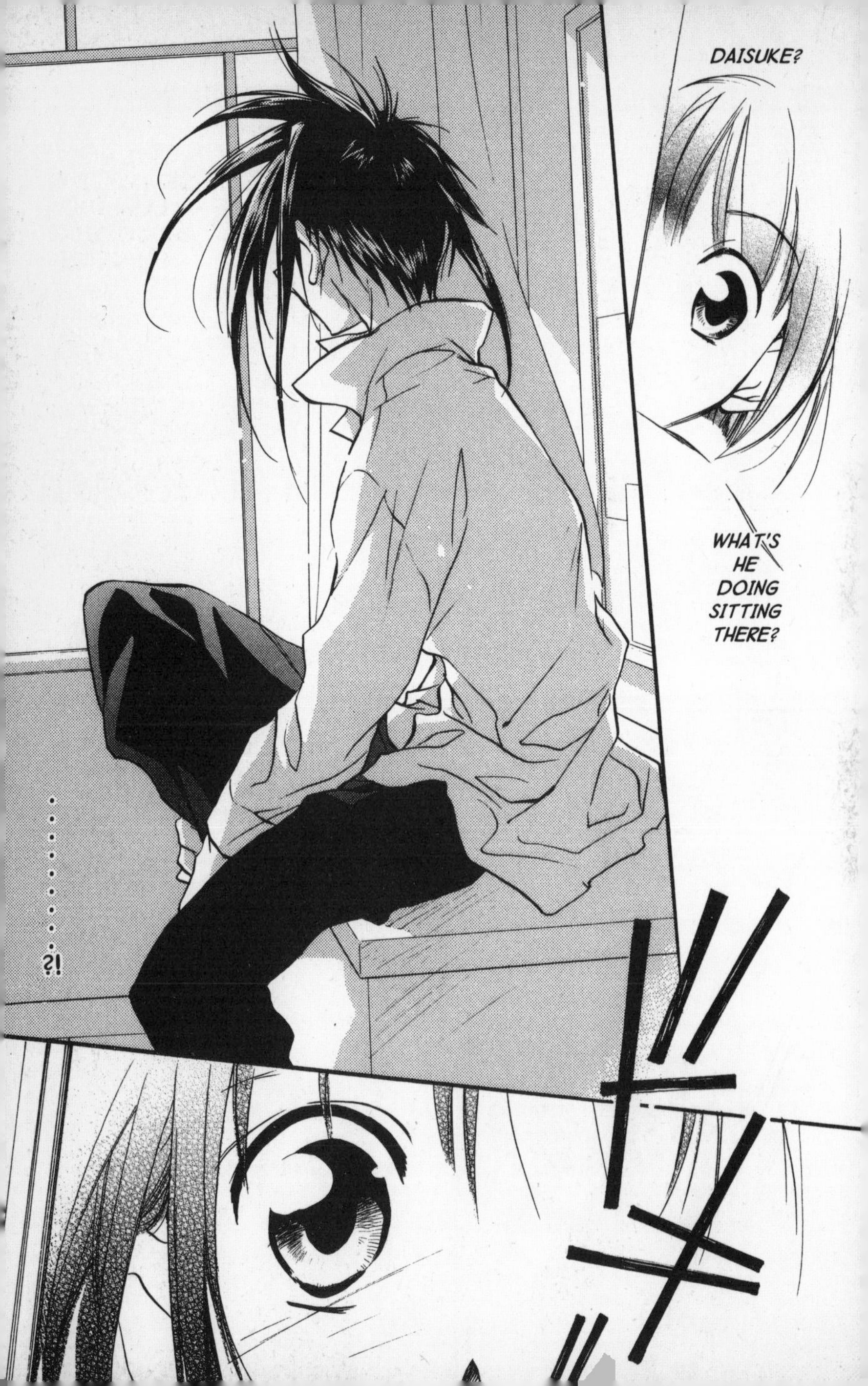
DAISUKE?
WHAT'S HE DOING SITTING THERE?
..........?!

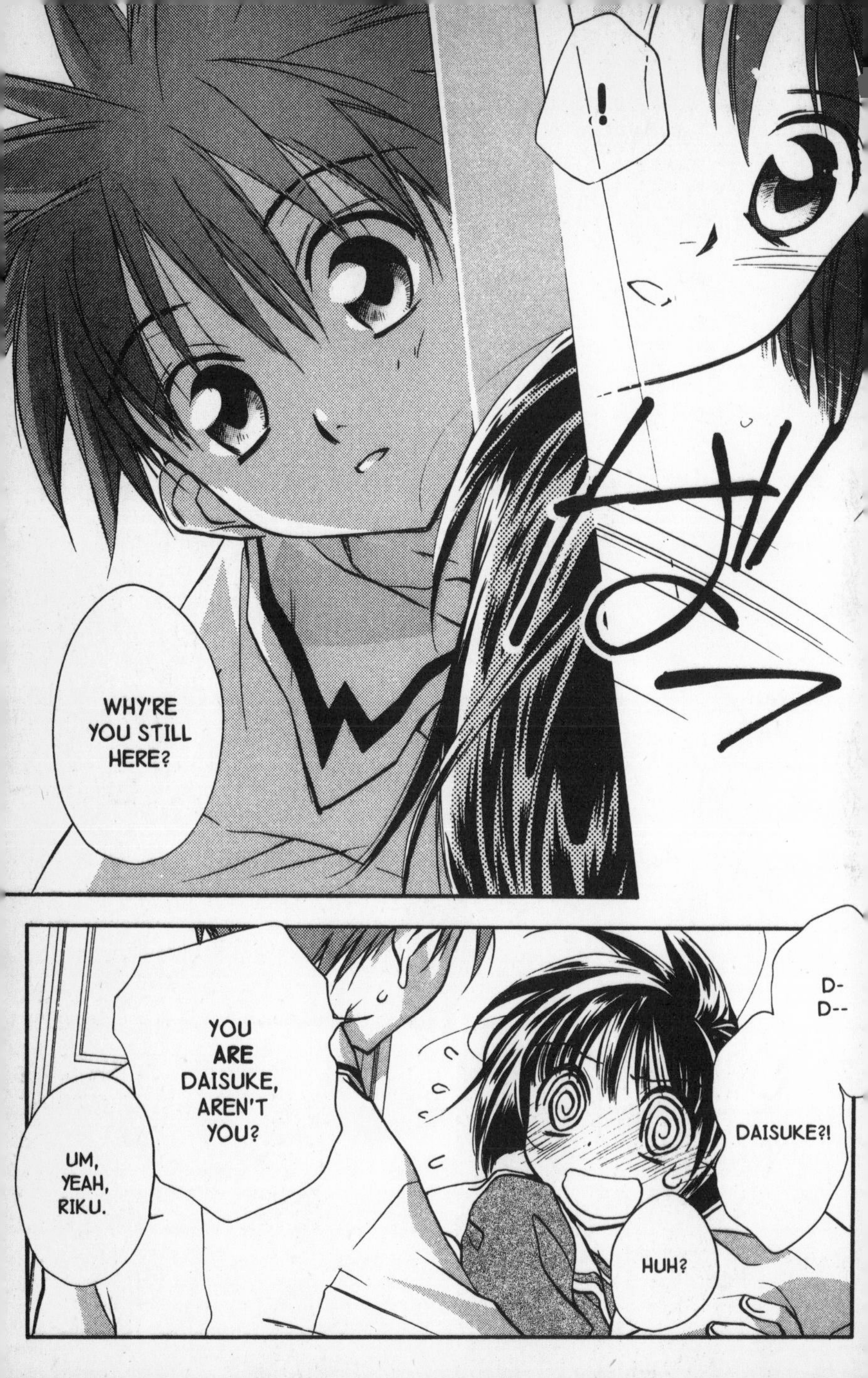
!
WHY'RE YOU STILL HERE?
D- D--
DAISUKE?!
HUH?
YOU ARE DAISUKE, AREN'T YOU?
UM, YEAH, RIKU.

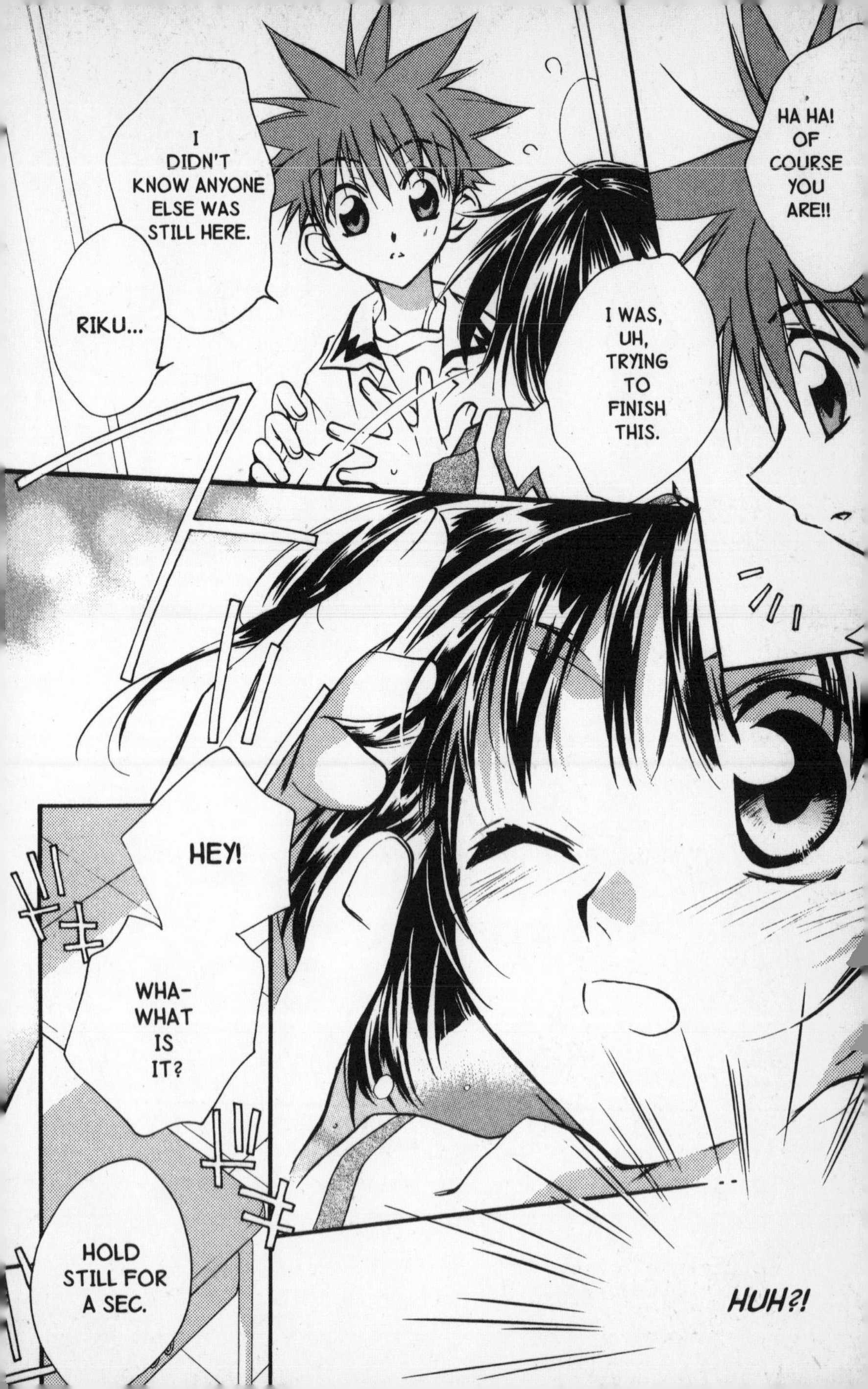
HA HA! OF COURSE YOU ARE!!
I WAS, UH, TRYING TO FINISH THIS.
I DIDN'T KNOW ANYONE ELSE WAS STILL HERE.
RIKU...
HEY!
WHA-WHAT IS IT?
HOLD STILL FOR A SEC.
HUH?!

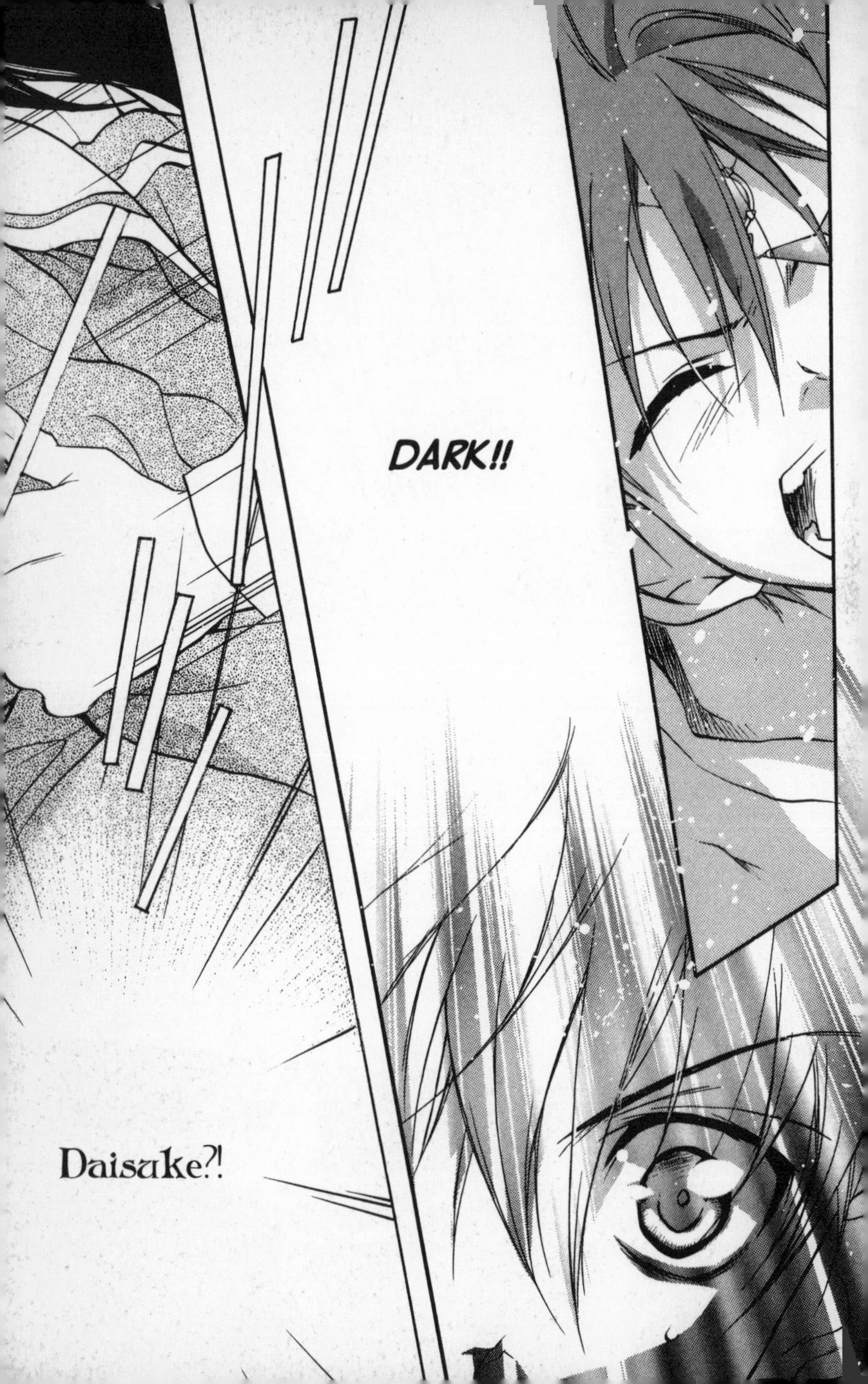
DARK!!
Daisuke?!

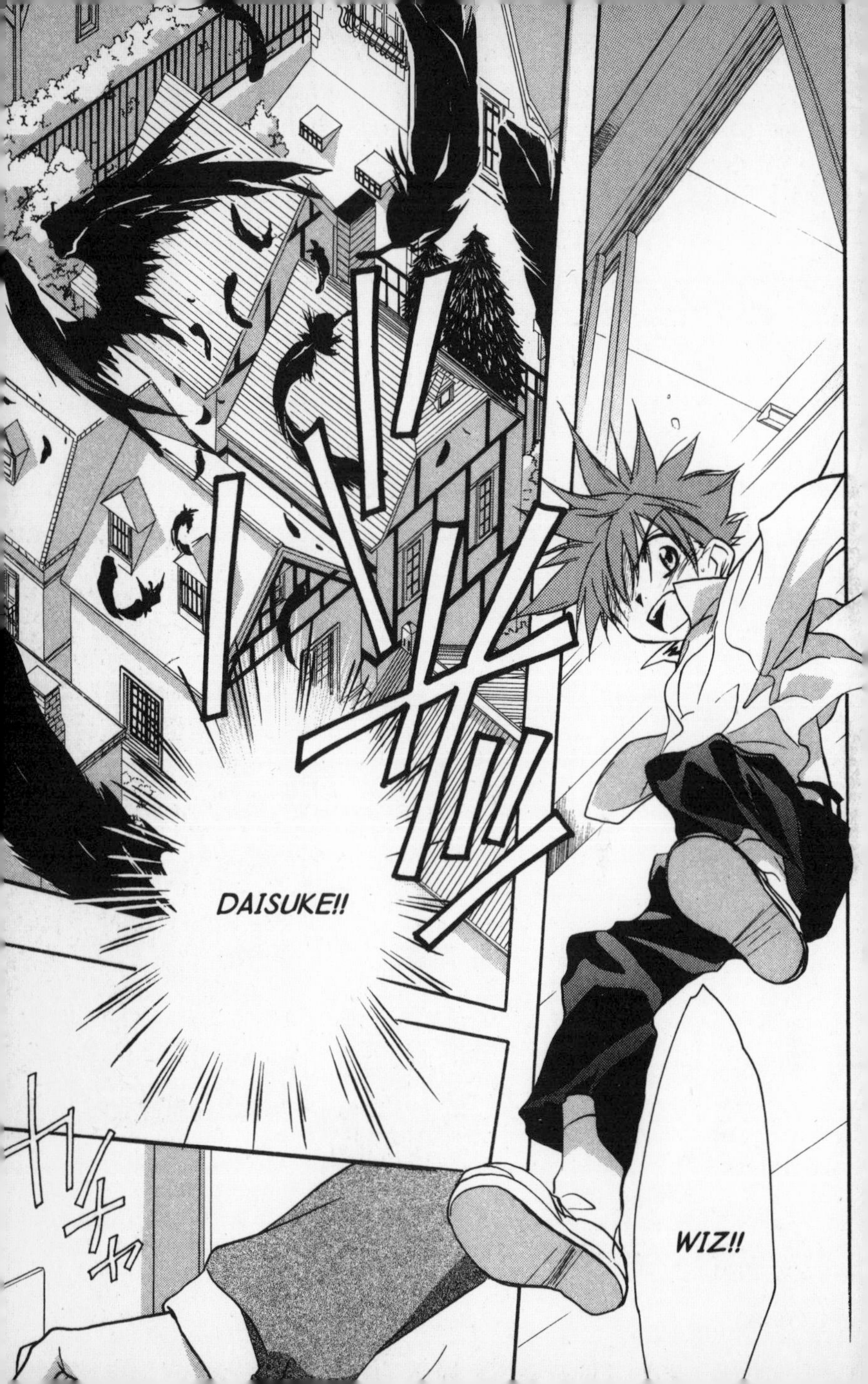
DAISUKE!!
WIZ!!

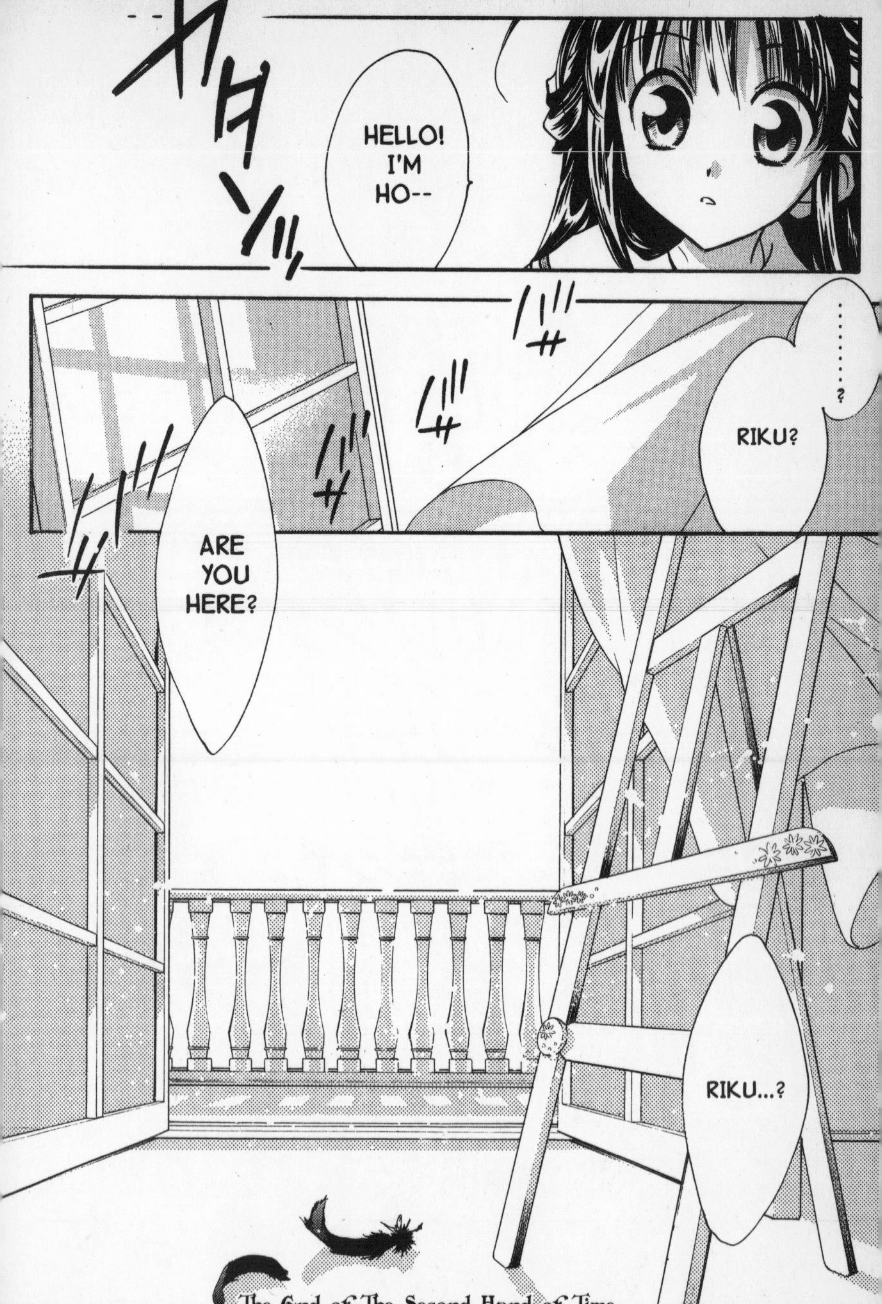

HELLO! I'M HO--
......?
RIKU?
ARE YOU HERE?
RIKU...?

The End of The Second Hand of Time, part 6

Messed up from struggling

T-shirt showing
through

Dark's Complaint

When we turn into my body, my clothes...

So...

I've been wanting to say this...

And here...

Here.

Here.

WELL, SORRY I'M SO MUCH SMALLER THAN YOU!

'Cause they're yours!

They get way too small and tight.

DON'T BE DISGUST- ING!!

But the tightest part of all is right—

AAAGH!!!

Don't look at him!!

...ooh...sorry!

GIRLS' mini-manga

GIRLS CUTE

RISA! DID YOU HIT YOUR HEAD AGAIN?

MY HEAD HURTS!!

OWWW!!

I BET YOU RAN INTO YOUR DESK OR SOMETHING, RIKU!

WHAT?

I'M THE ONE WHO'S IN PAIN--MY ARM HURTS!

Hurt her head herself.

But only Risa hit her head.

Hurt her arm.

But only Riku hurt her arm.

It's a twin mystery!

Twice the pain!!

OW OW OW OW OW OW OW OW !!

OW OW OW OW OW OW OW OW !!

One Night Magic

Fan Art Gallery

Thanks for all the fun postcards you've sent me!! Here are some of my favorite drawings of yours in this fan art gallery!

Kiri Futaba
Miyazaki Prefecture

D·N·ANGEL Daisuke's World

Dark version

Daisuke is so cute ♥

Note: it's a wig

Kyu?

Rabbit Daisuke?! Eh?!

Daisuke: Freedert version

Mika Hiromatsu
Fukuoka Prefecture

I'm the main character!

Hey, Daisuke!!

Dark

Daisuke

D·N·ANGEL

Yukie Akagawa
Niigata Prefecture

Double Freedert! No fair to Daisuke!

Fake

Real

DARK

RIKU

DAISUKE・SATOSI

DARK・KRAD

▲ "Krad" - Shizuoka Prefecture

▲ Ichigo Sawamura
- Ibaraki Prefecture

Izumiko Katori　Tochigi Prefecture

Daisuke Niwa

▶ "Uchu" Niigata Prefecture

D.N.ANGEL

Young Elliot

▼ "Aa-chin" - Wakayama Prefecture

LITTLE

RIKU

D.N.ANGEL

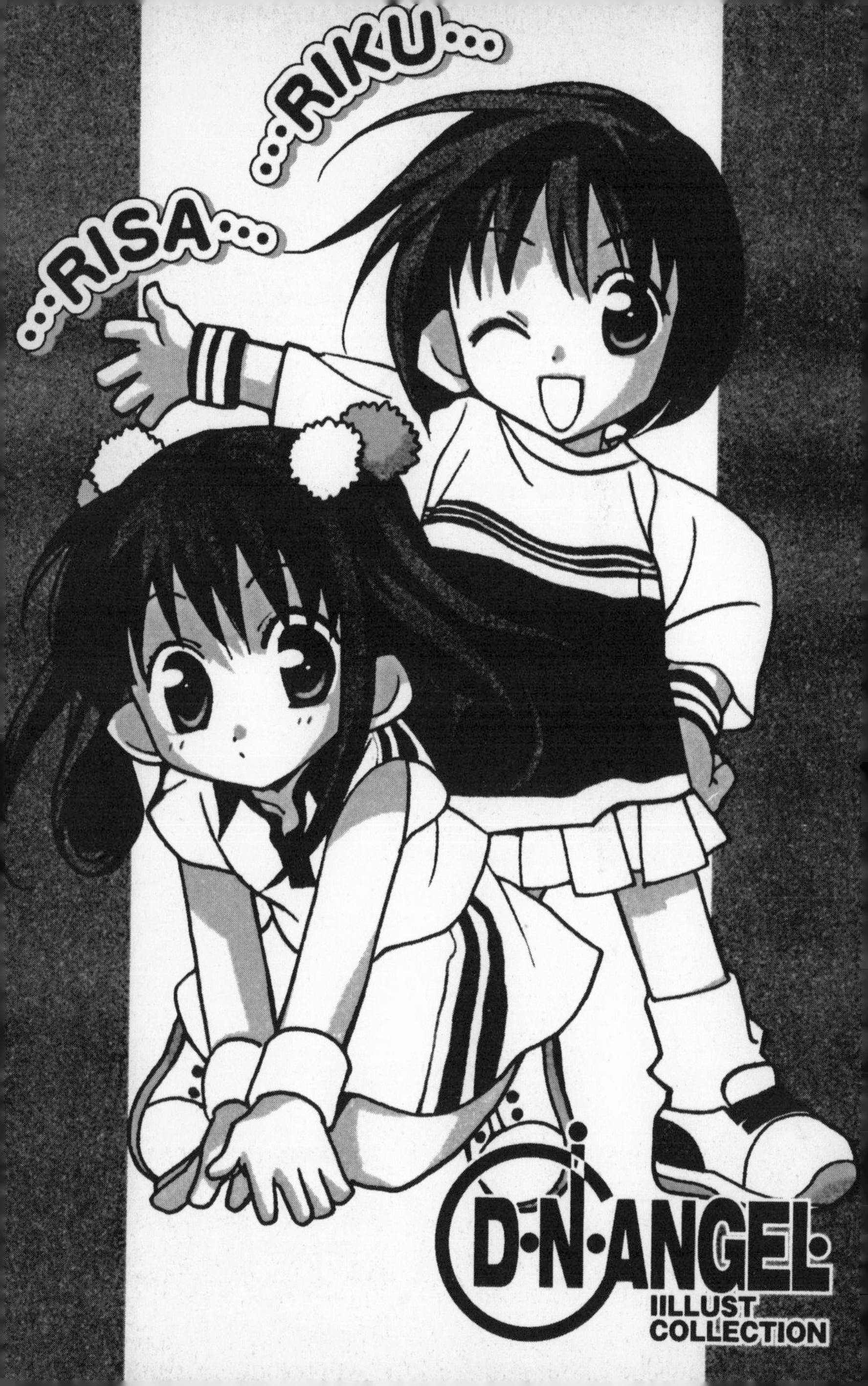

...RIKU...
...RISA...
D·N·ANGEL
ILLUST COLLECTION

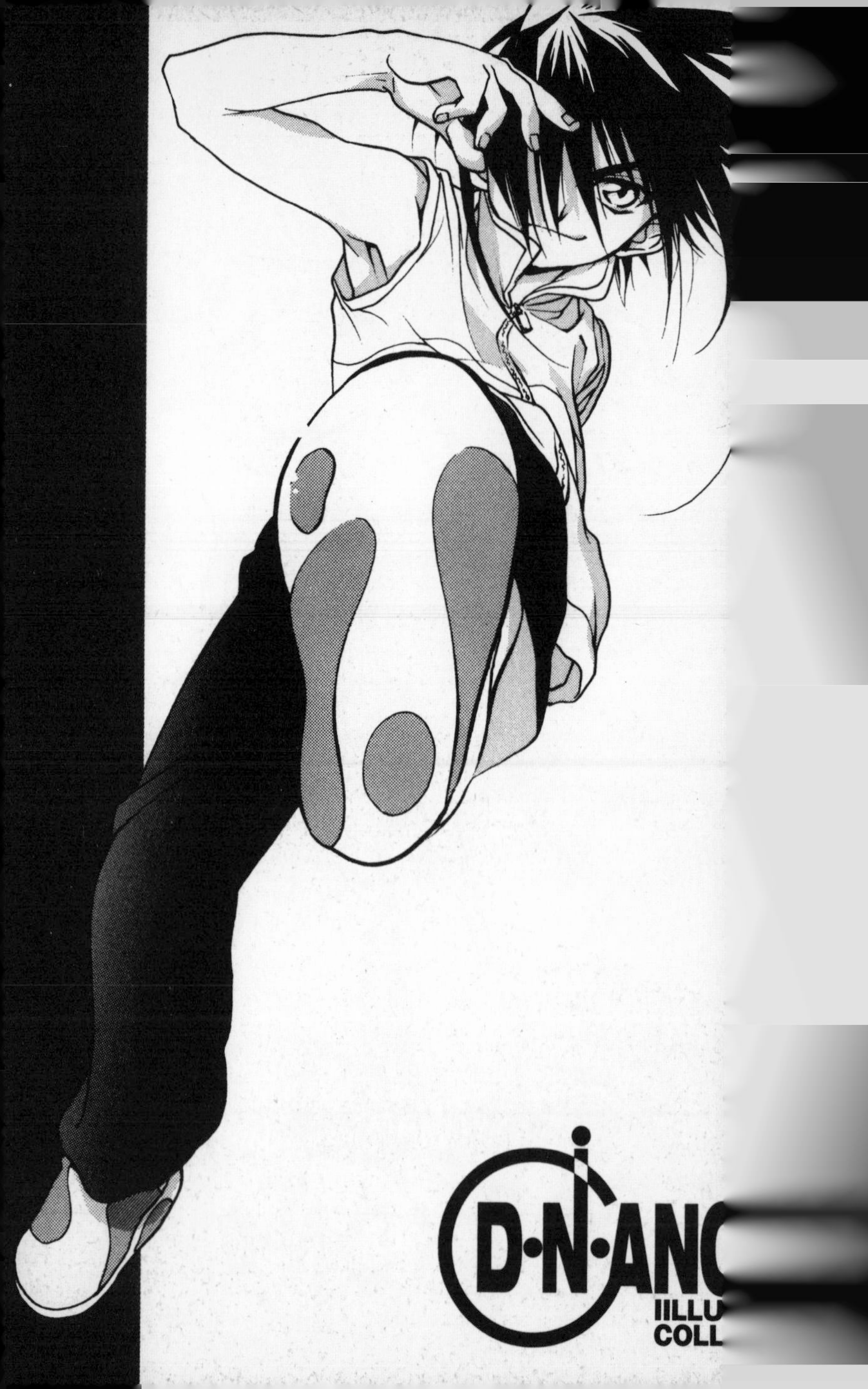

D•N•ANGEL
THINGS TO COME...

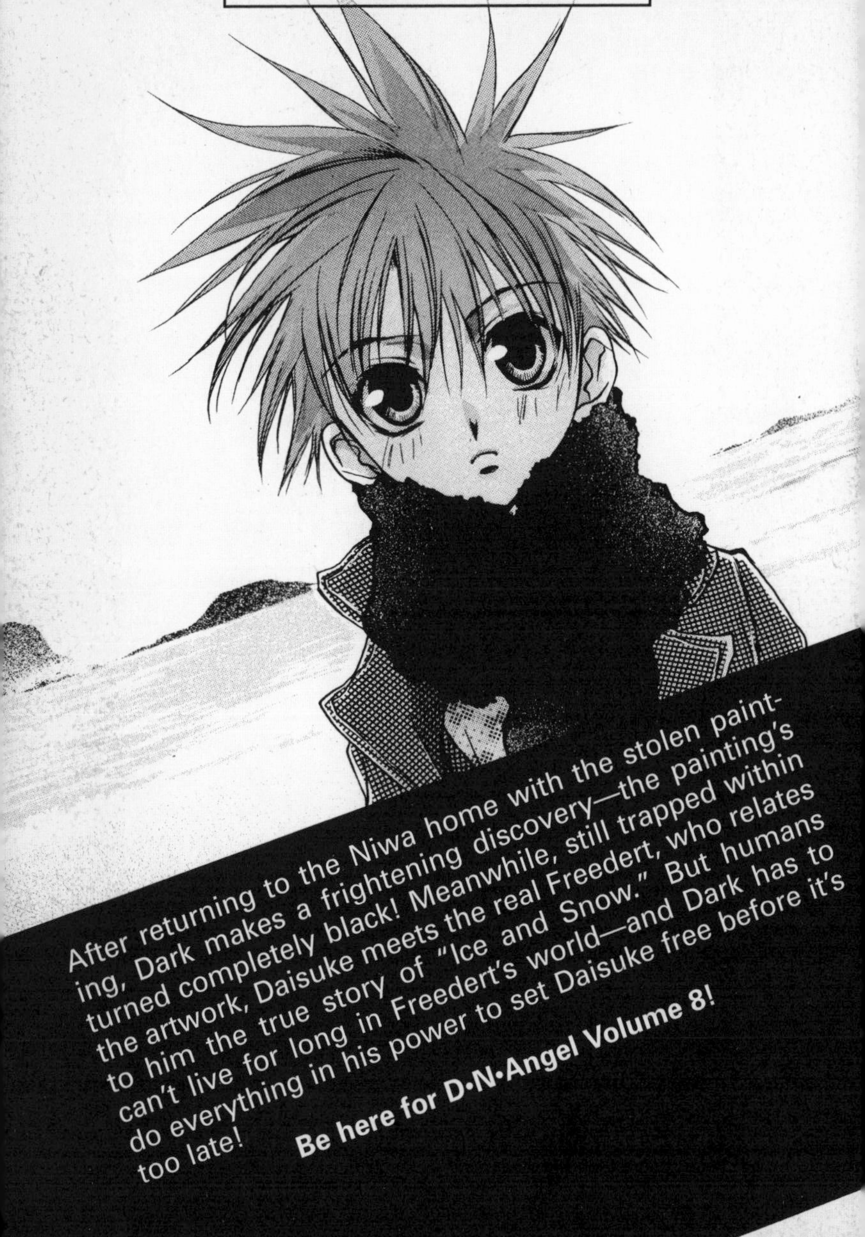

After returning to the Niwa home with the stolen painting, Dark makes a frightening discovery—the painting's turned completely black! Meanwhile, still trapped within the artwork, Daisuke meets the real Freedert, who relates to him the true story of "Ice and Snow." But humans can't live for long in Freedert's world—and Dark has to do everything in his power to set Daisuke free before it's too late!

Be here for D•N•Angel Volume 8!

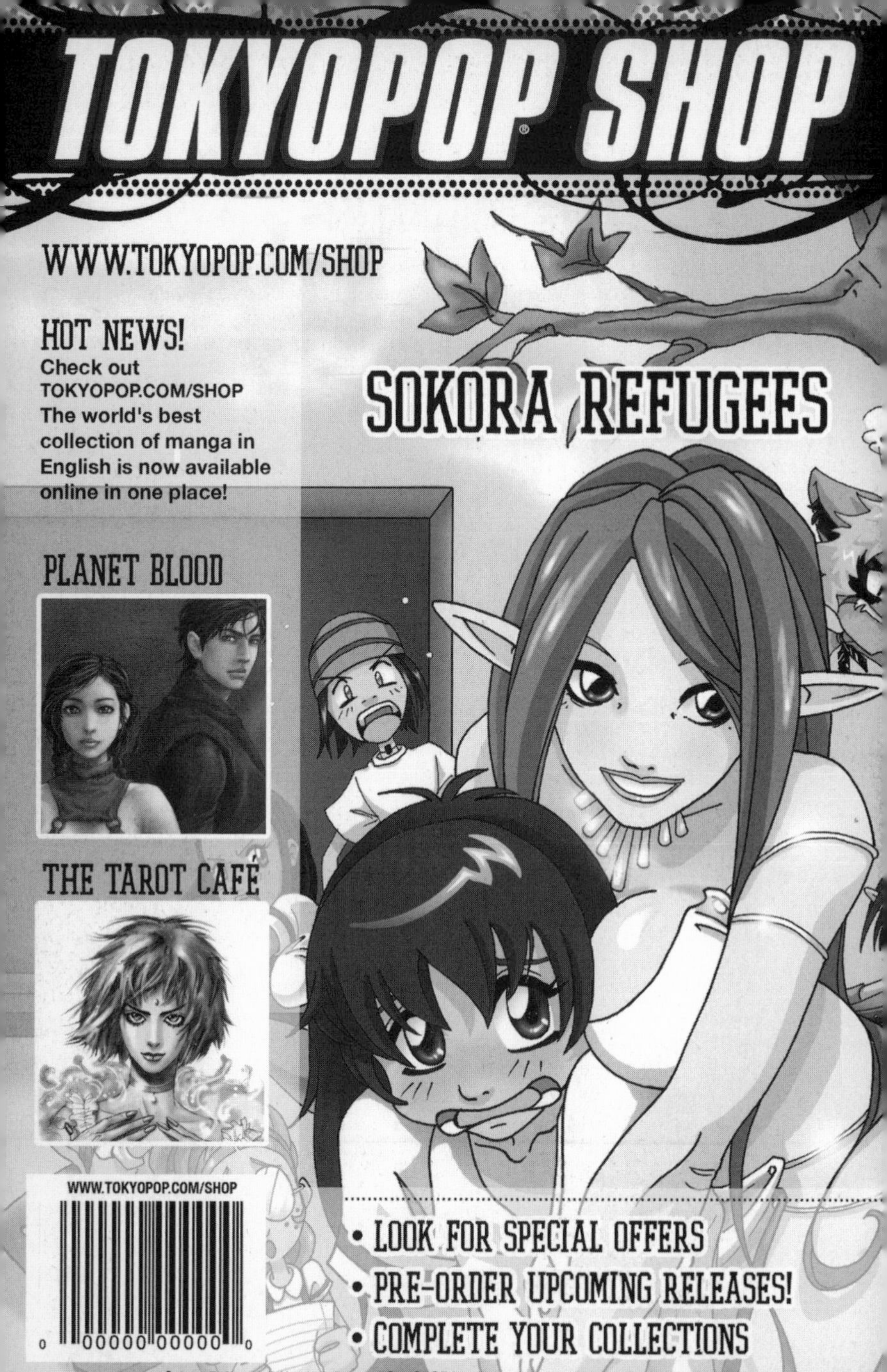
TOKYOPOP® SHOP
WWW.TOKYOPOP.COM/SHOP
HOT NEWS!
Check out TOKYOPOP.COM/SHOP The world's best collection of manga in English is now available online in one place!
PLANET BLOOD
THE TAROT CAFÉ
SOKORA REFUGEES
WWW.TOKYOPOP.COM/SHOP
0 00000 00000 0
• LOOK FOR SPECIAL OFFERS
• PRE-ORDER UPCOMING RELEASES!
• COMPLETE YOUR COLLECTIONS

SHOWCASE

PASSION FRUIT
BY MARI OKAZAKI

Passion Fruit is a unique, unforgettable collection of stylish stories that touch upon our most private inhibitions and examine our deepest desires. This uncompromising blend of realism and raw emotion focuses on women exploring the vulnerability and frailty of the human condition. With uninhibited authenticity and pathos, passion proves to be stranger than fiction.

OT OLDER TEEN AGE 16+

© Mari Okazaki

~~WITHDRAWN~~
YA (YAGRAPH)
D.N. ANGEL

PLANET BLOOD   335-9190
BY TAE-HYUNG KIM

Universal Century 0091. The Mars and Moon colonies fight for repatriation rights over the newly restored Earth. Amidst the bloody battle, one soldier, is rendered unconscious—only to awaken in an entirely different world enmeshed in an entirely different war...

T TEEN AGE 13+

© KIM TAE-HYUNG, DAIWON C.I. Inc.

LILING-PO
BY AKO YUTENJI

Master thief Liling-Po has finally been captured! However, the government offers a chance for Liling-Po to redeem himself. All he has to do is "retrieve" some special items—eight mystic treasures that are fabled to grant their owners any wish!

T TEEN AGE 13+

© Ako Yutenji